KU-359-351

ST. DEINIOL'S
HAWARDEN
LIBRARY

TRANSLATIONS OF CHRISTIAN LITERATURE

SERIES VI

SELECT PASSAGES

DOCUMENTS ILLUSTRATIVE OF THE HISTORY OF THE CHURCH

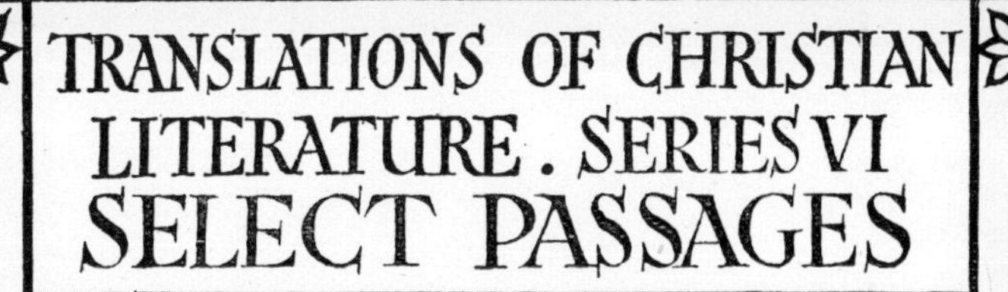

TRANSLATIONS OF CHRISTIAN LITERATURE. SERIES VI
SELECT PASSAGES

DOCUMENTS ILLUSTRATIVE OF THE HISTORY OF THE CHURCH

VOL. I TO A.D. 313

Edited by B. J. KIDD, D.D.

SOCIETY FOR PROMOTING CHRISTIAN KNOWLEDGE: London
The Macmillan Company: New York

First printed, 1920
Second Impression, 1928

Printed in Great Britain by Richard Clay & Sons, Limited,
Bungay, Suffolk.

CONTENTS

PREFACE

I WAS asked by S. P. C. K. to prepare a collection of extracts for the use of lecturers and students in colleges where it was not possible to assume such acquaintance, on the part of the students, with Greek and Latin as would enable them to profit by documents in the original languages. I happened, at the time, to be engaged upon *A History of the Church to A. D. 461*, and I selected the extracts to illustrate each chapter as it was written. So I hope the selection will cover the ground sufficiently; and, perhaps, be of use to the general reader as well as to the student.

My thanks are due to the following for permission to use extracts from their copyright works:—Messrs. Allen & Unwin for F. C. Conybeare, *Monuments of Early Christianity;* Messrs. Blackwood for Bishop Gregg, *The Decian Persecution;* Balliol College and the Delegates of the Oxford University Press for B. Jowett, *The Dialogues of Plato*, and *The Republic of Plato;* Messrs. T. & T. Clark for J. G. Cunningham, *Letters of Augustine*, J. R. King, *Works of Augustine*, G. Lewis, *The Philocalia of Origen*, and for numerous extracts from *The Ante-Nicene Christian Library;* the Delegates of the Oxford University Press for R. H. Charles, *The Apocalypse of Baruch;* C. R. Kennedy for *Demosthenes on the Crown;* Messrs. Heinemann for S. Gaselee, Apuleius, *The Golden Ass*, J. B. Firth, *Letters of the Younger Pliny*, J. C. Rolfe, *Suetonius;* Messrs. Longmans for A. J. Mason, *Historic Martyrs of the Primitive Church*, and D. Stone, *Episcopacy and Valid Orders;* Messrs. Longmans and the Rev. O. R. Vassall-Phillips for *St. Optatus;* Messrs. Macmillan for Church and Brodribb, *The Annals of Tacitus*, Hort and Mayor, *Miscellanies*, H. M. Gwatkin, *Selections;* Messrs. Macmillan and the Lightfoot Trustees for J. B. Lightfoot, *The Apostolic Fathers;* The Oxford and Cambridge University Presses, 2 *Esdras R.V.;* Messrs. Parker for the *Library of the Fathers;* Messrs. Parker and Messrs. Scribner for *Nicene and Post-Nicene Fathers.*

B. J. K.

Oxford, 1919.

NOTE

THANKS are due to the following for permission to use extracts from their copyright works :—the Delegates of the Oxford University Press for C. M. Dalton, *Letters of Sidonius ;* Messrs. W. Heinemann and Co. for W. C. Wright, *Works of the Emperor Julian ;* Messrs. G. Bell and Sons for C. W. King, *Julian, the Emperor ;* Messrs. Deighton Bell and Co. for G. H. Rendall, *The Emperor Julian ;* Rev. O. R. Vassall-Phillips for *The Works of St. Optatus ;* Rev. D. Stone, *Library of the Fathers ;* Mr. John Murray for *Dictionary of Christian Biography ;* Messrs. Bowes and Bowes for C. A. A. Scott, *Ulfilas ;* Rev. E. F. Morison for St. Basil ; Messrs. Longmans, Green and Co. for A. J. Mason, *Historic Martyrs ;* Messrs. T. and T. Clark for J. G. Cunningham, *Letters of St. Augustine*, P. Holmes, *Anti-Pelagian Writings of St. Augustine*, J. R. King, *Anti-Donatist Writings of St. Augustine*, and M. Dods, *The City of God ;* the Rt. Rev. A. Robertson, for *St. Athanasius on the Incarnation ;* Messrs. Parker for *Library of the Fathers* and *Nicene and Post-Nicene Fathers*, H. de Romestin, *Smaller Treatises of St. Augustine*, and C. A. Heurtley, *Faith and Creed ;* Messrs. Scribner for *Nicene and Post-Nicene Fathers*, and Ayers, *Source Book of Church History ;* Messrs. Williams and Norgate for W. Nevins, *Julian against the Christians.*

ABBREVIATIONS

N. & P.-N.F. = *Nicene & Post-Nicene Fathers*, Parker & Co.

A.-N.C.L. = *Ante-Nicene Christian Library*, T. & T. Clark.

L.F. = *Library of the Fathers*, Parker & Co.

E.C.C. = *Early Christian Classics*, S.P.C.K.

C.S.E.L. = *Corpus Scriptorum Ecclesiasticorum Latinorum*, Vindobonae.

J.T.S. = *Journal of Theological Studies*, Clar. Press.

DOCUMENTS ILLUSTRATIVE OF THE HISTORY OF THE CHURCH

No. 1.—Demons

From Plato [B.C. 429–†347], *Symposium*, c. xxiii.

Love "is a great spirit ['demon']; and, like all spirits, he is intermediate between the divine and the mortal." "And what," I said, "is his power?" "He interprets," she replied, "between gods and men, conveying to the gods the prayers and sacrifices of men, and to men the commands and replies of the gods; he is the mediator who spans the chasm which divides them, and in him all is bound together, and through him the arts of the prophet and the priest, their sacrifices and mysteries and charms, and all prophecy and incantation, find their way. For God mingles not with man; but through Love all the intercourse and speech of God with man, whether awake or asleep, is carried on. The wisdom which understands this is spiritual; all other wisdom, such as that of arts and handicrafts, is mean and vulgar. Now these spirits or intermediate powers are many and diverse, and one of them is Love."—B. Jowett, *The Dialogues of Plato*,[2] ii. 54.

No. 2.—The Orphic Mysteries

From Plato [B.C. 429–†347], *Republic*, II. c. vii.

But most extraordinary of all is their mode of speaking about virtue and the gods; they say that the gods apportion calamity and misery to many good men, and good and happiness to the wicked. And mendicant prophets go to rich men's doors and persuade them that they have a power committed to them by the gods of making an atonement for a man's own or his ancestors' sins by sacrifices or charms, with rejoicings and feasts; and they promise to harm an enemy, whether just or unjust, at a small cost; with magic arts and incantations binding heaven, as they say, to execute their will. And the poets are the authorities to whom they appeal, now smoothing the path of vice with the words of Hesiod:—"Vice may be had in abundance without trouble; the way is smooth and her dwelling-place is near. But before virtue the gods have set toil" and a tedious and uphill road; then citing Homer as a witness that the gods may be influenced by men; for he also says:—"The gods, too, may be turned from their purpose; and men pray to them and avert their wrath by sacrifices and soothing entreaties, and by libations and the odour of fat, when they have sinned and transgressed." And they produce a host of books written by Musæus and Orpheus, who were children of the Moon and the Muses—that is what they say—according to which they perform their ritual, and persuade not only individuals but whole cities, that expiations and atonements for sin may be made by sacrifices and amusements which fill a vacant hour, and are equally at the service of the living and the dead; the latter sort they call mysteries, and they redeem us from the pains of hell, but if we neglect them no one knows what awaits us.—B. Jowett, *The Republic of Plato*,[2] ii. 364–365.

No. 3.—The Mysteries of Dionysus

From Demosthenes [B.C. 385–†22], *De Corona*, §§ 258–60.

[§ 258] . . . As a boy, you [Æschines] were reared in abject poverty, waiting with your father on the school, grinding the ink, sponging the benches, sweeping the room, doing the duty of a menial rather than a freeman's son. [§ 259] After you were grown up, you attended your mother's initiations, reading her books and helping in all the ceremonies; at night wrapping the novitiates in fawn-skin, swilling, purifying and scouring them with clay and bran, raising them after the lustration, and bidding them say "Bad have I 'scaped, and better I have found"; priding yourself that no one ever howled so lustily—and I believe him! for don't suppose that he who speaks so loud is not a splendid howler! [§ 260] In the daytime you led your noble orgiasts, crowned with fennel and poplar, through the highways, squeezing the big-cheeked serpents, and lifting them over your head, and shouting "Evœ Sabœ," and capering to the words "Hyes Attes, Attes Hyes," saluted by the beldames as Leader, Conductor, Chest-bearer, Fan-bearer, and the like; getting as your reward tarts and biscuits and rolls; for which any man might well bless himself and his fortune!—C. R. Kennedy, Demosthenes, *On the Crown*, 94 *sq*.

No. 4.—The Principate

From the *Monumentum Ancyranum*, or *Res Gestæ* of Augustus, A.D. 14.

Below is a copy of the deeds of the divine Augustus, by which he subjected the whole world to the dominion of the Roman people, and of the amounts which he expended upon the commonwealth and the Roman people, as engraved upon two brazen columns which are set up at Rome . . . . [c. 34] In my sixth and seventh consulships (28–7 B.C.), when I had put an end to the civil wars, after having obtained complete control of affairs by universal consent, I transferred the commonwealth from my own dominion to the authority of the senate and Roman people. In return for this favour on my part, I received by decree of the senate the title Augustus, the door-posts of my house were publicly decked with laurels, a civic crown was fixed above my door, and in the Julian Curia was placed a golden shield, which, by its inscription, bore witness that it was given to me by the senate and Roman people on account of my valour, clemency, justice and piety. After that time I excelled all others in dignity, but of power I held no more than those also held who were my colleagues in any magistracy. — *Translations and reprints from the original sources of Europæan history*, Vol. V. no. 1.

No. 5.—Jewish Pessimism[1] after the Fall of Jerusalem

From *The Apocalypse of Baruch*, c. lxxxv. [70–100].

[1] Know ye, moreover, that in former times and in the generations of old those our fathers had helpers, righteous men and holy prophets; [2] Nay more, we were in our own land, and they helped us when we sinned, and they interceded for us to Him Who made us, because they trusted in their works, and the Mighty One heard their prayer and forgave us. [3] But now the righteous have been gathered, and the prophets have fallen asleep, and we also have gone forth from the land, and Zion hath been taken from us; and we have nothing now save the Mighty One and His law. [4] If, therefore, we direct and dispose our hearts, we shall receive everything that we lost, and much better things than we lost by many times. [5] For what we have lost was subject to corruption, and what we shall receive shall not be corruptible. [6] Moreover, also, I have written thus to our brethren to Babylon; that to them also I may attest these very things. [7] And let all those things aforesaid be always before your eyes, because we are still in the spirit and the power of our liberty. [8] Again, moreover, the Most High is long-suffering towards us here, and He hath shown to us that which is to be, and hath not concealed from us what shall befall in the end. [9] Before, therefore, judgment exact its own, and truth that which is its due, let us prepare our soul that we may enter into possession of, and not be taken possession, and that we may hope and not be put to shame, and that we may rest with our fathers and not be tormented with our enemies. [10] For the youth of the world is past, and the strength of the creation is already exhausted, and the advent of the times is very short, yea, they have passed by; and the pitcher is near to the cistern, and the ship to the port, and the course of the journey to the city, and life to its consummation. [11] And again, prepare your souls, so that when ye sail

[1] To be contrasted with the Christian outlook in *The Epistle to the Hebrews*.

and ascend from the ship ye may have rest and not be condemned when ye depart. [12] For lo! when the Most High shall bring to pass all these things, there shall not be there again a place of repentance, nor a limit to the times, nor a duration for the hours, nor a change of ways, nor place for prayer, nor sending of petitions, nor receiving of knowledge, nor giving of love, nor place of repentance for the soul, nor supplication for offences, nor intercession of the fathers, nor prayer of the prophets, nor help of the righteous. [13] There there is the sentence of corruption, the way of fire, and the path which bringeth to Gehenna. [14] On this account there is one Law by One, one age and an end for all who are in it. [15] Then He will preserve those whom He can forgive, and at the same time destroy those who are polluted with sins.—R. H. Charles, *The Apocalypse of Baruch.*

No. 6.—Jewish Pessimism

From *The Ezra Apocalypse*[1] [*c.* 100].

[22] Then answered I and said, I beseech thee, O Lord, wherefore is the power of understanding given unto me? [23] For it was not my mind to be curious of the ways above, but of such things as pass by us daily; because Israel is given up as a reproach to the heathen, and the people whom thou hast loved is given over unto ungodly nations, and the law of our forefathers is made of none effect, and the written covenants are nowhere regarded, [24] and we pass away out of the world as grasshoppers, and our life is as a vapour, neither are we worthy to obtain mercy. [25] What will he then do for his name whereby we are called? Of these things have I asked.

[26] Then he answered me, and said, If thou be alive, thou shalt see, and if thou livest long, thou shalt marvel; for the world hasteth fast to pass away. [27] For it is not able to bear the things that are promised to the righteous in the time to come: for this world is full of sadness and infirmities. [28] For the evil thereof thou askest me is sown, but the gathering thereof is not yet come. [29] If therefore

[1] Perhaps derived from *The Apocalypse of Salathiel:* see G. H. Box, *The Ezra-Apocalypse* on 2 Esdras iii. 1, for name and date.

that which is sown be not reaped, and if the place where the evil is sown pass not away, there cannot come the field where the good is sown. [30] For a grain of evil seed was sown in the heart of Adam from the beginning, and how much wickedness hath it brought forth unto this time! and how much shall it yet bring forth until the time of threshing come! [31] Ponder now by thyself, how great fruit of wickedness a grain of evil seed hath brought forth. [32] When the ears which are without number shall be sown, how great a floor shall they fill!

[33] Then I answered and said, How long? and when shall these things come to pass? wherefore are our years few and evil?

[34] And he answered me, and said, Thou dost not hasten more than the Most High: for thy haste is for thine own self, but he that is above hasteneth on behalf of many. [35] Did not the souls of the righteous ask question of these things in their chambers, saying, How long are we here? when cometh the fruit of the threshing time of our reward? [36] And unto them Jeremiel the archangel gave answer, and said, Even when the number is fulfilled of them that are like unto you. For he hath weighed the world in the balance; [37] and by measure hath he measured the times, and by number hath he numbered the seasons; and he shall not move nor stir them, until the said measure be fulfilled.—2 Esdras iv. 22–37 (R.V.).

No. 7.—The True Doctrine of the Sabbath

From *The Epistle of Barnabas*, ? 70–79.

[Ch. XV] Moreover concerning the sabbath likewise it is written in the Ten Words, in which He spake to Moses face to face on Mount Sinai: *And ye shall hallow the sabbath of the Lord with pure hands and with a pure heart.* And in another place He saith: *If My sons observe the sabbath, then I will bestow My mercy upon them.* Of the sabbath He speaketh in the beginning of the creation: *And God made the works of His hands in six days, and He endeth on the seventh day, and rested on it, and He hallowed it.* Give heed, children, what this meaneth; *He ended in six days.* He meaneth this, that in six thousand years the Lord shall bring all things to an end; for the day with him signifieth a thousand years; and this He Himself beareth me witness, saying: *Behold, the day of the Lord shall be as a thousand years.* Therefore, children, in six days, that is in six thousand years, everything shall come to an end. *And He rested on the seventh day.* This He meaneth; when His Son shall come, and shall abolish the time of the Lawless One, and shall judge the ungodly, and shall change the sun and the moon and the stars, then shall He truly rest on the seventh day. Yea, and furthermore He saith: *Thou shalt hallow it with pure hands and a pure heart.* If therefore a man is able now to hallow the day which God hallowed, though he be pure in heart, we have gone utterly astray. But if after all then and not till then shall we truly rest and hallow it, when we shall ourselves be able to do so after being justified and receiving the promise, when iniquity is no more and all things have been made new by the Lord, we shall be able to hallow it then, because we ourselves shall have been hallowed first. Finally He saith to them: *Your new moons and your sabbaths I cannot away with.* Ye see what is His meaning; it is not your present sabbaths that are acceptable [unto Me], but the sabbath which I have made, in the which, when I have set all things at rest, I will make the beginning of the eighth day which is the beginning of another world. Wherefore also we keep the eighth day for rejoicing, in the which also Jesus rose from the dead, and having been manifested ascended into the heavens.—J. B. Lightfoot, *Apostolic Fathers* (abridged edition), 283 *sq*.

No. 8.—The Burning of the Temple, August 10, A.D. 70

From Josephus [37–† *c.* 100], *Bellum Judaicum* [*c.* 75], VI. iv. 5–7.

[§ 5] So Titus retired into the tower of Antonia; and resolved to storm the Temple, the next day, early in the morning, with his whole army: and to encamp round about the holy house. But as for that house, God had, for certain, long ago, doomed it to the fire. And now that fatal day was come, according to the revolution of ages: it was the tenth day of the month *Lous* [*Ab*]; upon which it was formerly burnt by the King of Babylon. Although these flames took their rise from the Jews themselves, and were occasioned by them. For upon Titus's retiring, the seditious lay still for a little while, and then attacked the Romans again; when those that guarded the holy house fought with those that quenched the fire that was burning the inner [court of] the temple. But these Romans put the Jews to flight; and proceeded as far as the holy house itself. At which time, one of the soldiers, without staying for any orders and without any concern or dread upon him at so great an undertaking; and being hurried on by a certain divine fury, snatched somewhat out of the materials that were on fire, and being lift up by another soldier, he set fire to a golden window, through which there was a passage to the rooms that were round about the holy house, on the north side of it. As the flames went upward, the Jews made a great clamour, such as so mighty an affliction required; and ran together to prevent it. And now they spared not their lives any longer: nor suffered anything to restrain their force, since that holy house was perishing, for whose sake it was that they kept such guard about it.

[§ 6] And now a certain person came running to Titus, and told him of this fire; as he was resting himself in his tent, after the last battle. Whereupon he rose up in great haste; and, as he was, ran to the holy house; in order to have a stop put to the fire. After him followed all his commanders; and after them followed the several legions, in great astonishment. So there was a great clamour, and tumult raised, as was natural upon the disorderly motion of so great an army. Then did Cæsar, both by calling to the soldiers that were fighting, with a loud voice; and by giving a signal to them with his right hand, order them to quench the fire. But they did not hear what he said; though he spake so loud: having their ears already dinned by a greater noise another way. Nor did they attend to the signal he made with his hand neither: as still some of them were distracted with fighting, and others with passion. But as for the legions that came running thither, neither any persuasions, nor any threatenings could restrain their violence: but each one's own passion was his commander at this time. And as they were crowding into the Temple together, many of them were trampled on by one another; while a great number fell among the ruins of the cloisters, which were still hot and smoking; and were destroyed in the same miserable way with those whom they had conquered. And when they were come near the holy house, they made as if they did not so much as hear Cæsar's orders to the contrary; but they encouraged those that were before them to set it on fire. As for the seditious, they were in too great distress already to afford their assistance [towards quenching the fire]. They were everywhere slain, and everywhere beaten. And as for a great part of the people, they were weak, and without arms, and had their throats cut wherever they were caught. Now round about the altar lay dead bodies heaped one upon another; as at the steps going up to it, ran a great quantity of their blood; whither also the dead bodies that were slain above [on the altar] fell down.

[§ 7] And now, since Cæsar was no way able to restrain the enthusiastic fury of the soldiers, and the fire proceeded on more and more, he went into the holy place of the Temple, with his commanders; and saw it, with what was in it: which he found to be far superior to what the relations of foreigners contained; and not inferior to what we ourselves boasted of, and believed about it. But as the flame had not as yet reached to its inward parts, but was still consuming the rooms that were about the holy house only; and Titus supposing, what the fact was, that the house itself might yet be saved, he came up in haste, and endeavoured to persuade the soldiers to quench the fire; and gave order to Liberalius the centurion, and one of those spearmen that were about him, to beat the soldiers that were refractory with their staves; and to restrain them. Yet were their passions too hard for the regards they had for Cæsar, and the dread they had of him who forbade them; as was their hatred of the Jews, and a certain vehement inclination to fight them too hard for them also. Moreover, the hope of plunder induced many to go on; as having this opinion, that all the places within were full of money; and as seeing that all round about it was made of gold. And besides, one of those that went into the place prevented Cæsar, when he ran so hastily out to restrain the soldiers: and threw the fire upon the hinges of the gate, in the dark. Whereby the flame burst out from within the holy house itself immediately: when the commanders retired, and Cæsar with them; and when nobody any longer forbade those that were without to set fire to it. And thus was the holy house burnt down, without Cæsar's approbation.—William Whiston, *The Works of Josephus*, ii. 933 *sq.* (London, 1737).

No. 9.—St. James, the Lord's Brother

From Josephus, *Antiquities* [93–4], XX. ix. § 1.

And now Cæsar, upon hearing of the death of Festus, sent Albinus into Judæa as procurator. But the King deprived Joseph of the High Priesthood; and bestowed the succession to that dignity on the son of Ananus, who was also himself called Ananus. Now the report goes that this eldest Ananus proved a most fortunate man. For he had five sons who had all performed the office of an High Priest to God; and who had himself enjoyed that dignity a long time formerly: which had never happened to any other of our High Priests. But this younger Ananus who, as we have told you already, took the High Priesthood, was a bold man in his temper and very insolent. He was also of the sect of the Sadducees: who are very rigid in judging offenders above all the rest of the Jews: as we have already observed. When therefore Ananus was of this disposition, he thought he had now a proper opportunity [to exercise his authority]. Festus was now dead; and Albinus was but upon the road. So he assembled the sanhedrin of judges, and brought before them the brother of Jesus who was called Christ, whose name was James: and some others; [or, some of his companions]. And when he had formed an accusation against them as breakers of the law, he delivered them to be stoned. But as for those who seemed the most equitable of the citizens, and such as were the most uneasy at the breach of the laws, they disliked what was done. They also sent to the King [Agrippa], desiring him to send to Ananus that he should act so no more; for that what he had already done was not to be justified. Nay, some of them went also to meet Albinus, as he was upon his journey from Alexandria; and informed him that it was not lawful for Ananus to assemble a sanhedrin without his consent. Whereupon Albinus complied with what they said; and wrote in anger to Ananus; and threatened that he would bring him to punishment for what he had done. On which account King Agrippa took the High Priesthood from him when he had ruled but three months; and made Jesus the son of Damneus High Priest.—William Whiston, *The Works of Josephus*, i. 648 (London, 1737).

No. 10.—The Persecution of Domitian, *c.* 96

From Clement of Rome, *Epistle to the Corinthians* [*c.* 96], c. i.

The Church of God sojourning in Rome to the Church of God sojourning in Corinth, to them that are called and sanctified by the will of God through our Lord Jesus Christ. Grace to you and peace from Almighty God through Jesus Christ be multiplied.

I. By reason of the sudden and oft-repeated calamities and troubles which have befallen us, brethren, we consider that we have been slow in turning our attention to the questions in dispute among you, beloved, and to that disgraceful and unholy division, which is so alien to the spirit of the elect of God, and yet has been kindled by a few headstrong and reckless persons to such a pitch of folly, that it has caused very evil things to be spoken of your name, once so widely honoured and so rightly beloved of all men.

For who ever sojourned among you and did not prove the virtuousness and firmness of your faith or marvelled not at the sobriety and respectfulness of your Christian piety? or did not tell of your noble disposition of hospitality? or failed to congratulate you on your perfect and unshaken knowledge?

All that ye did was without respect of persons; ye walked after the ordinances of God; ye submitted yourselves to your rulers, and ye paid the honour that was due to the older men among you. Upon the young men ye enjoined sober and seemly thoughts; the women ye exhorted to fulfil all their duties with a blameless and seemly and pure conscience, rendering to their own husbands the love that was due to them; and ye taught them that they should observe the rule of obedience, and perform their household tasks with seemliness and wise discretion.—J. A. F. Gregg, *Epistle of St. Clement*, 21–23.

No. 11.—The Neronian Persecution, A.D. 64

From Clement of Rome, *Epistle to the Corinthians*, cc. v., vi.

V. But enough of examples from the days of old. Let us come to those great ones who are nearest to our time—let us take the grand examples which our own generation supplies.

It was for jealousy and envy that the greatest and most righteous pillars (of the Church) were persecuted and fought even to the death. Let us set before our eyes the good Apostles; Peter, who for unrighteous jealousy submitted to not one, nor two, but many labours, and who having thus borne witness, passed to the appointed place of glory; Paul, who by reason of jealousy and envy was able to point by his example to the prize of patience. Seven times was he thrown into prison; he was driven into exile, he was stoned; then when he had preached in the East and the West, he attained the noble renown which his faith won for him, teaching righteousness to the whole world, and coming to the furthest limits of the West. Lastly, he bore witness before rulers, and thus passed from the world, and went to the holy place, after proving himself a marvellous pattern of patience.

VI. To these men of holy conversation we must add a goodly company of elect souls who gathered round them, and who, when by reason of jealousy they were subjected to countless indignities and tortures, stood forth as a noble example among us. It was by reason of jealousy that women were persecuted, and were subjected, under the guise of Danaids and Dirces, to dreadful and unholy violence, until they won the goal for which their faith had struggled, and they received, despite their feebleness, a noble prize.—J. A. F. Gregg, *The Epistle of St. Clement*, 26 *sq.*

No. 12.—The Christian Ministry, *c.* A.D. 96.

From Clement of Rome, *Epistle to the Corinthians*, cc. xl.–xlii. and xliv.

XL. Seeing then that these things are plain, and that we have looked into the depths of the Divine knowledge, we are bound to do in due order all those things that the Master commanded us to accomplish at their appointed times. In respect of the offerings and ministrations, not only did He ordain that they should be performed at their appointed times and seasons; but also by His supreme will He Himself set forth the place and the ministers for their performance, that so all things might be done in holiness according to His pleasure and might be acceptable to His will. As many therefore as make their offerings at the appointed seasons are acceptable and blessed, for by following the ordinances of the Master, they are preserved from error. For the high priest is called to perform special ministrations, and the office to which the priests are appointed is special, and upon the Levites special services are laid, and the layman is bound by special ordinances.

XLI. Let each of you, brethren, in his own order, give thanks unto God, preserving a good conscience, and adhering to the appointed rule of his service with all reverence. Not in every place, brethren, but only in Jerusalem are the daily sacrifices offered, or the free-will offerings, or the sin offerings and trespass offerings. And even there the offering is made in only one place, in the court of the altar before the sanctuary; and that, not until the offering has been inspected by the high priest and the ministers aforesaid. All who make an offering contrary to the seemly appointment of His will are liable to be punished with death. Yet see, brethren, that according as we have been counted worthy to receive fuller knowledge, so is the danger greater to which we are exposed.

XLII. The Apostles were taught the Gospel for our sakes at the feet of the Lord Jesus Christ; Jesus Christ was sent out from God. Christ then is from God, and the Apostles from Christ. Both therefore issued from the will of God with due order. Having therefore received His instructions, and being finally stablished through the Resurrection of our Lord Jesus Christ, and being confident in the word of God, they went forth with full conviction from the Holy Spirit, and preached that the Kingdom of God was soon to come. And so, as they preached in the country and in the towns, they proved by the Spirit the first-fruits of their work in each place, and appointed them to be overseers and deacons among them that should believe. And this was no innovation, for from of old it had been written concerning bishops and deacons, as the Scripture says in a certain place, *I will set up their bishops in righteousness, and their deacons in faith.*

XLIV. No less did our Apostles know through our Lord Jesus Christ that there would be strife over the dignity of the overseer's office. For this very reason, having received complete foreknowledge, they appointed the aforesaid overseers and deacons, and ordained that at their death their ministry should pass into the hands of other tried men. We hold therefore that it is an act of injustice to thrust out from their ministry men who, with the good-will of the entire Church, received their position at the hands of Apostles, or of other honoured men at a later time, and who in all humility ministered to the flock of Christ without offence, peaceably and without presumption, and who have on many occasions been well reported of by all. For we shall be guilty of no small sin, if we reject men who have holily and without offence offered the gifts pertaining to the bishop's office. Blessed are the elders who have departed hence in time past, for they continued till their time was fulfilled and their work had borne fruit; they have no fear of being removed from their appointed place. We must needs beware; for ye have taken upon you to put some men out of their office, although they walk discreetly and have held their position without offence.—J. A. F. Gregg, *The Epistle of St. Clement*, 54-59.

No. 13.—A Church Order, *c.* 100

From *The Didache ;* or, *The Teaching of the Lord, through the Twelve Apostles, to the Gentiles.*

I. 1. There are two Ways, one of Life and one of Death, and there is much difference between the two Ways. 2. The Way then of Life is this: Firstly, thou shalt love God who made thee: secondly, thou shalt love thy neighbour as thyself: and whatsoever thou wouldest not have done to thyself, do not thou either to another. 3. Now the doctrine of these words is this: Bless them which curse you, and pray for your enemies, and fast for them which persecute you. For what thank have ye, if ye love them which love you? Do not even the Gentiles the same? But do ye love them which hate you, and ye shall have no enemy. 4. Abstain from fleshly and bodily lusts. If any one give thee a blow on the right cheek, turn to him the other also, and thou shalt be perfect. If any compel thee to go one mile, go with him two: if any take thy cloak, give him also thy tunic: if any take from thee what is thine, ask for it not again: for indeed thou canst not. 5. Give to every one that asketh thee, and ask it not again; for the Father wills that we should give to all from his own gifts. Blessed is he that giveth according to the commandment: for he is guiltless: woe to him that receiveth: for if one receiveth because he hath need, he shall be guiltless: but he that hath no need shall render account why he received and for what, and being cast into straits shall be examined concerning what he did, and shall not come out thence till he have paid the uttermost farthing. 6. But about this it hath also been said: Let thine alms sweat into thy hands, until thou know to whom thou art to give.

II. 1. And the second commandment of the doctrine is this: 2. Thou shalt not kill, thou shalt not commit adultery, thou shalt not corrupt boys, thou shalt not commit fornication, thou shalt not steal, thou shalt not use magic, thou shalt not practise sorcery, thou shalt not procure abortion, nor kill the new-born child. Thou shalt not covet thy neighbour's goods. 3. Thou shalt not forswear thyself, thou shalt not bear false witness, thou shalt not slander, thou shalt not bear malice. 4. Thou shalt not be double-minded nor double-tongued: for a double tongue is a deadly snare. 5. Thy word shall not be false, nor empty, but fulfilled in deed. 6. Thou shalt not be covetous, nor extortionate, nor a hypocrite, nor spiteful, nor arrogant. Thou shalt not take evil counsel against thy neighbour. 7. Thou shalt hate no man, but some thou shalt reprove, and for some thou shalt pray, and some thou shalt love more than thy soul.

III. 1. My child, flee from all evil and from all that is like it. 2. Be not wrathful: for wrath guideth to murder: nor a zealot, nor contentious, nor quick to anger: for from all these things murders are begotten. 3. My child, be not lustful, for lust guideth to fornication: nor a filthy talker, nor one of high looks: for from all these things adulteries are begotten. 4. My child, be not an augur: for it guideth to idolatry: nor an enchanter, nor an astrologer, nor a purifier, nor do thou consent to look on these things: for from all these things idolatry is begotten. 5. My child, be not a liar: for the lie guideth to theft: nor a lover of money, nor vainglorious: for from all these things thefts are begotten. 6. My child, be not a murmurer: for it guideth to blasphemy: nor self-willed; nor evil-minded; for from all these things blasphemies are begotten. 7. But be meek, for the meek shall inherit the earth. 8. Be long-suffering, and merciful, and harmless, and quiet, and good, and trembling always at the words that thou didst hear. 9. Thou shalt not exalt thyself, nor give boldness to thy soul. Thy soul shall not cleave to the lofty, but with the just and lowly shalt thou walk. 10. The providences that befall thee thou shalt welcome as good, knowing that without God nothing cometh to pass.

IV. 1. My child, night and day shalt thou remember him that speaketh to thee the Word of God, and thou shalt honour him as the Lord, for in him by whom the Lordship is spoken of is the Lord. 2. And daily shalt thou seek out the faces of the saints, that thou mayest rest on their words. 3. Thou shalt not desire division, but shalt set at peace them that strive: thou shalt judge justly; thou shalt not regard persons, when thou rebukest for transgressions. 4. Thou shalt not be double-minded, whether it shall be or not. 5. Be not one that holdeth out his hands to receive and shutteth them for giving. 6. If thou have aught in thy hands, thou shalt give a ransom for thy sins. 7. Thou shalt not doubt to give, nor shalt thou murmur when thou givest: for thou shalt know who is the good requiter of the reward. 8. Thou shalt not turn away from him that hath need, but shalt share all things with thy brother, and shalt not say that aught is thine own: for, if ye are partners in the eternal, how much more are ye partners in the perishable? 9. Thou shalt not remove thy hand from thy son, or from thy daughter, but from youth up shalt teach them the fear of God. 10. Thou shalt not command thy servant or thy handmaiden, who hope on the same God, in thy bitterness, lest they fear not the God who is over both: for he cometh not to call according to respect of persons, but on those whom the Spirit prepared. 11. And ye, servants, shall be subject to your masters, as to a type of God, in modesty and fear. 12. Thou shalt hate all hypocrisy, and all that is not pleasing to the Lord. 13. Thou shalt not forsake the commandments of the Lord, but shalt keep what thou didst receive, neither adding thereto nor taking aught away. 14. Thou shalt confess thy transgressions in church, and shalt not come to thy prayer in an evil conscience. This is the Way of Life.

V. 1. But the Way of Death is this: first of all it is wicked and full of curse: murders, adulteries, lusts, fornications, thefts, idolatries, witchcrafts, sorceries, ravenings, false witnesses, hypocrisies, a double heart, guile, arrogance, malice, self-will, covetousness, filthy talking, jealousy, boldness, pride, boasting. 2. Persecutors of good men, haters of truth, loving a lie, not knowing the recompense of righteousness, not cleaving to good, nor to just judgment, watching not for that which is good, but for that which is evil: from whom meekness is far off and patience, loving vanity, hunting after reward, not pitying the poor man, not sorrowing over him that is weighed down by sorrow, knowing not him that made them, murderers of children, destroyers of God's handiwork, turning aside from him that hath need, grinding down the afflicted, advocates of the rich, unjust judges of the poor, steeped in sin. May ye be delivered, my children, from all these.

VI. 1. See that no man lead thee astray from this Way of the doctrine, for he teacheth thee without God. 2. For, if thou canst bear the whole yoke of the Lord, thou shalt be perfect; but, if thou canst not, do what thou canst. 3. And as regards eating, bear what thou canst, but of meat offered to idols beware thou diligently: for it is a worship of dead gods.

VII. 1. And concerning baptism, baptize ye thus. Having first declared all these things, baptize in the name of the Father, and of the Son, and of the Holy Ghost in living water. 2. But if thou have not living water, baptize into other water; and, if thou canst not in cold, in warm. 3. But if thou have neither, pour water thrice upon the head in the name of Father, Son, and Holy Ghost. 4. And before the baptism let the baptizer and him that is baptized fast, and such others as can: and thou shalt enjoin the baptized to fast for one or two days before.

VIII. 1. And let not your fasts be with the hypocrites: for they fast on the second and fifth days of the week: but do ye fast on the fourth and on Friday. 2. Neither pray ye as do the hypocrites, but as the Lord commanded in His gospel, so pray ye. Our Father which art in heaven, hallowed be thy name, thy kingdom come, thy will be done on earth, as it is in heaven. Give us this day our daily bread, and forgive us our debt, as we also forgive our debtors, and lead us not into temptation, but deliver us from evil. For thine is the power and the glory for ever. 3. Thrice in the day pray ye thus.

IX. 1. And as regards the Eucharist, give thanks in this manner. 2. First for the cup. We thank thee, our Father, for the holy vine of David, thy servant, which thou didst make known to us through Jesus, thy servant. Glory be to thee for ever. 3. And for the broken bread. We thank thee, our Father, for the life and knowledge which thou didst make known to us through Jesus, thy servant. Glory be to thee for ever. 4. As this bread that is broken was scattered upon the mountains, and gathered together, and became one, so let thy Church be gathered together from the ends of the earth into thy kingdom: for thine is the glory and the power through Jesus Christ for ever. 5. And let none eat nor drink of your Eucharist, but they that are baptized into the name of the Lord; for as touching this the Lord hath said: Give not that which is holy to the dogs.

X. 1. And, after ye are filled, give thanks thus. We thank thee, Holy Father, for thy holy name, which thou hast made to dwell in our hearts, and for the knowledge, faith, and immortality, which thou didst make known to us through Jesus, thy servant. Glory be to thee for ever. 3. Thou, Almighty Lord, didst create all things for thy name's sake, and gavest meat and drink for men to enjoy, that they might give thanks unto thee, and to us didst vouchsafe spiritual meat and drink and life eternal, through thy servant. 4. Above all we thank thee because thou art mighty. Glory be to thee for ever. 5. Remember, Lord, thy Church, to deliver her from all evil, and to perfect her in thy love, and gather together from the four winds her that is sanctified into thy kingdom which thou didst prepare for her. For thine is the power and the glory for ever. 6. Come grace, and let this world pass away. Hosanna to the God of David. If any is holy, let him come: if any is unholy let him repent. Maranatha. Amen. 7. But suffer the prophets to give thanks as much as they will.

XI. 1. Whosoever then shall come and teach you all these things aforesaid, receive him. 2. But, if the teacher himself turn and teach another doctrine to pervert, hear him not. But unto the increase of righteousness and of the knowledge of the Lord, receive him as the Lord. 3. And as touching the apostles and prophets, according to the decree of the gospel, so do ye. 4. But let every apostle that cometh unto you be received as the Lord. 5. And he shall stay one day, and, if need be, the next also, but, if he stay three, he is a false prophet. 6. And, when the apostle goeth forth, let him take nothing save bread, till he reach his lodging, but if he asks money, he is a false prophet. 7. And every prophet that speaketh in the spirit ye shall not try nor judge: for every sin shall be forgiven, but this sin shall not be forgiven. 8. But not every one that speaketh in the spirit is a prophet, but if he have the manners of the Lord. By their manners then shall the false prophet and the prophet be known. 9. And no prophet that † orders † a table in the spirit shall eat of it, else is he a false prophet. 10. And every prophet that teacheth the truth if he doeth not what he teacheth is a false prophet. 11. But every approved true prophet, who † doeth for an earthly mystery of the church,† but teacheth not others to do what he himself doeth, shall not be judged among you, for he hath his judgment with God: for even so did the ancient prophets also. 12. But whosoever shall say in the spirit: Give me money, or any other thing, ye shall not hearken to him: but, if he bid you give for others that are in need, let no man judge him.

XII. 1. Let every one that cometh in the name of the Lord be received, and then, when ye have proved him, ye shall know, for ye shall have understanding [to distinguish] between the right hand and the left. 2. If he that cometh is a passer-by, succour him as far as ye can; but he shall not abide with you longer than two or three days unless there be necessity. 3. But if he be minded to settle among you, and be a craftsman, let him work and eat. 4. But, if he hath no trade, according to your understanding provide that he shall not live idle among you, being a Christian. 5. But, if he will not do this, he is a Christmonger: of such men beware.

XIII. 1. But every true prophet, who is minded to settle among you, is worthy of his maintenance. 2. In like manner a true teacher also is worthy, like every workman, of his maintenance. 3. Thou shalt take, therefore, all first fruits of the produce of winepress and threshing floor, of oxen and sheep, and give them to the prophets; for they are your high priests. 4. But if ye have no prophet, give to the poor. 5. If thou art making bread, take the first fruits and give according to the commandment. 6. In like manner, when thou openest a jar of wine or oil, take the first fruits and give to the prophets. 7. And of money, and raiment, and of every chattel, take the first fruits, as seemeth thee good, and give according to the commandment.

XIV. 1. And on the Lord's day of the Lord come together and break bread and give thanks, having † first † confessed your transgressions, that our sacrifice may be pure. 2. But whoso hath a dispute with his fellow, let him not come together with you, until they be reconciled, that our sacrifice be not polluted. 3. For this is that which was spoken of by the Lord. In every place and time offer me a pure sacrifice: for I am a great King, saith the Lord, and my name is wonderful among the Gentiles.

XV. 1. Elect therefore for yourselves bishops and deacons worthy of the Lord, men meek and not covetous, and true and approved: for they also minister unto you the ministry of the prophets and teachers. 2. Therefore despise them not: for these are they which are honoured of you with the prophets and teachers. 3. And reprove one another, not in wrath but in peace, as ye have it in the gospel: and to him that behaveth amiss against another let no man speak, neither let him hear a word from you, until he repent. 4. But your prayers and alms and all that ye do, do so as ye have it in the gospel of our Lord.

XVI. 1. Watch over your life: let not your lamps be extinguished, neither let your loins be ungirt, but be ye ready: for ye know not the hour in which our Lord doth come. 2. But ye shall be frequently gathered together, seeking the things that belong unto your souls. For the whole time of your faith shall not profit you, except ye be perfected in the last time. 3. For in the last days false prophets and corrupters shall abound, and the sheep shall be turned into wolves, and love shall be turned into hate. 4. For, as lawlessness increases, they shall hate and persecute and deliver up one another; and then shall appear the World-deceiver as son of God, and shall do signs and wonders, and the earth shall be delivered up into his hands, and he shall commit iniquities which have never been seen from the beginning. 5. Then shall the race of man come into the fiery trial of testing, and many shall be offended and perish, but they who endure in their faith shall be saved by the Curse himself. 6. And then shall appear the signs of the truth: first a sign of spreading out in heaven, then a sign of the sound of the trumpet, and the third the resurrection of the dead. 7. But not of all, but as it was said: The Lord shall come and all the saints with Him. 8. Then shall the world behold the Lord coming on the clouds of heaven.
—C. Bigg, *The Doctrine of the Twelve Apostles*, 45–76, in *Early Church Classics*. S.P.C.K. 1898.

No. 14.—The Christians in Bithynia, *c.* 112

Pliny [62–†113] to Trajan (Pliny, *Epp.* X. xcvi.).

[§ 1] It is my custom, Sire, to refer to you in all cases where I do not feel sure, for who can better direct my doubts or inform my ignorance? I have never been present at any legal examination of the Christians, and I do not know, therefore, what are the usual penalties passed upon them, or the limits of those penalties, or how searching an inquiry should be made. [§ 2] I have hesitated a great deal in considering whether any distinctions should be drawn according to the ages of the accused; whether the weak should be punished as severely as the more robust; whether if they renounce their faith they should be pardoned, or whether the man who has once been a Christian should gain nothing by recanting; whether the name itself, even though otherwise innocent of crime, should be punished, or only the crimes that gather round it.

In the meantime, this is the plan which I have adopted in the case of those Christians who have been brought before me. [§ 3] I ask them whether they are Christians; if they say yes, then I repeat the question a second time and a third time, warning them of the penalties it entails, and if they still persist, I order them to be taken away to prison. For I do not doubt, that whatever the character of the crime may be which they confess, their pertinacity and inflexible obstinacy certainly ought to be punished. [§ 4] There were others who showed similar mad folly whom I reserved to be sent to Rome, as they were Roman citizens. Subsequently, as is usually the way, the very fact of my taking up this question led to a great increase of accusations, and a variety of cases were brought before me. [§ 5] A pamphlet was issued anonymously, containing the names of a number of people. Those who denied that they were or had been Christians and called upon the gods in the usual formula, reciting the words after me, those who offered incense and wine before your image, which I had given orders to be brought forward for this purpose, together with the statues of the deities—all such I considered should be discharged, especially as they cursed the name of Christ, which, it is said, those who are really Christians cannot be induced to do. [§ 6] Others, whose names were given me by an informer, first said that they were Christians and afterwards denied it, declaring that they had been but were so no longer, some of them having recanted many years before, and more than one so long as twenty years back. They all worshipped your image and the statues of the deities, and cursed the name of Christ. [§ 7] But they declared that the sum of their guilt or their error only amounted to this, that on a stated day they had been accustomed to meet before daybreak and to recite a hymn among themselves to Christ, as though he were a god, and that so far from binding themselves by oath to commit any crime, their oath was to abstain from theft, robbery, adultery, and from breach of faith, and not to deny trust-money placed in their keeping when called upon to deliver it. When this ceremony was concluded, it had been their custom to depart and meet again to take food; but it was of no special character and quite harmless, and they had ceased this practice after the edict in which, in accordance with your orders, I had forbidden all secret societies. [§ 8] I thought it the more necessary, therefore, to find out what truth there was in these statements by submitting two women, who were called deaconesses, to the torture, but I found nothing but a debased superstition carried to great lengths. So I postponed my examination, and immediately consulted you. [§ 9] The matter seems to me worthy of your consideration, especially as there are so many people involved in the danger. Many persons of all ages and of both sexes alike are being brought into peril of their lives by their accusers, and the process will go on. For the contagion of this superstition has spread not only through the free cities, but into the villages and the rural districts, and yet it seems to me that it can be checked and set right. [§ 10] It is beyond doubt that the temples, which have been almost deserted, are beginning again to be thronged with worshippers, that the sacred rites which have for a long time been allowed to lapse are now being renewed, and that the food for the sacrificial victims is once more finding a sale, whereas, up to recently, a buyer was hardly to be found. From this it is easy to infer what vast numbers of people might be reclaimed if only they were given an opportunity of repentance.—J. B. Firth, *Letters of the Younger Pliny*, ii. 270–2.

No. 15.—Trajan's Policy towards the Christians

Trajan [98–†117] to Pliny (Pliny, *Epp.* X. xcvii.).

[§ 1] You have adopted the proper course, my dear Pliny, in examining into the cases of those who have been denounced to you as Christians, for no hard and fast rule can be laid down to meet a question of such wide extent. [§ 2] The Christians are not to be hunted out; if they are brought before you and the offence is proved, they are to be punished, but with this reservation—that if any one denies that he is a Christian and makes it clear that he is not, by offering prayers to our deities, then he is to be pardoned because of his recantation, however suspicious his past conduct may have been. But pamphlets published anonymously must not carry any weight whatever, no matter what the charge may be, for they are not only a precedent of the very worst type, but they are not in consonance with the spirit of our age.—*Ibid.* ii. 273.

No. 16.—The Person of Christ

From Ignatius, †*c.* 110–7, *Epistle to the Ephesians*, c. vii.

[§ 1] For some are wont, out of malicious cunning, to bear about with them the Name, while they practise certain other deeds unworthy of God. These you must needs avoid as wild beasts. For they are mad dogs, biting stealthily, against whom you must be on your guard, for their bite is hard to heal. [§ 2] There is one Physician, of flesh and of Spirit, originate and unoriginate, God in man, true Life in death, son of Mary and Son of God, first passible and then impassible, Jesus Christ our Lord.—J. H. Srawley, *Epistles of St. Ignatius*, i. 46 *sq.*

No. 17.—Judaism

From Ignatius, *Epistle to the Magnesians*, cc. viii., ix.

[§ 1] Be not deceived by strange doctrines nor by ancient fables, seeing that they are profitless. For if, until now, we live after the rule of Judaism, we confess that we have not received grace. [§ 2] For the divine prophets lived a life in accordance with Christ Jesus. For this cause too they were persecuted, being inspired by [His] grace, so that unbelievers might be fully convinced that there is One God, who manifested Himself through Jesus Christ His Son, who is His Word, coming forth from silence, who in all things did the good pleasure of Him that sent Him.

[§ 1] If therefore those who lived in ancient observances attained unto newness of hope, no longer keeping the Sabbath, but living a life ruled by the Lord's day, whereon our life too had its rising through Him and His death—[§ 2] which some deny, a mystery through which we have received the power to believe, and therefore we endure, that we may be found disciples of Jesus Christ, our only Teacher—how shall we be able to live apart from Him? For the prophets also became His disciples, and awaited in the spirit His coming to teach them. And therefore He, for whom they rightly waited, came and raised them from the dead—*Ibid.* i. 66–8.

No. 18.—Docetism

From Ignatius, *Epistle to the Trallians*, cc. ix., x.

[§ 1] Stop your ears then when any one speaks unto you apart from Jesus Christ, who is of the race of David, the child of Mary, who was truly born, and ate and drank, was truly persecuted under Pontius Pilate, was truly crucified and died, before the eyes of those in heaven and those on earth and those under the earth; [§ 2] who also was truly raised from the dead, since His Father raised Him up, who in like manner will also raise up us who believe on Him—even His Father will raise us in Christ Jesus, apart from whom we have not that life, which is life indeed.

[§ 1] But if it be, as some godless men, *i.e.* unbelievers, assert, that He suffered in phantom only—it is they that are phantoms—why am I in bonds? Why, moreover, do I pray that I may fight with the wild beasts? Then I die for naught. Then I lie against the Lord.—*Ibid.* i. 77 *sq.*

No. 19.—The Ministry and the Sacraments

From Ignatius, *Epistle to the Smyrnæans*, c. viii.

[§ 1] Avoid divisions, as the beginning of evil. Follow, all of you, the bishop, as Jesus Christ followed the Father; and follow the presbytery as the Apostles. Moreover, reverence the deacons as the commandment of God. Let no man do aught pertaining to the Church apart from the bishop. Let that eucharist be considered valid which is under the bishop or him to whom he commits it. [§ 2] Wheresoever the bishop appears, there let the people be, even as wheresoever Christ Jesus is, there is the Catholic Church. It is not lawful apart from the bishop either to baptize, or to hold a love-feast. But whatsoever he approves, that also is well-pleasing to God, that everything which you do may be secure and valid.—*Ibid.* ii. 40 *sq.*

No. 20.—St. Polycarp

From Polycarp (bishop of Smyrna, 110–†56), *Epistle to the Philippians*, *c.* 110–7.

Polycarp and the Presbyters that are with him to the Church of God that is sojourning at Philippi, mercy to you and peace from Almighty God and Jesus Christ our Saviour "be multiplied" (1 Pet. i. 2; 2 Pet. i. 2; Jude 2).

I. I rejoiced greatly with you in our Lord Jesus Christ on your receiving the copies of the true Love, and escorting on their way, as it fell to your lot to do, the men enwrapped in their chains, seemly ornament of Saints, in that they are diadems of them that are truly chosen by God and by our Lord: and because the firm root of your faith, proclaimed from times of old, abides unto this present time, and "brings forth fruit" (Col. 1. 6) unto our Lord Jesus Christ, Who endured to come so far as to death for our sins, Whom God raised, "having loosed the pains of death" (Acts ii. 24), in "whom, not having seen, ye" trust "with joy unspeakable and full of glory" (1 Pet. i. 8). Into this joy many long to enter, knowing that "by grace ye are saved," "not of works" (Eph. ii. 5, 8, 9), but by God's will through Jesus Christ.

II. Therefore "gird up" your "loins" (1 Pet. i. 13 (and

"serve" God "in fear" (Ps. ii. 11) and truth; leave the vain talking and the error of the many; "trust in God Who raised" our Lord Jesus Christ "from the dead, and gave Him glory" (1 Pet. i. 21) and a Throne on His right hand; to Whom were subjected all things in heaven and on earth; Whom "everything that hath breath" (Ps. cl. 6) serves; Who is coming as "Judge of quick and dead" (Acts x. 42); Whose blood God will require of them that disobey Him. But He that raised Him from the dead will raise us also, if we do His will and walk in His commandments, and love what He loved, holding off from all unrighteousness, covetousness, love of money, backbiting, false witness, "not rendering evil for evil or railing for railing" (1 Pet. iii. 9), or cuff for cuff, or curse for curse, remembering what the Lord said, teaching "Judge not, that ye be not judged" (Matt. vii. 1); forgive and it shall be forgiven unto you; be ye merciful, that ye be shown mercy; "With what measure ye mete it shall be measured to you again" (Matt. vii. 2); and "Blessed are the poor" (Matt. v. 3) and they that are being "persecuted for righteousness' sake, for theirs is the kingdom of God" (Matt. v. 10).

III. Not, brethren, in concession to my own inclination, but because you challenged me, am I writing to you concerning righteousness. For neither have I nor has any other like me ability to follow hard on the wisdom of the blessed and glorious Paul, who, when he had come among you, in the presence of them of that time, taught accurately and constantly the word of truth and, when absent, wrote to you letters, into which if you examine carefully you will be enabled to be built up into the faith given to you, "which is the Mother of us all" (Gal. iv. 26), with hope following after, and love towards God and Christ and our neighbour going before. For if any one be surrounded by, and occupied in these, he hath fulfilled (Rom. xiii. 8 and Gal. v. 14) the commandment of righteousness. For he that hath love is far from all sin.

IV. Now love of money is the beginning of all difficulties. Knowing then that "we brought nothing into the world" and "neither can we carry anything out" (1 Tim. vi. 7), let us arm ourselves with "the arms of righteousness" (2 Cor. vi. 7), and teach ourselves first to walk in the commandment of the Lord; next also your wives, in the faith given unto them, and in love and in chastity, cherishing their own husbands in all truth, and loving all men alike in all continency, to train up their children too in the training of the fear of the Lord. [Let us teach] the widows too to be temperate concerning the faith of the Lord, making supplication unceasingly for all, being far removed from all calumny, backbiting, false witness, love of money, and every evil; knowing that they are God's Altar, and that all things are examined to see if there be blemish in them, and that there is hid from Him nor thought nor intention nor any of "the secrets of our heart" (1 Cor. xiv. 25).

V. Knowing then that "God is not mocked" (Gal. vi. 7), we ought to walk worthily of His commandment and glory. In like manner should the deacons be blameless before His righteousness, as deacons of God and Christ, and not of men; not slanderers, not double-tongued, not lovers of money, continent in all things, tender-hearted, careful, walking according to the truth of the Lord, Who was made "deacon" of all. To Him if we be well pleasing in this present world we shall also receive as our reward the world to come, in accordance with His promise to us to raise us from the dead, and because, if our conversation be worthy of Him, "we shall also reign with Him" (2 Tim. ii. 12), if indeed we believe. In like manner let the younger men be blameless in all things, above everything taking heed for purity, bridling themselves from every evil. For it is good to be checked from following the lusts in the world, for every lust warreth against the Spirit, and "neither fornicators nor effeminate, nor abusers of themselves with mankind shall inherit the kingdom of God" (1 Cor. vi. 9, 10), nor they that do iniquity. Wherefore they are bound to abstain from all these things, being subject to the presbyters and deacons as to God and Christ. And the virgins must walk in a blameless and pure conscience.

VI. And that the presbyters be tender-hearted, compassionate to all, turning homeward the strayed sheep, visiting all that are sick, not neglecting widow or orphan or poor man, but providing ever what is good before God and man, abstaining from all wrath, respect of persons, unjust judgment, being far removed from all love of money, not quickly believing anything against any one, not hasty in judgment, knowing that we are all debtors of sin. If then we ask of the Lord to forgive us, we ought also to forgive. For we are before the eyes of the Lord and God, and we must "all stand before the judgment seat of Christ" (Rom. xiv. 10), and give each an account for himself. Thus then let us serve Him with fear and reverence as He Himself charged us, and the Apostles who evangelized us and the prophets who preached beforehand the coming of our Lord, zealous for what is good, abstaining from things which make to offend, and from false brethren and from them that bear the name of the Lord in hypocrisy, who make vain men to err.

VII. "For every one that confesseth not that Jesus Christ is come in the flesh is anti-Christ" (1 John iv. 3). And whosoever confesseth not the witness of the Cross is of the devil, and whosoever perverts the oracles of the Lord to his own lusts, and says that there is neither resurrection nor judgment, this man is the first begotten of Satan. Wherefore let us leave the vanity of the many, and their false teaching, and let us turn to the word delivered to us from the beginning, "watching unto prayer" (1 Pet. iv. 7), continuing in fastings, in supplications asking the all-seeing God not to "lead us into temptation" (Matt. vi. 13; Luke xi. 4), as the Lord said, "The Spirit indeed is willing, but the flesh is weak" (Matt. xxvi. 41 and Mark xiv. 38).

VIII. Unfailingly then let us continue in our hope, and in the pledge of our righteousness, which is Christ Jesus, "Who bare our sins in His own body on the tree" (1 Pet. ii. 24), "Who did no sin, neither was guile found in His mouth" (1 Pet. ii. 22), but on our account, that we may live in Him Who endured all things. Let us then become imitators of His patience, and if we be suffering on account of His name, let us glorify Him. For this example He appointed for us through Himself, and this was the profession of our faith.

IX. I therefore call on you all to obey the "word of righteousness" (Heb. v. 13) and to practise all patience. This patience you saw face to face not only in the blessed Ignatius and Zosimus and Rufus, but also in others of your own folk, and in Paul himself and the rest of the Apostles.

I call upon you as men persuaded that these did not "run in vain" (Phil. ii. 16) but in faith and righteousness, and that they are in the place due to them by the side of the Lord, Whose sufferings they shared. For they did not "love this present world" (2 Tim. iv. 10), but Him Who on our behalf died, and on our account by God was raised.

X. In these things then stand, following the example of the Lord, "steadfast" (1 Cor. xv. 58) in the faith and "unmovable," "kindly affectioned one to another with brotherly love" (Rom. xii. 10), partners in the truth, forestalling one another in the gentleness of the Lord, despising no one. While you are able to do good put it not off, because "Almsgiving delivereth from death" (Tobit iv. 10; xii. 9). "All of you be subject one to another" (1 Pet. v. 5), "having your conversation" blameless "among the Gentiles, in order that from your good works" (1 Pet. ii. 12) both you may receive praise, and your Lord may not be blasphemed in you. But woe unto him by whom the name of the Lord is blasphemed. Teach therefore all men temperance, in which you yourselves have your conversation.

XI. I have been much distressed for Valens, who was once upon a time made a Presbyter among you, that he should be so ignorant of the place assigned him. I exhort you therefore that ye abstain from covetousness, and that ye be chaste and true. "Abstain from every evil" (1 Thess. v. 22). How can he who is not able to rule himself in these things preach this to another? If any man have not abstained from covetousness he shall be defiled by idolatry and judged among the Gentiles, who have not known the judgment of the Lord, or do we not know that "the saints shall judge the world" (1 Cor. vi. 2), as Paul teacheth? Not that I have perceived or heard of anything of this kind in you among whom the blessed Paul laboured and who were in the beginning his "epistles" (2 Cor. iii. 2). Concerning you he boasts in all the Churches which alone in those days had known the Lord: for we had not yet known Him. Deeply, brethren, am I grieved for him and for his wife. The Lord grant them genuine repentance. Be ye too, therefore, moderate in this matter, and "count not" folk of this sort as "enemies" (2 Thess. iii. 15), but call them back as weak and wandering members, that you may keep whole the body of you all, for thus doing ye edify yourselves.

XII. For I am assured that you are well trained in the Holy Scriptures, and that nothing has escaped your attention. This has not been granted to me. Only, as is said in these Scriptures, "Be ye angry and sin not" (Ps. iv. 4, LXX), and "Let not the sun go down on your wrath" (Eph. iv. 26).

Happy is he who remembers, as I believe you do. But God and the Father of our Lord Jesus Christ and the Eternal High Priest Himself, Jesus Christ the Son of God, edify you in faith and truth and in all gentleness and meekness; in forbearance, in long-suffering, in patience, in purity; may He grant you part and lot among His Saints, and to us with you, and to all under heaven which are ordained to believe in our Lord and God Jesus Christ, and in His Father "who raised Him from the dead" (Gal. i. 1; Col. ii. 12). "Pray for all Saints" (Eph. vi. 18). Pray also for kings and for powers and rulers, and "for them that persecute" and "hate you" (Matt. v. 44), and for the "enemies of the Cross" (Phil. iii. 18), that your fruit may be manifest in all, that ye may be perfect in Him.

XIII. Both you and Ignatius have written to me that, if any one go to Syria, he is to convey the letter also from you. I shall carry out your wish, if I find a favourable opportunity; whether I go myself, or find some one to act the envoy also for you. The letters of Ignatius sent to us by him, and all the rest which we had by us, we have sent to you, as you enjoined. They are attached to this letter. From them you will be able to be greatly benefited, for they embrace faith, patience, and every kind of edification which regards our Lord. If ye have any more certain knowledge concerning Ignatius himself, and those with him, inform us.

XIV. This letter I have written you by Crescens, whom I but now commended to you, and am still commending; for his conversation with us was blameless, and so I believe was his conversation with you. His sister you shall have commended to you when she comes to you.

Fare ye well in the Lord Jesus Christ, in grace, with all yours. Amen.—B. Jackson, *St. Polycarp*, 28–48. S.P.C.K.

No. 21.—The Trial of Pomponia Graecina, 57

From Tacitus, *Annales* [116–7], XIII. xxxii. §§ 3–5.

Pomponia Graecina, a distinguished lady, wife of the Plautius who returned from Britain[1] with an ovation, was accused of some foreign superstition and handed over to her husband's judicial decision. Following ancient precedent, he heard his wife's cause in the presence of kinsfolk, involving, as it did, her legal status and character, and he reported that she was innocent. This Pomponia lived a long life of unbroken melancholy. After the murder of Julia, Drusus's daughter,[2] by Messalina's treachery, for forty years[3] she wore only the attire of a mourner, with a heart ever sorrowful. For this, during Claudius's reign, she escaped unpunished, and it was afterwards counted a glory to her.—A. J. Church and W. J. Brodribb, *The Annals of Tacitus*, 242.

No. 22.—The Neronian Persecution, 64

From Tacitus, *Annales*, XV. xliv.

But all human efforts, all the lavish gifts of the emperor, and the propitiations of the gods, did not banish the sinister belief that the conflagration was the result of an order. Consequently, to get rid of the report, Nero fastened the guilt and inflicted the most exquisite tortures on a class hated for their abominations, called Christians by the populace. Christus, from whom the name had its origin, suffered the extreme penalty during the reign of Tiberius at the hands of one of our procurators, Pontius Pilatus, and a most mischievous superstition thus checked for the moment, again broke out not only in Judæa, the first source of the evil, but even in Rome, where all things hideous and shameful from every part of the world find their centre and become popular. Accordingly, an arrest was first made of all who pleaded guilty; then, upon their information, an immense multitude was convicted, not so

[1] Aulus Plautius conquered Britain in A.D. 43.

[2] She married Rubellius Blandus, Tac., *Ann.* VI. xxvii. 1, and died, according to Suetonius, *Vita Claudii*, xxix. § 1, in A.D. 42.

[3] Pomponia therefore died in A.D. 82.

much of the crime of firing the city, as of hatred against mankind. Mockery of every sort was added to their deaths. Covered with the skins of beasts, they were torn by dogs and perished, or were nailed to crosses, or were doomed to the flames and burnt, to serve as a nightly illumination when daylight had expired. Nero offered his gardens for the spectacle, and was exhibiting a show in the circus, while he mingled with the people in the dress of a charioteer or stood aloft on a car. Hence, even for criminals who deserve extreme and exemplary punishment, there arose a feeling of compassion; for it was not, as it seemed, for the public good, but to glut one man's cruelty, that they were being destroyed.—*Ibid.* 304 *sq.*

No. 23.—Docetism

From *The Gospel according to Peter* [*c.* 120], §§ 4, 5

[§ 4] And they brought two malefactors, and they crucified the Lord between them. But he held his peace, as though having no pain. And when they had raised the cross, they wrote the title: This is the King of Israel. And having set his garments before him, they parted them among them and cast lots for them. And one of these malefactors reproached them, saying: We, for the evils that we have done, have suffered thus; but this man, who hath become the Saviour of men, what wrong hath he done to you? And they, being angered at him, commanded that his legs should not be broken, that he might die in torment.

[§ 5] And it was noon, and darkness came over all Judæa. And they were troubled and distressed, lest the sun had set, whilst he was yet alive: [for] it is written for them that the sun set not on him that hath been put to death. And one of them said, Give him to drink gall with vinegar. And they mixed and gave him drink, and fulfilled all things, and accomplished their sins against their own head. And many went about with lamps, supposing that it was night, and fell down. And the Lord cried out, saying: My power, my power, thou hast forsaken me. And when he had said it, he was taken up. And in that hour the vail of the temple of Jerusalem was rent in twain.—*A.-N.C.L.*, additional volume, ed. A. Menzies, p. 7.

No. 24.—Apology of Quadratus, 125

From Quadratus, *Apology to Hadrian*.

But the works of our Saviour were always present, for they were genuine: those that were healed, and those that were raised from the dead, who were seen not only when they were healed and when they were raised, but were always present; and not merely while the Saviour was on earth, but also after His death, they were alive for a long time, so that some of them lived even to our day.—Eus., *H.E.* IV. iii. 2, in *N.* & *P.-N.F.* i. 175 (slightly altered).

No. 25.—The *Rescript* of Hadrian to Caius Minucius Fundanus, Proconsul of Asia, *c.* 125

From the original as given by Tyrannius Rufinus, 345–†410, in his translation of Eus., *H.E.* IV. ix.

[§ 1] I received the letter written to me by your predecessor, the most illustrious Serenius Granianus, and it is not my pleasure to pass by without enquiry the matter referred to me, lest both the inoffensive should be disturbed, and an opportunity afforded to slanderous informers of practising their vile traffic. [§ 2] Now, if our subjects of the Provinces are able to sustain by evidence this their demand against the Christians, so as to answer before a Court of Justice, I have no objection to their taking this course. But to mere clamorous demands and outcries for this purpose, I do not allow them to have recourse. For it is much more equitable, if any one wishes to accuse them, for you to take cognizance of the matters laid to their charge. [§ 3] If therefore any one accuses and proves that the aforesaid men do anything contrary to the laws, you will also determine their punishments in accordance with their offences. As on the other hand, by Hercules, have an especial regard; that if any one demand a writ of accusation against any of these Christians, merely for the sake of libelling them as such, you proceed against that man with heavier penalties, in proportion to his heinous guilt.—*L.F.* xl. 53.

26.—The Apology of Aristides, 125

From Aristides, *The History of Barlaam and Josaphat* [in Greek], cc. xv., xvi.

[c. xv.] Now the Christians trace their origin from the Lord Jesus Christ. And He is acknowledged by the Holy Spirit to be the Son of the Most High God, who came down from heaven for the salvation of men. And being born of a pure virgin, unbegotten and immaculate, He assumed flesh and revealed Himself among men that He might recall them to Himself from their wandering after many gods. And having accomplished His wonderful dispensation, by a voluntary choice He tasted death on the Cross, fulfilling an august dispensation. And after three days He came to life again, and ascended into heaven. And if you would read, O King,[1] you may judge the glory of His presence from the holy Gospel writing, as it is called among themselves. He had twelve disciples who, after His ascension to heaven, went forth into the provinces of the whole world, and declared His greatness. As for instance one of them traversed the countries about us, proclaiming the doctrine of the truth. From this it is, that they who still observe the righteousness enjoined by their preaching are called Christians.

And these are they who more than all the nations on the earth have found the truth. For they know God, the Creator and Fashioner of all things through the only-begotten Son and the Holy Spirit; and beside Him they worship no other God. They have the commands of the Lord Jesus Christ Himself graven upon their hearts; and they observe them, looking forward to the resurrection of the

[1] The King, in *The Romance of Barlaam and Josaphat* (Joasaph), is an Indian prince, Abenner, the father of Josaphat: in the original *Apology*, the Emperor Hadrian. The speaker, in the *Romance*, Barlaam, personated by Nachor: but, originally, the author, Aristides: Eus., *H.E.* IV. iii. 3.

dead and life in the world to come. They do not commit adultery nor fornication, nor bear false witness, nor covet the things of others; they honour father and mother, and love their neighbours; they judge justly, and they never do to others what they would not wish to happen to themselves; they appeal to those who injure them, and try to win them as friends; they are eager to do good to their enemies; they are gentle and easy to be entreated; they abstain from all unlawful conversation and from all impurity; they despise not the widow, nor oppress the orphan; and he that has, gives ungrudgingly for the maintenance of him who has not.

If they see a stranger, they take him under their roof, and rejoice over him as over a very brother; for they call themselves brethren not after the flesh but after the Spirit.

And they are ready to sacrifice their lives for the sake of Christ; for they observe His commandments without swerving, and live holy and just lives, as the Lord God enjoined upon them.

And they give thanks unto Him every hour, for all meat and drink and other blessings.

[c. xvi.] Verily then this is the Way of the truth which leads those who travel therein to the everlasting kingdom promised through Christ in the life to come. And that you may know, O King, that in saying these things I do not speak at my own instance, if you deign to look into the writings of the Christians, you will find that I state nothing beyond the truth. Rightly then did thy son[1] apprehend, and justly was he taught to serve the living God and to be saved for the age that is destined to come upon us. For great and wonderful are the sayings and deeds of the Christians; for they speak not the words of men but those of God. But the rest of the nations go astray and deceive themselves; for they walk in darkness and bruise themselves like drunken men.—W. D. M. Kay, in *A.-N.C.L.*, additional volume, ed. A. Menzies, 276 *sqq.*

[1] Josaphat, the son of King Abenner. He was converted by the monk Barlaam.

No. 27.—The Traditions of the Elders

From Papias, *Expositions of Oracles of the Lord* [c. 130], in Eus., *H.E.* III. xxxix. §§ 3, 4, 15, 16.

[§ 3] But I will not scruple also to give a place for you along with my interpretations to everything that I learnt carefully and remembered carefully in time past from the elders, guaranteeing its truth. For, unlike the many, I did not take pleasure in those who have so very much to say, but in those who teach the truth; nor in those who relate foreign commandments, but in those (who record) such as were given from the Lord to the Faith, and are derived from the Truth itself. [§ 4] And again, on any occasion when a person came (in my way) who had been a follower of the Elders, I would enquire about the discourses of the Elders—what was said by Andrew, or by Peter, or by Philip, or by Thomas or James, or by John or Matthew or any other of the Lord's disciples, and what Aristion and the Elder John, the disciples of the Lord, say. For I did not think that I could get so much profit from the contents of books as from the utterances of a living and abiding voice.

[§ 15] And the Elder said this also: Mark, having become the interpreter of Peter, wrote down accurately everything that he remembered, without, however, recording in order what was either said or done by Christ. For neither did he hear the Lord nor did he follow Him; but afterwards, as I said, (attended) Peter, who adapted his instructions to the needs (of his hearers), but had no design of giving a connected account of the Lord's oracles. So then Mark made no mistake, while he thus wrote down some things as he remembered them; for he made it his one care not to omit anything that he heard, or to set down any false statement therein.

[§ 16] So then Matthew composed the oracles in the Hebrew language, and each one interpreted them as he could.—J. B. Lightfoot, *The Apostolic Fathers* (Abridged Edition), 527 *sq.*

No. 28.—Millenarianism of Papias, as seen in Fragments Preserved by Irenæus

From Irenæus, *Adv. Hær.* (α) V. xxxiii. §§ 3, 4; (β) xxxvi. §§ 1, 2.

(α) The days will come in which vines shall grow, each having ten thousand shoots, and on each shoot ten thousand branches, and on each branch again ten thousand twigs, and on each twig ten thousand clusters, and on each cluster ten thousand grapes, and each grape when pressed shall yield five-and-twenty measures of wine. And when any of the saints shall have taken hold of one of their clusters, another shall cry, I am a better cluster; take me, bless the Lord through me. Likewise also a grain of wheat shall produce ten thousand heads, and every head shall have ten thousand grains, and every grain ten pounds of fine flour, bright and clean, and the other fruits, seeds, and the grass shall produce in similar proportions, and all the animals, using these fruits which are products of the soil, shall become, in their turn, peaceable and harmonious, obedient to man in all subjection. . . . But these things are credible to them that believe. And when Judas the traitor did not believe, and asked, How shall such growths be accomplished by the Lord? he relates that the Lord said, They shall see, who shall come to these (times).

(β) As the Elders say, then also shall they which have been deemed worthy of the abode in heaven go thither, while others shall enjoy the delight of paradise, and others again shall possess the brightness of the city; for in every place the Saviour shall be seen, according as they shall be worthy who see Him. They say moreover that this is the distinction between the habitation of them that bring forth a hundred-fold, and them that bring forth sixty-fold, and them that bring forth thirty-fold; of whom the first shall be taken up into the heavens, and the second shall dwell in paradise, and the third shall inhabit the city; and that therefore our Lord has said, *In my Father's abode are many mansions;* for all things are of God, who giveth to all their appropriate dwelling.—*Ibid.* 527 *sq.*, 529, 533, 562.

No. 29.—Christian Life in the Second Century

From *The Epistle to Diognetus* [*c.* 140], cc. v., vi., vii.

V. For Christians are not distinguished from the rest of mankind by country, or by speech, or by customs. 2. For they do not dwell in cities of their own, or use a different language, or practise a peculiar life. 3. This knowledge of theirs has not been discovered by the thought and effort of inquisitive men; they are not champions of a human doctrine, as some men are. 4. But while they dwell in Greek or barbarian cities according as each man's lot was cast, and follow the customs of the land in clothing and food, and other matters of daily life, yet the condition of citizenship which they exhibit is wonderful, and admittedly beyond all expectation. 5. They live in countries of their own, but simply as sojourners; they share the life of citizens, they endure the lot of foreigners; every foreign land is to them a fatherland, and every fatherland a foreign land. 6. They marry like the rest of the world, they beget children, but they do not cast their offspring adrift. 7. They have a common table, but not a common bed. 8. They exist in the flesh, but they live not after the flesh. 9. They spend their existence upon earth, but their citizenship is in heaven. 10. They obey the established laws, but in their own lives they surpass the laws. 11. They love all men, and are persecuted by all. 12. They are unknown, and yet they are condemned; they are put to death, and yet they give proof of new life. 13. They are poor, and yet make many rich; they lack everything, and yet in everything they abound. 14. They are dishonoured, and their dishonour becomes their glory; they are reviled, and yet are vindicated. 15. They are abused, and they bless; they are insulted, and repay insult with honour. 16. They do good, and are punished as evil-doers; and in their punishment they rejoice as finding new life therein. 17. The Jews war against them as aliens; the Greeks persecute them; and yet they that hate them can state no ground for their enmity.

VI. In a word, what the soul is in the body Christians are in the world. 2. The soul is spread through all the members of the body; so are Christians through all the cities of the world. 3. The soul dwells in the body, and yet it is not of the body; so Christians dwell in the world, and yet they are not of the world. 4. The soul, itself invisible, is detained in a body which is visible; so Christians are recognized as being in the world, but their religious life remains invisible. 5. The flesh hates the soul, and fights against it, though suffering no wrong, because it is prevented by the soul from indulging in its pleasures; so too the world, though suffering no wrong, hates the Christians because they set themselves against its pleasures. 6. The soul loves the flesh that hates it, and the members thereof; so Christians love them that hate them. 7. The soul is enclosed within the body, and itself holds the body together; so too Christians are held fast in the world as in a prison, and yet it is they who hold the world together. 8. Immortal itself, the soul abides in a mortal tenement; Christians dwell for a time amid corruptible things, awaiting their incorruption in heaven. 9. The soul when it is stinted of food and drink thrives the better; so Christians when they are punished increase daily all the more. 10. So great is the position to which God has appointed them, and which it is not lawful for them to refuse.

VII. For this is no earthly discovery, as I said, which was delivered into their charge; it is no mortal idea which they regard themselves bound so diligently to guard; it is no stewardship of merely human mysteries with which they have been entrusted. 2. But God Himself in very truth, the almighty and all-creating and invisible God, Himself from heaven planted among men and established in their hearts the Truth and the Word, the holy, incomprehensible Word, sending to men not a servant, as one might imagine, or an angel or ruler, or one of those who administer earthly things, or of those who have been entrusted with the ordering of things in heaven, but the very Artificer and Creator of the universe Himself, by whom He made the heavens, by whom He enclosed the sea within bounds of its own, whose mysteries all the elements faithfully observe, from whom the sun has received the measure of his daily courses to keep, whom the moon obeys as He bids her shine at night, whom the stars obey as they follow the course of the moon, by whom all things have been ordered and defined and placed in subjection, the heavens and things in the heavens, the earth and things in the earth, the sea and things in the sea, fire, air, abyss, things in the heights above, things in the depths beneath, things in the space between—He it was whom God sent to men. 3. Did He send Him, as a man might think, on a mission of domination and fear and terror? 4. Indeed He did not, but in gentleness and meekness He sent Him, as a king sending his own son who is himself a king; He sent Him as God, He sent Him as man to men, He sent Him with the idea of saving, of persuading, not of forcing; for force is no part of the nature of God. 5. He sent Him as inviting, not as pursuing man; He sent Him in love, not in judgment. 6. For He will send Him in judgment; and who shall stand before His presence? . . . 7. (Dost thou not see them) flung to the wild beasts, to make them deny their Lord, and yet unconquered? 8. Dost thou not see that the more of them are punished the more their numbers increase? 9. These things look not like the achievements of man; they are the power of God; they are the proofs of His presence.—L. B. Radford, *The Epistle to Diognetus*, 61 *sq*.

No. 30.—Penance

From Hermas [c. 140–50], *The Shepherd*, Vis. II. ii. §§ 4, 5.

II. 4. After thou hast made known to them these words, which the Master commanded me to reveal unto thee, then shall all their sins which they committed before be forgiven them; yea, and all the saints who have sinned unto this day shall be forgiven, if they repent with their whole heart and remove doubts from their minds. 5. For the Master hath sworn by His glory touching His elect, that if there be more sinning after this day which He hath limited, they shall not obtain salvation. For the repentance of the righteous hath an end; the days of repentance for all saints are fulfilled; but for the heathen there is repentance unto the last day.—C. Taylor, *The Shepherd of Hermas*, i. 67 *sq*.

No. 31.—Divorce and Re-marriage

From Hermas, *The Shepherd*, Mandate IV. i. §§ 1–10.

I. I charge thee, quoth he, to observe purity, and to let no thought about another man's wife or about any fornication or the likeness of any such evil things enter thy heart, for by doing this thou committest great sin; whereas if thou remember always thine own wife, thou shalt never fall into sin. 2. But if this imagination enter thy heart, thou wilt fall into sin; or should other like evil thought, thou committest sin. For this imagination is great sin to a servant of God; and if one do this evil thing, he worketh death to himself. 3. See therefore that thou keep thyself from this thought; for where modesty dwelleth, there iniquity should not come into the heart of a righteous man. 4. I said to him, Sir, suffer me to ask thee a few things. Say on, quoth he. Sir, quoth I, if one have a wife that is faithful in the Lord, and he find her in some adultery, doth then the husband sin if he live with her? 5. During ignorance, quoth he, he sinneth not; but if the man come to know of her sin, and the wife repent not but continue in her fornication, and the man live with her, he becometh guilty of her sin and a partner in her adultery. 6. What then, sir, quoth I, should the man do if the woman continue in this passion? Let him put her away, quoth he, and let the husband abide alone; but if when he hath put away his wife he marry another, then he likewise committeth adultery. 7. But if, sir, quoth I, after the wife hath been put away, she repent and desire to return to her own husband, shall she not be received? 8. Yea, verily, quoth he, if the husband receive her not he sinneth, and bringeth great sin upon himself. He that hath sinned and repenteth must be received; yet not often, for to the servants of God there is but one repentance. For the sake of her repentance therefore the husband ought not to marry. Thus the case standeth with both wife and husband. 9. And not only, quoth he, is it adultery if a man defile his flesh, but whoso doeth things after the similitude of the heathen likewise committeth adultery. So then, if a man continue in such deeds and repent not, refrain from him and company not with him; otherwise thou also art a partaker of his sin. 10. For this cause ye are bidden to abide alone, whether husband or wife, for in such matters there may be repentance.—*Ibid.* i. 118–21.

No. 32.—Penance

From Hermas, *The Shepherd*, Mandate IV. iii. §§ 1–6.

III. I will ask yet something more, sir, quoth I. Say on, quoth he. I have heard, sir, quoth I, from certain teachers that there is no other repentance than that one, when we went down into the water and received remission of our former sins. 2. He said to me, Thou didst rightly hear, for so it is. He who hath received remission of sins must sin no more, but dwell in purity. 3. Howbeit, seeing thou enquirest diligently about all things, I will show thee this also, not as giving occasion to such as are about to believe or have now believed on the Lord. For they who have now believed or are about to believe have no more repentance from sins, but have only remission of their former sins. 4. For them that were called before these days the Lord appointed repentance. Because the Lord, knowing the heart and foreknowing all things, knew the weakness of men and the cunning craftiness of the devil, how that he would do the servants of God some hurt and deal wickedly with them. 5. The Lord therefore being full of compassion had compassion upon His handiwork, and appointed this repentance, and to me was given the power over this repentance. 6. But I say unto thee, quoth he, that after that great and solemn calling, should any man being sorely tempted of the devil sin, he hath one repentance. But if he sin oft and repent it advantageth not such an one, for hardly shall he live.—*Ibid.* i. 123 *sq.*

No. 33.—Prophets, False and True

From Hermas, *The Shepherd*, Mandate XI. i. §§ 1–13.

I. He showed me men sitting on a bench, and another man sitting on a chair. And he said to me, Seest thou them that sit on the bench? I see them, sir, quoth I. These, quoth he, are faithful, but he that sitteth on the chair is a false prophet who destroyeth the servants of God; to wit, of the double-minded, but not of the faithful. 2. These men of two minds then come to him as to a soothsayer, and ask him what haply shall befall them; and the false prophet, having in himself no power of the divine Spirit, answereth them according to their demands and according to their unholy desires, and filleth their souls even as they wish. 3. For being himself void, he giveth void answers to the void; because, whatsoever he be asked, he answereth according to the emptiness of the man. Yet he speaketh some true words also; for the devil filleth him with his spirit, that peradventure he may be able to break some one of the righteous. 4. As many therefore as have put on the truth and are strong in the faith of the Lord cleave not to such spirits but keep away from them. But men who are of two minds and often repent use divination like the heathen, and bring upon themselves the greater sin by their idolatry; for he that enquireth of a false prophet about any matter is an idolater and void of the truth and foolish. For any Spirit given of God is not enquired of, but having the power of the Godhead, it speaketh all things of itself, because it is from above, from the power of the divine Spirit. 6. But the Spirit that is enquired of and speaketh according to the desires of men is earthly and light and hath no power, and it speaketh not all except it be enquired of. 7. How then, sir, quoth I, shall a man know which of them is a prophet and which a false prophet? Hear, quoth he, concerning both the prophets; and as I will now tell thee, so shalt thou prove the prophet and the false prophet. From his life prove thou the man that hath the divine Spirit. 8. First he that hath the divine Spirit which is from above is meek and peaceable and lowly, and refraineth himself from every wickedness and vain desire of this world, and he maketh himself more needy than all men, and answereth nothing to any when enquired of, and speaketh not solitarily, neither when a man would speak doth the Holy Spirit speak; but when God willeth that he should speak, then he speaketh. 9. Whensoever therefore the man who hath the divine Spirit cometh into a synagogue of just men who have faith in the divine Spirit, and the congregation of those men make their prayer unto God, then the Angel of the prophetic spirit which besetteth him filleth the man, and the man being filled with the Holy Spirit speaketh to the multitude as the Lord willeth. 10. Thus then shall the Spirit of the Godhead be manifest. Concerning the divine Spirit of the Lord, such is its power. 11. Hear now, quoth he, about the spirit that is earthly and void and hath no power, but is foolish. 12. First the man who thinketh that he hath the Spirit exalteth himself and wisheth to have the pre-eminence, and straightway he is heady and shameless and full of talk and conversant among many luxuries and other deceits; and he receiveth hire for his prophecy, and if he receive not he prophesieth not. Can then a divine Spirit receive hire and prophesy? It cannot be that a prophet of God should do this, but the spirit of such prophets is earthly. 13. And then he never at all approacheth an assembly of righteous men, but fleeth from them. And he joineth himself to the double-minded and empty, and prophesieth unto them in corners, and deceiveth them by speaking in all things emptily according to their lusts; for it is to the empty that he replieth. Because an empty vessel set with empty ones is not crushed, but they agree with one another.—*Ibid.* i. 149–152.

No. 34.—The Trinity and the Person of Christ

From Hermas, *The Shepherd*, Similitude V. v. §§ 1–5, vi. §§ 1–8.

V. I told thee, even now, quoth he, that thou art knavish and bold in demanding the interpretations of the parables. But since thou art so persistent, I will interpret to thee the parable of the field and all the accompaniments thereof, that thou mayest make them known to all. Hearken, quoth he, and understand them. 2. The field is this world; and the owner of the field is He who created all things and ordered and strengthened them. The slave is the Son of God; and the vines are this people which He planted. 3. The stakes are the holy angels of the Lord which hold His people together; the weeds that were plucked out of the vineyard are the iniquities of the servants of God; the meats sent to the slave from the supper are the commandments which He gave to His people through His Son; the friends and counsellors are the holy angels which were first created; and the going abroad of the master is the time that remaineth over until His coming. 4. I said to him, Sir, all these things are of great and wondrous and glorious sort: could I then possibly have understood them? No, nor can any other man, though he were exceeding prudent, understand them. Yet further, sir, quoth I, declare unto me that which I am about to ask of thee. 5. Say, quoth he, what thou wilt. Wherefore, sir, quoth I, is the Son of God set in the character of a slave in the parable?

VI. Hearken, quoth he. The Son of God is not set in the character of a slave, but in great authority and lordship. How, sir? quoth I; I understand not. 2. Because, quoth he, God planted the vineyard, that is to say He created the people, and He delivered them to His Son. And the Son gave the angels charge over them to keep them, and Himself purged their sins when He had laboured much and borne many toils; for none can dig without toil or trouble. 3. Having then Himself purged the sins of the people He shewed them the paths of life, giving them the law which He had received from His Father. 4. Thou seest, quoth he, that He is Lord of the people, having received all authority from His Father. Hear also how that the Lord took counsel with His Son and the holy angels about the inheritance of the slave. 5. The pre-existent Holy Spirit, which created the whole creation, did God make to dwell in flesh which He chose. This flesh then wherein the Holy Spirit dwelt served the Spirit rightly, walking in sanctity and purity and in no wise defiling the Spirit. 6. When therefore it had lived orderly and purely, and laboured and wrought with the Spirit in every matter, quitting itself stoutly and valiantly, He chose it for a partner with the Holy Spirit; for the way of this flesh pleased the Lord, because it defiled not itself upon the earth when it had the Holy Spirit. 7. Accordingly He took the Son and the glorious angels for counsellors, that this flesh also when it had served the Spirit blamelessly might have some abiding place, and might not seem to have lost the reward of its service; for all flesh found undefiled and spotless, wherein the Holy Spirit hath dwelt, shall receive a reward. 8. Thou hast the interpretation of this parable also.—*Ibid.* ii. 29–32.

No. 35.—The Mysteries of Isis

From Apuleius of Madaura [*c.* 150], *Metamorphoses*, xi. §§ 22, 23.

[§ 22] . . . Then I saluted him [*sc.* Mithras, the chief priest of Isis] and thought with myself to ask and demand with a bold courage that I should be initiate, as a thing now due; but as soon as he perceived me, he began first to say: "O Lucius, now know I well that thou art most happy and blessed, whom the divine goddess doth so greatly accept with mercy. Why dost thou stand idle and delay? Behold the day which thou didst desire with prayer, when as thou shalt receive at my hands the order of the most secret and holy religion, according to the divine commandment of this goddess of many names." Thereupon the old man took me by the hand and led me courteously to the gate of the great temple, where, after that it was religiously opened, he made a solemn celebration, and after the morning sacrifice was ended, he brought out of the secret place of the temple certain books, written with unknown characters, partly painted with figures of beasts declaring briefly every sentence, partly with letters whose tops and tails turned round in fashion of a wheel, joined together above like unto the tendrils of a vine, whereby they were wholly strange and impossible to be read of the profane people; thence he interpreted to me such things as were necessary to the use and preparation of mine order.

[§ 23] This done, I diligently gave in charge to certain of my companions to buy liberally whatsoever was needful and convenient; but part thereof I bought myself. Then he brought me, when he found that the time was at hand, to the next baths, accompanied with all the religious sort, and demanding pardon of the gods, washed me and purified my body according to the custom: after this, when two parts of the day was gone, he brought me back again to the temple and presented me before the feet of the goddess, giving me a charge of certain secret things unlawful to be uttered, and commanding me generally before all the rest to fast by the space of ten days; without eating of any beast or drinking of any wine: which things I observed with a marvellous continency. Then behold the day approached, when as the sacrifice of dedication should be done; and when the sun declined and evening came, there arrived on every coast a great multitude of priests, who, according to their ancient order, offered me many presents and gifts. Then was all the laity and profane people commanded to depart; and when they had put on my back a new linen robe, the priest took my hand and brought me to the most secret and sacred place of the temple. Thou wouldest, peradventure, demand, thou studious reader, what was said and done there: verily I would tell thee, if it were lawful for me to tell, thou wouldest know if it were convenient for thee to hear; but both thy ears and my tongue should incur the like pain of rash curiosity. Howbeit, I will not torment thy mind, which, peradventure, is somewhat religious and given to some devotion; listen, therefore, and believe it to be true. Thou shalt understand that I approached near unto hell, even to the gates of Proserpine, and after that I was ravished through all the elements, I returned to my proper place; about midnight I saw the sun brightly shine, I saw likewise the gods celestial and the gods infernal, before whom I presented myself and worshipped them. Behold now, I have told thee, which although thou hast heard, yet it is necessary that thou conceal it: wherefore this only will I tell, which may be declared without offence for the understanding of the profane.—Apuleius, *The Golden Ass*, tr. W. S. Gaselee, 577 *sq.*

No. 36.—The Martyrdom of Polycarp, February 22, 156

From the *Martyrium Polycarpi*.

The Church of God sojourning at Smyrna to the Church of God sojourning at Philomelium, and to all the dioceses of the Holy Catholic Church in every place, mercy and peace and love of God the Father and of our Lord Jesus Christ be multiplied.

I. We write to you, brethren, the events which befell them that suffered martyrdom, and the blessed Polycarp, who, as it were, by his martyrdom set his seal upon the persecution, and put an end to it. For nearly all the preceding events came to pass in order that to us the Lord might once again give an example of the martyrdom which resembles the Gospel story.

For he waited that he might be betrayed, just as was the Lord, to the end that we too may become imitators of Him, regarding not only what concerns ourselves but also what concerns our neighbours.

For it is the part of true and constant love that a man should wish not only himself, but also all the brethren, to be saved.

II. Now blessed and noble were all the martyrdoms which took place in accordance with the will of God; for we are bound to be very reverent and to ascribe the power over all things to God. And who could fail to marvel at their nobility, their endurance, their love for their Master? Some were so torn by the scourges that the structure of their flesh to the inner veins and arteries was exposed to view; but they endured it, so that even the bystanders were moved to pity and lamentation. Some reached such a pitch of noble endurance that not one of them let cry or groan escape him, while they showed to us all that tortured as they were at that time Christ's martyrs were absent from the flesh; or rather that standing by their side their Lord was in close converse with them. So, giving heed to the grace of Christ, they were despising the torments of the world, redeeming themselves at the cost of one short season from everlasting punishment. Cold to them was the fire of the inhuman tormentors; for they kept before their eyes their escape from the fire that is everlasting and is never quenched, while with the eyes of the heart they looked up at the good things reserved for them that have endured, which "neither ear hath heard nor eye seen, neither have entered into the hearts of man" (1 Cor. ii. 9, slightly varied), but were being shown by the Lord to those who were now already no longer men but angels. In like manner they that were condemned to the beasts underwent awful punishments, being made to lie on prickly shells and buffeted, with various other forms of torture, to the end that, if it were possible, by means of their protracted punishment they might be turned to denial by him who was devising so many wiles against them—the devil.

III. But thanks be to God, for He verily prevailed against all. For the right noble Germanicus, by means of his endurance, turned their cowardice into courage. With signal distinction did he fight against the beasts. While the Proconsul, wishful to persuade him, was urging him to have compassion on his youth, in his eagerness to be released the sooner from their unrighteous and careless mode of life he used force to the wild beast and pulled it on himself. Now it was on this that all the multitude, amazed at the noble conduct of the Godbeloved and Godfearing race of the Christians, shouted out, "Away with the Atheists. Let search be made for Polycarp."

IV. But one of them, Quintus by name, a Phrygian, lately arrived from his native province, when he saw the beasts, was afraid. It was he who had forced both himself and certain others to come forward of their own accord. After very earnest entreaty he had been persuaded by the Proconsul to take the oath and offer incense. Now, brethren, we do not commend those who surrender themselves, for not such is the teaching of the Gospel.

V. Now the most admirable Polycarp so soon as he heard [that he was being sought for] at first showed no dismay, but wished to remain in town. The majority, however, prevailed on him to withdraw. And withdraw he did, to a little estate not far from the city. There he spent his time with a few companions, occupied night and day in nothing but prayer for all men, and for the Churches throughout the world, as indeed was his constant habit. And while praying he fell into a trance three days before his apprehension, and he saw his pillows being burned by fire. And he turned and said to them that were with him, "I must needs be burned alive."

VI. Now his pursuers were persistent, so he shifted his quarters to another farm. Then straightway the pursuers arrived on the spot and, on failing to find him, they seized two slave-boys. One of these confessed under torture; for indeed it was impossible for him to evade pursuit, since they that betrayed him were of his own household. And the head of the police, who, as it befell, bore the same name [as our Lord's judge], being called Herod, made haste to bring him into the stadium, in order that he might be made a partner of Christ, and so fulfil his own appointed lot, and that his betrayers might undergo the punishment of Judas himself.

VII. Accordingly, having the lad with them, on Friday at about supper-time forth sallied constables and mounted men, with their usual equipment, hurrying as though "against a thief" (Matt. xxvi. 55). Late in the day they came up together and found him in a cottage lying in an upper room. It was within his power to go away thence to another place, but he refused to do so, saying, "God's will be done." So, on hearing of their arrival, he came down and conversed with them, they all the while wondering at his age and his constancy, and at there being so much ado about the arrest of such an old man. Upon this he gave orders for something to be served for them to eat and drink, at that hour, as much as they would. He besought them withal to give him an hour that he might pray freely; and on their granting him this boon he stood up and prayed, being so full of the grace of God, that for the space of two hours he could not hold his peace, while the hearers were smitten with amazement, and many were sorry that they had come after so venerable an old man.

VIII. After remembering all, both small and great, high and low, who had ever been brought into communication with him, and all the Catholic Church throughout the world, at last he brought his prayer to an end. The time had come for him to depart. They set him on an ass and brought him into the city, it being a high Sabbath. He was met by the eirenarch Herodes, and by his father, Nicetes, who shifted him into their carriage, and tried to persuade him as they sate by his side, urging, "Why, what harm is there in saying Cæsar is Lord, and sacrificing, and the rest of it, and so saving thyself?" At first he made no reply, but, as they were persistent, he said, "I do not intend to do what you advise me." On their failing to persuade him they began to use terrible language and to drag him hurriedly down, so that as he was getting down from the carriage he grazed his shin. Without turning back, as though he had suffered no hurt, he fared on with speed, and was conducted to the stadium, where there was so great a tumult that it was impossible for any one to be heard.

IX. Now as Polycarp was entering into the stadium, there came a voice to him from heaven, "Be strong, Polycarp, and play the man." The speaker indeed no one saw, but the voice was heard by those of our friends who were present. Then he was dragged forward, and great was the din of them that heard that Polycarp was arrested. So he was brought before the Proconsul, who asked him if he were the man himself? He assented, and the Proconsul tried to persuade him, urging, "Have respect to thine old age," and the rest of it, according to the customary form, "Swear by the genius of Cæsar; repent; say, 'Away with the Atheists!'" Then Polycarp looked with a serious countenance on the multitude of lawless heathen gathered in the stadium, and he beckoned with his hand, and looked up to heaven with a groan, and said, "Away with the Atheists." The Proconsul continued insisting and saying, "Swear, and I release thee; revile the Christ." And Polycarp said, "Eighty and six years have I served Him, and He hath done me no wrong: how then can I blaspheme my King Who saved me?"

X. The Proconsul continuing to persist, and to urge, "Swear by the genius of Cæsar," he answered, "If thou vainly fanciest that I would 'swear by the genius of Cæsar,' as thou sayest, pretending that thou art ignorant who I am, hear plainly that I am a Christian. And if thou art willing to learn the doctrine of Christianity, appoint a day, and grant me a hearing." The Proconsul said, "Persuade the people." Polycarp then said, "Thee, indeed, I should have deemed worthy of argument, for we have been taught to render to authorities and powers ordained by God, honour as is meet, so long as it does us no harm, but I deem not yon multitude worthy of my making my defence to them."

XI. The Proconsul said, "I have wild beasts; if thou wilt not change thy mind I will throw thee to them." Then he said, "Bid them be brought: change of mind from better to worse is not a change that we are allowed; but to change from wrong to right is good." Then again said the Proconsul to him, "As thou despisest the beasts, unless thou change thy mind, I make thee to be destroyed by fire." Then Polycarp: "Thou threatenest the fire that burns for a season, and after a little while is quenched; for thou art ignorant of the fire of the judgment to come, and of everlasting punishment reserved for the ungodly. But for what art thou waiting? Bring what thou wilt."

XII. While speaking these words and many more he was filled with courage and gladness: his face grew full of grace, so that not only did it not fall, agitated at all that was being said to him, but on the contrary the Proconsul was amazed, and sent his own crier to make proclamation in the middle of the stadium thrice, "Polycarp has confessed himself to be a Christian." No sooner was this proclaimed by the crier than the whole multitude, both of Gentiles and of Jews dwelling at Smyrna, with ungovernable rage and a loud voice began to shout—"This is the teacher of Asia, the father of the Christians, the destroyer of our Gods, the man who teaches many not to sacrifice nor even to worship." With these words they kept up their shout and continued asking Philip the Asiarch to let loose a lion at Polycarp. "But," said he, "that is no longer in my power: the sports are over." Thereupon it was their pleasure to yell with one accord that he should burn Polycarp alive. For the [prediction] of the vision about his pillow must needs be fulfilled, on the occasion of his seeing it burning while he was at prayer, and turning round and saying prophetically to his faithful friends, "I must needs be burnt alive."

XIII. This then was no sooner said than done, the mob in a moment getting together logs and fagots from the workshops and baths, the Jews as usual showing themselves specially zealous in the work. When the pyre had been made ready, Polycarp took off all his upper garments, and untied his girdle. He endeavoured also to take off his shoes, though he had never been in the habit of doing this, because every one of the faithful was eager to be the first to touch his bare body. For his good life's sake he had been treated with every honour even before his head was white. Forthwith then all the gear adapted for the pyre was put about him. They were on the point of fastening him with nails, but he said, "Let me be as I am: He that gave me power to abide the fire will grant me too without your making me fast with nails to abide untroubled at the pyre."

XIV. So they did not nail him, but they bound him to [the stake]. He put his hands behind him and was bound, like a goodly ram out of a great flock for an offering, a whole burnt offering made ready and acceptable to God. Then he looked up to heaven and said, "O Lord God Almighty, Father of Thy beloved and blessed Son Jesus Christ, by Whose means we have received our knowledge of Thee, God of Angels and Powers and of all creation and of the whole race of the just who live before Thy face, I bless Thee in that Thou hast deemed me worthy of this day and hour; that I might take a portion in the number of the martyrs in the cup of Christ, to the resurrection of eternal life both of soul and body in the incorruption of the Holy Ghost. Among these may I to-day be welcome before Thy face as a fat and acceptable sacrifice as Thou didst prepare and manifest beforehand and didst bring about its fulfilment, Thou the faithful and true God. For this cause, yet and for all things I praise Thee, I bless Thee, I glorify Thee through the everlasting and heavenly High Priest Jesus Christ Thy beloved Son, through Whom to Thee with Him and with the Holy Ghost be glory now and for the ages to come. Amen."

XV. When he had offered up his Amen and completed his prayer, the firemen kindled the fire. A great flame flashed out, and we to whom it was granted to see saw a marvel; and we moreover were preserved to the end that we might tell to the rest the tidings of what came to pass. The fire made the appearance of a vaulted roof, like a ship's sail filling out with the wind, and it walled about the body of the martyr in a ring. There was it in the midst, not like flesh burning, but like a loaf baking, or like gold and silver being fired in a furnace. Moreover we were aware of a fragrance as great as of frankincense or some other of the precious spices breathing forth [its perfume].

XVI. In the end, when the wicked ones had seen that his body could not be consumed by the fire they commanded an executioner to come up to him and to drive in a dagger. When he had so done there came out [a dove and] abundance of blood so that it put out the fire, and all the multitude marvelled at the mighty difference between the unbelievers and the elect, of whom one was this man, the most admirable Polycarp, who in our times was an apostolic and prophetic teacher, bishop of the Holy Church in Smyrna; for every word which he uttered from his mouth was accomplished and will be accomplished.

XVII. But when the jealous, envious evil one, the adversary of the race of the righteous, saw both the majesty of his martyrdom and his blameless conversation from the beginning, and that he was crowned with the crown of incorruption and had carried off a prize which could not be gainsaid, he contrived that not even his poor body should be taken up by us, though many were desirous so to do and to come into communion with his most holy flesh. So he prompted Nicetes, father of Herodes and brother of Alce, to entreat the magistrate not to grant his body, lest, as he said, we should forsake the Crucified, and begin to worship this man. This was done at the prompting and persistence of the Jews. They moreover watched, when we were about to try to take him out of the fire, ignorant that it will never at any time be possible for us to abandon the Christ,—Who, blameless on behalf of sinners, suffered for the salvation of the whole world of them that are being saved,—and to worship some other. Him, in that He is Son of God, we adore; the martyrs, as disciples and imitators of the Lord, we reverence as they deserve on account of their unsurpassable good will to their own King and Teacher. With them may it be granted to us to be made sharers alike of lot and of learning!

XVIII. When the centurion saw the opposition raised by the Jews, he put him in the midst, and, as their custom is, burned him. So we afterwards took up his bones, more valuable than precious stones, and finer than fine gold, and laid them where it was fitting. There the Lord will permit us, as shall be possible to us, to assemble ourselves together in joy and gladness, and to celebrate the birthday of his martyrdom, alike in memory of them that have fought before, and for the training and preparation of them that are to fight hereafter.

XIX. Thus it befell the blessed Polycarp, who was martyred with them that came from Philadelphia, himself and eleven others, in Smyrna, and is himself alone held in all men's memory, so that even among the heathen is he everywhere spoken of as one who was not merely an illustrious teacher, but also a conspicuous martyr. His martyrdom all men are eager to copy, in that it came to pass according to the gospel of Christ. Through his patience he overcame the unrighteous ruler, and thus received the crown of incorruption. Rejoicing with Apostles and all just men, he glorifies our Almighty God and Father, and blesses our Lord Jesus Christ, Saviour of our souls, and Helmsman of our bodies, and Shepherd of the Catholic Church throughout the world.

XX. You did indeed request that the circumstances might be narrated to you more fully. We have, however, for the present, sent you concise information through our brother Marcian. On becoming acquainted with these events, send on our letter to brethren also beyond, that they may glorify the Lord who makes choice of His own servants. Now unto Him that is able by His grace and gift to bring us all into His heavenly kingdom, through His only-begotten Son, Jesus Christ, be glory, honour, might, majesty, for ever. Salute all the saints. They that are with us, and Euarestus, who wrote the letter, with his whole house, salute you.

XXI. The blessed Polycarp was martyred on the second day of the first part of the month Xanthicus, on the seventh day before the Kalends of March, at the eighth hour, on a great Sabbath. He was apprehended by Herodes in the Chief Priestship of Philip of Tralles, in the proconsulship of Statius Quadratus, but in the reign of the eternal King, Jesus Christ; to Whom be honour, glory, dominion through the eternal from generation to generation. Amen.—B. Jackson, *St. Polycarp*, 49–74.

No. 37.—The Expulsion of the Jews from Rome, *c.* 52

From Suetonius [*c.* 75–160], *Vita Claudii*, c. xxv. §§ 4, 5.

[§ 4] Since the Jews constantly made disturbances at the instigation of Chrestus, he expelled them from Rome. . . ,

[§ 5] He utterly abolished the cruel and inhuman religion of the Druids among the Gauls, which under Augustus had merely been prohibited to Roman citizens; on the other hand he even attempted to transfer the Eleusinian rites from Attica to Rome, and had the temple of Venus Erycina in Sicily, which had fallen to ruin through age, restored at the expense of the treasury of the Roman people.—J. C. Rolfe, *Suetonius*, ii. 53.

No. 38.—The Neronian Persecution, 64

From Suetonius, *Vita Neronis*, xvi. § 2.

During his reign many abuses were severely punished and put down, and no fewer new laws were made; a limit was set to expenditures; the public banquets were confined to a distribution of food; the sale of cooked viands in the taverns was forbidden, whereas before every sort of dainty was exposed for sale. Punishment was inflicted on the Christians, a class of men given to a new and mischievous superstition. He put an end to the diversions of the chariot drivers, who from immunity of long standing claimed the right of ranging at large and amusing themselves by cheating and robbing the people. The pantomimic actors and their partisans were banished from the city.—*Ibid.* ii. 111.

No. 39.—Heathenism the Work of Demons

From Justin [† 163], *Apology* [*c.* 150–5], I. v.

[§ 1] What then? On us who profess to do no evil, and not to hold the above godless doctrines, you make no judicial enquiry; but, impelled by unreasonable passion, and through the instigation of evil demons, you punish us without judgment and reflection. [§ 2] But the truth shall be spoken: these evil demons formerly appeared and defiled women, polluted boys, and made such dreadful exhibitions to men as to amaze those who did not consider the acts that were done, with judgment; but who, struck with fear and not knowing them to be evil demons, termed them gods, and bestowed on them the name which each of them chose for himself. [§ 3] When Socrates endeavoured by true reason and judgment to bring these things to light, and to deliver men from these demons, these demons themselves laboured through the agency of such men as delight in evil, to have him put to death as a godless and profane person; saying that he introduced new gods. [§ 4] And in like manner they do the same against us; for not only among the Greeks did Socrates these things by word of reason, but also among the barbaric nations the very Word Himself, who took a form, and became man, and was called Jesus Christ; taught by whom we say that those who have acted thus are not only not good spirits, but wicked and unholy demons, whose actions are not equal even to those of men that aim at virtue.—*L.F.* xl. 4.

No. 40.—Christian Life in the Second Century

From Justin, *Apology*, I. xvi.

[xvi.] . . . For we ought not to be guilty of strife, nor would He have us followers of the wicked, but He has urged us by patience and meekness, to convert all from shame and the lust of evil; and this I can show to have taken place in the case of many that have come in contact with us, who were overcome, and changed from violent and tyrannical characters, either from having watched the constancy of their neighbours' lives, or from having observed the wonderful patience of fellow travellers under unjust exactions, or from the trial they made of those with whom they were concerned in business.—*L.F.* xl. 12.

No. 41.—Christians before Christ

From Justin, *Apology*, I. xlvi. §§ 1–4.

[§ 1] But lest any should unreasonably urge, to turn men away from our doctrines, that we assert Christ to have been born one hundred and fifty years ago, under Cyrenius, and to have taught what we affirm that He did teach subsequently, in the time of Pontius Pilate; and should urge it against us as if all men who were born before Him were irresponsible, I will, by anticipation, answer this difficulty. [§ 2] We are taught that Christ is the first-born of God, and we have shown above that He is the Word of whom the whole human race are partakers, [§ 4] and those who lived according to reason are Christians, even though accounted Atheists. Such among the Greeks were Socrates and Heraclitus, and those who resembled them; of the Barbarians, Abraham, and Ananias, and Azarias, and Misæl, and Elias, and many others; whose actions, or names, would, I know, be tedious to relate; and for the present I refrain from so doing.—tr. *L.F.* xl. 35.

No. 42.—Christian Worship

From Justin, *Apology*, I. lxv.–lxvii.

[c. lxv. § 1] But after thus washing him who has professed, and given his assent, we bring him to those who are called brethren, where they are assembled together, to offer prayers in common both for ourselves, and for the person who has received illumination, and all others everywhere, with all our hearts, that we might be vouchsafed, now we have learnt the truth, by our works also to be found good citizens and keepers of the commandments, that we may obtain everlasting salvation. [§ 2] We salute one another with a kiss when we have concluded the prayers. [§ 3] Then is brought to the president of the brethren bread, and a cup of water and wine, which he receives; and offers up praise and glory to the Father of all things, through the Name of His Son, and of the Holy Ghost; and he returns thanks at length, for our being vouchsafed these things by Him. When he has concluded the prayers and thanksgiving, all the people who are present express their assent by saying *Amen*. [§ 4] This word *Amen* in the Aramaic language means "So be it"; and when the president has celebrated the Eucharist, and all the people have assented, they whom we call deacons give to each of those who are present a portion of the Eucharistic bread and wine and water; and carry them to those who are absent.

[c. lxvi. § 1] And this food was called by us the Eucharist, of which no one is allowed to partake but he who believes the truth of our doctrines; and who has been washed in the laver for the forgiveness of sins, and to regeneration; and who so lives as Christ has directed. [§ 2] For we do not receive them as ordinary food, or ordinary drink; but as by the Word of God Jesus our Saviour was made flesh, and had both flesh and blood for our salvation; so also the food which was blessed by the prayer of the Word which proceeded from Him, and from which our flesh and blood, by assimilation, receives nourishment, is, we are taught, both the flesh and blood of that Jesus who was made flesh. [§ 3] For the Apostles in the records which they made, and which are called Gospels, have declared that Jesus commanded them to do as follows: "He took bread and gave thanks and said, 'This do in remembrance of me: this is my body.' And in like manner He took the cup, and blessed it, and said, 'This is my blood,' and gave it to them alone." [§ 4] The same thing in the mysteries of Mithra also, the evil demons imitated, and commanded to be done; for bread and a cup of water are placed in the mystic rites for one who is to be initiated, with the addition of certain words, as you know or may learn.

[c. lxvii. § 1] But we, after these things, henceforward always reminded one another of them; and those of us who have the means assist all who are in want; and we are always together; [§ 2] and in all our oblations we bless the maker of all things through His Son Jesus Christ and through the Holy Ghost. [§ 3] And on the day which is called Sunday, there is an assembly in the same place of all who live in cities, or in country districts; and the records of the Apostles, or the writings of the Prophets, are read as long as we have time. [§ 4] Then the reader concludes, and the president verbally instructs and exhorts us to the imitation of these excellent things. [§ 5] Then we all together rise and offer up our prayers; and, as I said before, when we have concluded our prayer, bread is brought and wine and water; and the president in like manner offers up prayers and thanksgivings with all his strength; and the people give their assent by saying *Amen*, and there is a distribution, and a partaking by every one, of the Eucharistic elements; and to those who are not present they are sent by the hands of the deacons. [§ 6] And such as are in prosperous circumstances and wish to do so, give what they will, each according to his choice, and what is collected is placed in the hands of the president. [§ 7] He assists the orphans and widows and such as through sickness or any other cause are in want; and to those who are in bonds, and to strangers from afar, and, in a word, to all who are in need, he is a protector. [§ 8] But Sunday is the day on which we all hold our common assembly, because it is the first day on which God, when He changed the darkness and matter, made the world; and Jesus Christ our Saviour on the same day rose from the dead; for the day before that of Saturn He was crucified; and on the day after it, which is Sunday, He appeared to His Apostles and Disciples, and taught them these things, which we have given to you also, for your consideration.—*L.F.* xl. 50–2.

No. 43.—The Martyrdom of Ptolemy and Lucius

From Justin, *Apology*, II. ii.

[§ 1] A certain woman had a husband who was intemperate, she herself also formerly being intemperate. [§ 2] But when she knew the doctrines of Christ, she was brought to self-control; and endeavoured to persuade her husband to the same, relating these doctrines, and teaching him that there would be a future punishment in eternal fire, for all who did not govern their lives by moderation and right reason. [§ 3] But he continued in the same excesses, and by his conduct alienated his wife from him. [§ 4] And she, thinking it wrong to live any longer with one who, against the law of nature, and contrarily to right, laboured to procure by every device the means of gratification, wished for a divorce. [§ 5] And when she yielded to the entreaties of those about her who wished her to remain with him still, as her husband would come by and by to the hope of a change, she constrained herself and remained with him. [§ 6] But when her husband went into Alexandria and was said to be acting worse, she, that she might not be a partaker in his sins and impieties, by remaining in her connection with him, and continuing to share his table and his bed, gave him what you call the bill of divorce, and was separated. [§ 7] But this good and admirable husband, who ought to have rejoiced that the deeds which she formerly used to commit recklessly with the servants and hirelings, taking delight in drunkenness and every kind of wickedness, she now ceased to do, and wished him to abstain from doing as well; when she had parted from him against his will, laid an accusation against her declaring that she was a Christian. [§ 8] And she addressed a petition to you, O Emperor, praying that she might first be permitted to arrange her affairs, and then, after they were set in order, she would defend herself on the subject of the accusation. And you granted her petition. [§ 9] Her former husband then, being now unable to reply to her, turned, in the following manner, on a certain Ptolemæus, who was her teacher in the Christian doctrines, whom Urbicus punished; [§ 10] he persuaded the centurion who threw Ptolemæus into prison, and who was his friend, to take him and ask him this single question alone: Was he a Christian? [§ 11] And Ptolemæus, who was a lover of truth, and nowise disposed to be a deceiver or falsifier, confessed himself to be a Christian; on which the centurion caused him to be put in bonds, and confined him for a long time in the prison. [§ 12] At last, when he came before Urbicus, he was likewise asked this same question only—If he were a Christian. [§ 13] And he again knowing the blessing he had derived through the doctrine of Christ, confessed the school of divine virtue. [§ 14] For he who denies anything, either does so from condemning it, or, knowing himself to be unworthy of, and alien to it, avoids the confession of it; none of which conditions apply to the true Christian. [§ 15] And when Urbicus commanded him to be led away to execution, a certain Lucius, who was also himself a Christian, seeing the decision that was thus unreasonably given, said to Urbicus: [§ 16] "What is the reason of your punishing this man, who is neither an adulterer, nor a fornicator, nor a murderer, nor a thief, nor a robber, and who is not convicted of having committed any offence whatever, but who confesses himself to bear the name of a Christian? You judge not, O Urbicus, as becomes the Emperor Pius, or the Philosopher the son of Cæsar, or the sacred Senate." [§ 17] He gave no other reply to Lucius than merely this: "You yourself also appear to me to be such an one." [§ 18] And when Lucius answered, "Certainly I am," he commanded him also, in return, to be led away. [§ 19] He acknowledged it with thanks, knowing that he would be liberated from such wicked masters and would go to the Father, and King of the Heavens. [§ 20] And some other third person coming up, was in like manner condemned to punishment.—*L.F.* xl. 58 *sq.*

No. 44.—The Light that Lighteth Every Man

From Justin, *Apology*, II. xiii.

[§ 1] For I myself, when I discovered the evil disguise that was thrown around the divine doctrines of Christians by the evil demons, to deter others from them, laughed, both at the authors of these falsehoods, and their disguise, and the popular opinion; [§ 2] and I confess that I both prayed, and strove with all my might, to be found a Christian; not because the doctrines of Plato are entirely different from those of Christ, but because they are not in all respects like them; no more, in fact, are those of the others, the Stoics, for example, and poets and prose-writers. [§ 3] For each, seeing through a part of the Seminal Divine Word, that which was kindred to those, discoursed rightly. But they who contradict them on more important points, appear not to have possessed the hidden wisdom and the knowledge which cannot be spoken against. [§ 4] Whatever all men have uttered aright, then, belongs to us Christians; for we worship and love, next to God, the Word which is from the Unbegotten and Ineffable God: for it was even for us that He was made man, that He might be a partaker of our very sufferings, and bring us healing. [§ 5] For all writers through the engrafted seed of the Word, which was planted in them, were able to see the truth darkly; [§ 6] for the seed and imitation of a thing, which is given according to capability, is one thing, and the thing itself, of which the communication and imitation are given according to His grace, is another.—*L.F.* xl. 68.

No. 45. Justin's Conversion

From Justin, *Dialogue with Trypho* [*c.* 160], §§ 7, 8.

[§ 7] "Whom, then," I asked, "shall a man take as his master, or whence shall he derive any instruction, if the truth is not with these philosophers?"

"There once lived men," he replied, "called Prophets, who were anterior to any of those who are considered philosophers, and who were blessed, just, and beloved by God. These spoke of the Holy Ghost, and foretold what should happen thereafter, and what is now taking place. And they alone knew and taught the truth, neither regarding nor fearing any man, nor being themselves carried away by the love of glory, but declaring those things alone which they saw and heard when filled with the Holy Ghost. And their writings still remain to us, and whoever reads them will derive much instruction about the first principles and the end of things, together with all that a philosopher ought to know when he believes them. They have not indeed given demonstrations in their writings, for they are in fact above all demonstration as faithful witnesses of the truth; but the events that have happened already, and those which are taking place even now, compel you to receive their testimony. Even indeed for the miracles which they performed are they worthy of our belief, and especially since they glorified God, the Father and Maker of all things, and taught of Christ His Son, who was sent by Him; which the false prophets, who were filled with a spirit of falsehood and uncleanness, neither did nor do; but these presume to perform certain wonders to astonish mankind, and set forth the praises of lying spirits and devils. But do you above all things pray that the gates of light may be opened to you; for these things are not to be seen or comprehended, except by him to whom God and His Christ give the grace of understanding."

[§ 8] When he had said this, and much more which we have not now time to repeat, he left me, bidding me attend to what he had said, and I saw him no more.

But a flame was immediately kindled in my mind, and I was seized with an ardent love of the Prophets, and of these men who are the friends of Christ; and reflecting with myself on what I had heard, I saw that theirs was the only sure and valuable philosophy; thus it was that I became a Philosopher, and I could wish that all men were of the same mind as myself, not to turn from the doctrines of the Saviour; for they inspire a certain dread, and possess a power to overawe those who are turned from the right way; but they become the most pleasant resting-place to such as fully practise them. If therefore you have any regard for your own welfare, and desire of salvation, and trust in God, you may now have an opportunity, if you are not averse to the task, of attaining happiness by knowledge of the Christ of God, and by being made a perfect disciple.—*L.F.* xl. 80 *sq.*

No. 46.—Judaistic Christianity, *c.* 100-35

From Justin, *Dialogue with Trypho,* § 47.

Trypho then enquired, "But if any one has gained the knowledge that these things are so, and besides holding for certain that this is the Christ, has in fact both believed in and obeyed Him, yet wishes to keep these ordinances as well, shall he be saved?"

"As it appears to me, Trypho," I replied, "he shall be saved, provided that he do not on any account strive to persuade other men. I mean such of the Gentiles as are circumcised through Christ from their errors, to keep the same rites as himself, affirming that they cannot be saved except they do so, which you yourself did in the beginning of our conversation, saying that I could not be saved unless I kept them."

"But why," said Trypho, "do you say 'in my opinion' such an one shall be saved, except there are any who hold the contrary?"

"There are such, Trypho," I replied, "who are bold enough to refuse to hold communion, either in conversation or domestic life, with men of this description, with whom I do not agree. But if any through weakness of judgment wish to keep as many of these ordinances of the Mosaic Law as possible, which we consider to have been given because of the hardness of your hearts, whilst they place their hope in the same Christ, and observe the eternal and natural practices of justice and righteousness; and choose to live with those who are Christians, and faithful, as I said, without persuading them to be circumcised like themselves, or to keep the Sabbaths or other similar observances; I consider that we ought to receive them, and communicate with them in everything, as kinsmen and brothers; but if, I said, any of your nation, Trypho, profess to believe in this Christ, and yet at the same time endeavour to compel the faithful Gentile Christians to live according to the Law of Moses, or refuse to hold the above kind of communication with them, these also equally with the former I do not admit; but those Gentiles who have been persuaded by the Jews to adopt the observance of the Law, together with their confession of the Christ of God, may also, I think, be possibly saved. Those, however, who have once confessed and acknowledged that this is Christ, and yet have, for whatever reasons, gone over to the Jewish Law, denying that this is the Christ, and not repenting before their death, cannot, in my opinion, by any means whatever be saved: and I think the same of those of the seed of Abraham, who live according to the Law, and believe not in this Christ, to the very end of their lives. And so, too, especially of these who have cursed, or who now in the synagogues curse both Christ, and every other means by which they may both obtain salvation, and escape the punishment of the fire; for the goodness and the love of God and the immensity of His riches, accounts the man who repents of his sins, as righteous and spotless, according to His declarations by Ezekiel; and him who has departed from holiness and righteousness to injustice and ungodliness, as sinful, unrighteous and profane. Hence our Lord Jesus Christ has said: 'In whatsoever things I find you, in the same will I judge you.'"—*L.F.* xl. 127 *sq.*

No. 47.—The Jewish Interpretation of *Isaiah* vii. 14

From Justin, *Dialogue with Trypho*, § 67.

[§ 67] To this Trypho replied: "The Scripture does not say, 'Behold, a Virgin shall conceive and bring forth a Son': but 'Behold, a young woman shall conceive and bring forth a Son': what follows, being as you have cited it; and the whole prophecy was spoken of Hezekiah, to whom subsequent events befel in agreement with it. And as in the fables of the Greeks it is related how Perseus was born of Danæ, who was a virgin, he whom they call Jupiter, showering on her in the form of gold; you, who state the same things as these men, ought to be ashamed of yourselves, and should rather confess this Jesus to be a man born of men; and if you can show from the Scriptures that He is the Christ, assert that He was held worthy of being chosen to be such, from His having lived according to the Law and perfectly; but do not venture to utter your present marvels, lest you be convicted of mere folly, like the Greeks."—*L.F.* xl. 156.

No. 48.—The Christian Interpretation of *Daniel* vii. 13

From Justin, *Dialogue with Trypho,* § 76.

[§ 76] And when Daniel calls Him who received the eternal Kingdom, "one like the Son of Man" (Dan. vii. 13), does he not signify the same thing? For the words, "like the Son of Man," show that He should appear and be made man, but that He should not be of human seed; and when he calls Him "a Stone cut out without hands" (Dan. ii. 34), he declares the same thing in a figure; for to say that He is cut out without hands, shows He is not a human production, but is of the will of God the Father of all things, who sendeth Him forth. These words of Isaiah also, "Who shall declare His generation?" (Is. liii. 8), show that He has a generation that is ineffable; for no one who is a man of men has a generation that cannot be declared; and are not those words of Moses, "He shall wash His robes in the blood of the grape" (Gen. xlix. 11), that, as I have already affirmed to you, which He has mysteriously foretold? He foretold that He should have blood, but not of men, as it is not man who engenders the blood of the grape, but God; and when Isaiah called Him "The Angel of the great Counsel" (Is. ix. 6; lxx.), did he not foretell that He should be a teacher of those things which He taught when He did come? For the great thing which the Father had purposed to do to those who either were or should be pleasing to Him, and to all who revolted against His will, Angels and men alike, He alone taught without disguise. . . .—*L.F.* xl. 167 *sq.*

No. 49.—The Martyrdom of Justin and his Companions, 163

From *Acta Justini et Sociorum.*

[c. i] In the time of the lawless partisans of idolatry, wicked decrees were passed against the godly Christians in town and country, to force them to offer libations to vain idols; and accordingly the holy men having been apprehended, were brought before the prefect of Rome, Rusticus by name. And when they had been brought before his judgment-seat [c. ii], Rusticus the prefect said to Justin, "Obey the gods at once, and submit to the Emperors." Justin said, "To obey the commandments of our Saviour Jesus Christ is worthy neither of blame nor of condemnation." Rusticus the prefect said, "What kind of doctrines do you profess?" Justin said, "I have endeavoured to learn all doctrines, but I have acquiesced at last in the true doctrines, those namely of the Christians, even though they do not please those who hold false opinions." Rusticus the prefect said, "Are those the doctrines that please you, you wretched fellow?" Justin said, "Yes, since I adhere to them with right dogma." Rusticus the prefect said, "What is the dogma?" Justin said, "That according to which we worship the God of the Christians, whom we reckon to be one from the beginning, the maker and fashioner of the whole creation, visible and invisible; and the Lord Jesus Christ the Son of God, who had also been preached beforehand by the prophets as about to be present with the race of men, the herald of salvation and teacher of good disciples. And I, being a man, think that what I can say is insignificant in comparison with the boundless divinity, acknowledging a certain prophetic power, since it was prophesied concerning Him of whom I now say that He is the Son of God. For I know that of old the prophets foretold His appearance among men."

[c. iii] Rusticus the prefect said, "Where do you assemble?" Justin said, "Where each one chooses and can; for do you fancy that we all meet in the very same place? Not so, because the God of the Christians is not circumscribed by place; but, being invisible, fills heaven and earth, and everywhere is worshipped and glorified by the faithful." Rusticus the prefect said, "Tell me where you assemble, or into what place do you collect your followers?" Justin said, "I live above one Martinus, at the Trinothinian Bath; and during the whole time (and I am now living in Rome for the second time) I am unaware of any other meeting than his. And if any one wished to come to me, I communicated to him the doctrines of truth." Rusticus said, "Are you not then a Christian?" Justin said, "Yes; I am a Christian."

[c. iv] Then said the prefect Rusticus to Chariton, "Tell me further, Chariton, are you also a Christian?" Chariton said, "I am a Christian by the command of God." Rusticus the prefect asked the woman Charito, "What say you, Charito?" Charito said, "I am a Christian by the grace of God." Rusticus said to Euelpistus, "And what are you?" Euelpistus, a servant of Cæsar, answered, "I, too, am a Christian, having been freed by Christ, and by the grace of Christ, I partake of the same hope." Rusticus the prefect said to Hierax, "And you, are you a Christian?" Hierax said, "Yes, I am a Christian, for I revere and worship the same God." Rusticus the prefect said, "Did Justin make you Christians?" Hierax said, "I was a Christian, and will be a Christian." And Pæon stood up and said, "I too am a Christian." Rusticus the prefect said, "Who taught you?" Pæon said, "From our parents we received this good confession." Euelpistus said, "I willingly heard the words from Justin. But from my parents also I learned to be a Christian." Rusticus the prefect said, "Where are your parents?" Euelpistus said, "In Cappadocia." Rusticus says to Hierax, "Where are your parents?" And he answered and said, "Christ is our true father, and faith in Him is our mother; and my earthly parents died; and I, when I was driven from Iconium in Phrygia, came here." Rusticus the prefect said to Liberianus, "And what say you? Are you a Christian, and unwilling to worship [the gods]?" Liberianus said, "I too am a Christian, for I worship and reverence the only true God."

[c. v] The prefect says to Justin, "Hearken, you who are called learned, and think that you know true doctrines; if you are scourged and beheaded, do you believe that you will ascend into heaven?" Justin said, "I hope that if I endure these things, I shall have His gifts. For I know that to all who have thus lived, there abides the divine favour until the completion of the whole world." Rusticus the prefect said, "Do you suppose, then, that you will ascend into heaven to receive some recompense?" Justin said, "I do not suppose it, but I know and am fully persuaded of it." Rusticus the prefect said, "Let us then now come to the matter in hand, and which presses. Having come together, offer sacrifice with one accord to the gods." Justin said, "No right-thinking person falls away from piety to impiety." Rusticus the prefect said, "Unless ye obey, ye shall be mercilessly punished." Justin said, "Through prayer we can be saved on account of our Lord Jesus Christ, even when we have been punished, because this shall become to us salvation and confidence at the more fearful and universal judgment-seat of our Lord and Saviour." Thus also said the other martyrs: "Do what you will; for we are Christians and do not sacrifice to idols."

[c. vi] Rusticus the prefect pronounced sentence, saying: "Let those who have refused to sacrifice to the gods and to yield to the command of the Emperor be scourged, and led away to suffer the punishment of decapitation, according to the laws." The holy martyrs having glorified God, and having gone forth to the accustomed place, were beheaded, and perfected their testimony in the confession of the Saviour. And some of the faithful having secretly removed their bodies, laid them in a suitable place, the grace of our Lord Jesus Christ having wrought along with them, to whom be glory for ever and ever. Amen.—*A.-N.C.L.* ii. 367–70.

No. 50.—Conversion of Tatian

From Tatian [*fl. c.* 160–70], *Oratio adv. Græcos,* c. xxix.

Wherefore having seen these things, and moreover also having been admitted to the Mysteries, and having everywhere examined the religious rites performed by the effeminate and the pathic, and having found among the Romans the Latiarian Jupiter delighting in human gore and the blood of slaughtered men, and Artemis not far from the great city sanctioning acts of the same kind, and one demon here and another there instigating to the perpetration of evil—retiring by myself, I sought how I might be able to discover the truth. And while I was giving my most earnest attention to the matter, I happened to meet with certain barbaric writings, too old to be compared with the opinions of the Greeks, and too divine to be compared with their errors; and I was led to put faith in these by the unpretending cast of the language, the inartificial characters of the writers, the foreknowledge displayed of future events, the excellent quality of the precepts, and the declaration of the government of the universe as centred in one Being. And my soul being taught of God, I discerned that the former class of writings lead to condemnation, but that these put an end to the slavery that is in the world, and rescue us from a multiplicity of rulers and ten thousand tyrants, while they give us, not indeed what we had not before received, but what we had received but were prevented by error from retaining.—*A.-N.C.L.* iii. 33 *sq.*

No. 51.—Christian Life in the Sub-Apostolic Age

From Lucian, *De morte Peregrini* [*c.* 165–70], §§ 12, 13.

[§ 12] When [Peregrinus] was imprisoned, the Christians, taking the matter to heart, left no stone unturned in the endeavour to rescue him. Then, when this was found to be impossible, they looked after his wants in every other respect with unremitting care and zeal. And from the first break of day old women—widows they are called—and orphan children might been seen waiting about the doors of the prison; while their officers, by bribing the keepers, succeeded in passing the night inside with him. Then various meals were brought in, and sacred formulas of theirs were repeated; and this fine fellow Peregrinus—for he still bore this name—was entitled a new Socrates by them. [§ 13] Moreover there came from certain of the cities in Asia deputies sent by the Christian communities to assist and advise and console the man. Indeed the alacrity they display is incredible, when any matter of the kind is undertaken as a matter of public concern; for in short they spare for nothing. Accordingly, large sums of money came to Peregrinus at that time from them, on the plea of his bonds, and he made no inconsiderable revenue out of it. For the poor wretches have persuaded themselves that they will be altogether immortal and will live for ever, and with this end in view they actually despise death and the greater part of them give themselves up voluntarily.—J. B. Lightfoot, *Apostolic Fathers*,[2] II. i. 345 *sq*.

No. 52.—Bad Emperors the only Persecutors

From the *Apology* of Melito, Bishop of Sardis, *c*. 170, to M. Aurelius, in Eusebius, *H.E.* IV. xxvi. §§ 5–11.

[§ 5] For what never before happened, the race of the pious is now suffering persecution, being driven about in Asia by new decrees. For the shameless informers and coveters of the property of others, taking occasion from the decrees, openly carry on robbery night and day, despoiling those who are guilty of no wrong. . . . If these things are done by thy command, well and good. For a just ruler will never take unjust measures; and we indeed gladly accept the honour of such a death. [§ 6] But this request alone we present to thee, that thou wouldst thyself first examine the authors of such strife, and justly judge whether they be worthy of death and punishment, or of safety and quiet. But if, on the other hand, this counsel and this new decree, which is not fit to be executed even against barbarian enemies, be not from thee, much more do we beseech thee not to leave us exposed to such lawless plundering by the populace.

[§ 7] For our philosophy formerly flourished among the barbarians; but having sprung up among the nations under thy rule, during the great reign of thy ancestor Augustus, it became to thine empire especially a blessing of auspicious omen. For from that time the power of the Romans has grown in greatness and splendour. To this power thou hast succeeded as the desired possessor, and such shalt thou continue with thy son, if thou guardest the philosophy which grew up with the Empire and which came into existence with Augustus; that philosophy which thy ancestors also honoured along with the other religions.

[§ 8] And a most convincing proof that our doctrine flourished for the good of an Empire happily begun, is this — that there has no evil happened since the reign of Augustus; but that, on the contrary, all things have been splendid and glorious, in accordance with the prayers of all.

[§ 9] Nero and Domitian, alone, persuaded by certain calumniators, have wished to slander our doctrine, and from them it has come to pass that the falsehood has been handed down [§ 10] in consequence of an unreasonable practice which prevails of bringing slanderous accusations against the Christians. But thy pious fathers corrected their ignorance, having frequently rebuked in writing many who dared to attempt new measures against them. Among them thy grandfather Hadrian appears to have written to many others, and also to Fundanus the proconsul and governor of Asia. And thy father, when thou wast also ruling with him, wrote to the cities, forbidding them to take any new measures against us; among the rest to the Larissæans, to the Thessalonians, to the Athenians, and to all the Greeks.

[§ 11] And as for thee—since thy opinions respecting the Christians are the same as theirs, and indeed much more benevolent and philosophic—we are the more persuaded that thou wilt do all that we ask of thee.—*N. & P.-N.F.* i. 205 *sq.*

No. 53.—St. Peter and St. Paul in Rome, *c.* 64

From Dionysius, Bishop of Corinth, *c.* 170, and Gaïus, a Roman Presbyter under Pope Zephyrinus, 199–217, *ap.* Eusebius, *H.E.* II. xxv. §§ 5–8.

[§ 5] Thus publicly announcing himself as the first among God's chief enemies, he [Nero] was led on to the slaughter of the apostles. It is therefore recorded that Paul was beheaded in Rome itself, and that Peter likewise was crucified under Nero. This account of Peter and Paul is substantiated by the fact that their names are preserved in the cemeteries of that place even to the present day. [§ 6] It is confirmed likewise by Gaïus, a member of the Church who arose under Zephyrinus, bishop of Rome. He in a public disputation with Proclus, the leader of the Phrygian heresy, speaks as follows concerning the places where the sacred corpses of the aforesaid apostles are laid:—

[§ 7] "But I can show the trophies of the apostles. For if you will go to the Vatican or to the Ostian Way, you will find the trophies of those who laid the foundations of this church."

[§ 8] And that they both suffered martyrdom at the same time is stated by Dionysius, bishop of Corinth, in his epistle to the Romans, in the following words:—

"You have thus, by such an admonition, bound together the planting of Peter and of Paul at Rome and Corinth. For both of them planted and likewise taught us in our Corinth. And they taught together in like manner in Italy, and suffered martyrdom at the same time."—*N. & P.-N.F.* i. 129 *sq.*

No. 54.—The Letter of Dionysius, Bishop of Corinth, *c.* 170, to Soter, Bishop of Rome

From Eusebius, *H.E.* IV. xxiii. §§ 9–12.

[§ 9] There is extant also another epistle written by Dionysius to the Romans, and addressed to Soter, who was bishop at that time. We cannot do better than to subjoin some passages from this epistle, in which he commends the practice of the Romans which has been retained down to the persecution in our own days. His words are as follows: [§ 10] "For from the beginning it has been your practice to do good to all the brethren in various ways, and to send contributions to many churches in every city. Thus relieving the want of the needy, and making provision for the brethren in the mines by the gifts which you have sent from the beginning, you Romans keep up the hereditary customs of the Romans, which your blessed bishop Soter has not only maintained, but also added to, furnishing an abundance of supplies to the saints, and encouraging the brethren from abroad with blessed words, as a loving father his children." [§ 11] In this same epistle he makes mention of Clement's epistle to the Corinthians, showing that it had been the custom from the beginning to read it in the church. His words are as follows: "To-day we have passed the Lord's holy day, in which we have read your epistle. From it, whenever we read it, we shall always be able to draw advice, as also from the former epistle, which was written to us through Clement." [§ 12] The same writer also speaks as follows concerning his own epistles, alleging that they had been mutilated: "As the brethren desired me to write epistles, I wrote. And these epistles the apostles of the devil have filled with tares, cutting out some things and adding others. For them a woe is reserved. It is therefore not to be wondered at if some have attempted to adulterate the Lord's writing also, since they have formed designs even against writings which are of less account."—*N. & P.-N.F.* i. 201 *sq.*

No. 55.—Heaven and Hell

From *The Apocalypse of Peter* [*c.* 170], §§ 15–33.

[§ 15] And the Lord showed me a very great country outside of this world, exceeding bright with light, and the air there lighted with the rays of the sun, and the earth itself blooming with unfaded flowers and full of spices and plants, fair-flowering and incorruptible and bearing blessed fruit. [§ 16] And so great was the perfume that it was borne thence even unto us. [§ 17] And the dwellers in that place were clad in the raiment of shining angels, and their raiment was like unto their country; and the angels hovered about them there. [§ 18] And the glory of the dwellers there was equal, and with one voice they sang praises alternately to the Lord God, rejoicing in that place. [§ 19] The Lord saith to us: This is the place of your high-priests, the righteous men.

[§ 20] And over against that place I saw another, squalid, and it was the place of punishment; and those who were punished there and the punishing angels had their raiment dark like the air of the place.

[§ 21] And there were certain there hanging by the tongue: and these were the blasphemers of the way of righteousness; and under them lay fire, burning and punishing them.

[§ 22] And there was a great lake full of flaming mire, in which were certain men that pervert righteousness, and tormenting angels afflicted them.

[§ 23] And there were also others, women, hanged by their hair over that mire that bubbled up; and these were they who adorned themselves for adultery; and the men who mingled with them in the defilement of adultery were hanging by the feet and their heads in that mire. And I said: I did not believe that I should come into this place.

[§ 24] And I saw the murderers and those who conspired with them cast into a certain strait place, full of evil snakes, and smitten by those beasts, and thus turning to and fro in that punishment; and worms, as it were clouds of darkness, afflicted them. And the souls of the murdered stood and looked upon the punishment of these murderers and said: O God, thy judgment is just.

[§ 25] And near that place I saw another strait place into which the gore and the filth of those who were being punished ran down and became there as it were a lake: and there sat women having the gore up to their necks, and over against them sat many children who were born to them out of due time, crying; and there came forth from them sparks of fire and smote the women in the eyes; and these were the accursed who conceived and caused abortion.

[§ 26] And other men and women were burning up to the middle and were cast into a dark place and were beaten by evil spirits, and their inwards were eaten by restless worms; and these were they who persecuted the righteous and delivered them up.

[§ 27] And near those there were again women and men gnawing their own lips, and being punished and receiving a red-hot iron in their eyes; and these were they who blasphemed and slandered the way of righteousness.

[§ 28] And over against these again other men and women gnawing their tongues and having flaming fire in their mouths; and these were the false witnesses.

[§ 29] And in a certain other place there were pebbles sharper than swords or any spit red hot, and women and men in tattered and filthy raiment rolled about on them in punishment; and these were the rich who trusted in their riches and had no pity for orphans and widows, and despised the commandment of God.

[§ 30] And in another lake, full of pitch and blood and mire bubbling up, there stood men and women up to their knees; and these were the usurers and those who take interest on interest.

[§ 31] And other men and women were being hurled down from a great cliff and reached the bottom, and again were driven by those who were set over them to climb up upon the cliff, and hence were hurled down again, and had no rest from this punishment; and these were they who defiled their bodies acting as women; and the women who were with them were those who lay with one another as a man with a woman.

[§ 32] And alongside of that cliff there was a place full of much fire, and there stood men who with their own hands had made for themselves carven images instead of God. And alongside of these were other men and women, having rods and striking each other and never ceasing from such punishment.

[§ 33] And others again near them, women and men, burning and turning themselves and roasting; and these were they that leaving the way of God . . .—*A.-N.C.L.;* additional volume, ed. A. Menzies, 145 *sq.*

No. 56.—Montanism

From Miltiades, *c.* 160–80, as summarized by the Anonymous, *ap.* Eus., *H.E.* V. xvii. §§ 1–4.

[§ 1] . . . Having found these things in a certain work of theirs in opposition to the work of the brother Miltiades [*v.l.* Alcibiades], in which he shows that a prophet ought not to speak in ecstasy, I made an abridgment. [§ 2] . . . But the false prophet falls into an ecstasy in which he is without shame or fear. Beginning with supposed ignorance, he passes on, as has been stated, to involuntary madness of soul. [§ 3] They cannot show that one of the old or one of the new prophets was thus carried away in spirit. Neither can they boast of Agabus, or Judas, or Silas, or the daughters of Philip, or Ammia in Philadelphia, or Quadratus, or any others not belonging to them. [§ 4] . . . For if, after Quadratus, and Ammia in Philadelphia, as they assert, the women with Montanus received the prophetic gift, let them shew who among them received it from Montanus and the women. For the apostle thought it necessary that the prophetic gift should continue in all the Church until the final coming. But they cannot show it, though this is the fourteenth year [*sc.* 193] since the death of Maximilla [? 179].—*N. & P.-N.F.* i. 233 *sq.*

No. 57.—The Persecution at Lyons and Vienne, 177

From *The Epistle of the Gallican Churches*, *ap.* Eusebius, *H.E.* V. i.

The servants of Christ who sojourn in Vienna and Lugdunum of Gallia to the Brethren throughout Asia and Phrygia who hold the same faith and hope with us of redemption, peace, and grace and glory from God the Father and Christ Jesus our Lord.

* * * * *

The magnitude, however, of the tribulation in these parts, and the intensity of the fury of the Gentiles against the saints, and the variety of the sufferings which the blessed martyrs endured, we are neither able to state with accuracy nor indeed is it possible for them to be embraced in writing.

For the adversary darted upon us with all his might, preluding thus soon his fearless coming which is about to be. He practised withal every device, accustoming and training his own agents against the servants of God, so that not only were we excluded from houses and baths and markets, but actually the mere appearance of any one of us in any place whatever was forbidden.

But the grace of God was our general in the fight, rescuing the weak and ranging them in battle-array as strong pillars, enabling them through patient endurance to draw upon themselves all the violence of the Evil One; and indeed they advanced to close quarters with him, enduring every form of reproach and punishment; finally, making light of their sufferings, they hasted to Christ, truly showing that the sufferings of this present time are not worthy to be compared with the glory that shall be revealed to us-ward (Rom. viii. 18).

First, they nobly endured all that had to be borne at the hands of the mob and rabble; they were hooted, assaulted, pulled about, plundered, stoned, and forced to barricade themselves in; in fact they suffered every indignity which an infuriated mob is accustomed to inflict upon its supposed adversaries and foes. At length, being brought into the forum by the chiliarch and chief men of the city, they were examined in the presence of the whole multitude, and having confessed (their Christianity), were put into prison to await the arrival of the governor. Subsequently, when they were brought before him and he was treating us with great harshness, Vettius Epagathus, one of the brethren, a man filled with the fulness of love towards God and towards his neighbour, whose life as a citizen was so upright that, although so young a man, he equalled the testimony borne to the aged Zacharias, for indeed he walked in all the commandments and ordinances of the Lord blameless (Luke i. 6), being also tireless in every act of service to his neighbour, very zealous towards God, and fervent in spirit (Rom. xii. 11); Vettius, I say, being of such a character, could not endure that such unreasonable judgment should be given against us; and so, being highly indignant, he claimed himself also to give evidence in defence of the brethren, to the effect that "there is nothing impious or sacrilegious amongst us." But those around the judgment-seat shouted him down (for he was a man of note), and the governor refused the just claim which he thus put forward, merely asking if he were himself also a Christian; and when he confessed it with a clear voice, he was himself also taken into the order of the witnesses, being designated "the Christians' Advocate," having the Advocate (cf. John xiv. 16) in himself, the Spirit (cf. Luke i. 67) in greater measure than Zacharias, as he showed by the fulness of his love, being well pleased to lay down even his own life for the defence of the brethren. For he was, and is, a genuine disciple of Christ, following the Lamb whithersoever He goeth (Rev. xiv. 4).

Thereupon the rest were scrutinized, and the first witnesses were forward and ready, who with all eagerness completed the confession of their witness. Likewise the unready and untrained were made manifest, moreover also the weak, who were unable to bear the strain of a great contest. Of these about ten miscarried, who both caused us great grief and sorrow unmeasured, and also hindered the eagerness of the others who were unarrested, and who, although suffering all terrors, were nevertheless constantly present with the confessors, and would not leave them. Then, indeed, were we all greatly anxious, through uncertainty as to their confession, not dreading the punishments to be endured, but fixing our gaze on the end, and fearing lest any might fall away. Each day, however, those who were worthy were arrested, and filled up the others' places, so that there were gathered together from the two Churches all the zealous ones through whose instrumentality especially our affairs had been established. They arrested also certain heathen domestic slaves of ours, for the governor ordered that we should all be examined in public; and these falling into a plot of Satan, and fearing the tortures which they saw the saints suffering, on being instigated to this course by the soldiers, falsely accused us of Thyestean banquets and Œdipodean intercourse, and of other deeds of which it is not lawful for us either to speak or think, nor even to believe that the like is ever done amongst mankind. These statements being reported, all were infuriated against us, so that if there were any who from ties of kinship had hitherto been lenient, even these were now greatly enraged and mad with anger against us. Then that was fulfilled which was spoken by our Lord: "The time shall come wherein every one that killeth you will think that he doeth God service" (John xvi. 2). Hereupon the holy witnesses endured punishments beyond all description, Satan being ambitious that some of the slanders might be admitted by them also. The whole wrath of the populace and of the governor and of the soldiers was directed in excessive measure against Sanctus, a deacon from Vienna, and against Maturus, a very recent convert but a noble warrior, and against Attalus, a Pergamene by race, who had ever been a pillar and a foundation (1 Tim. iii. 15) of our Church, and against Blandina, through whom Christ showed how what appears to men worthless and uncomely and despicable is deemed worthy of great glory by God, because of that love toward Him which is manifested in power and not boasted of in mere show (cf. 1 Cor. i. 25 f.). For while we were all afraid for her, and her earthly mistress, who was herself also one of the witnessing combatants, dreaded lest she should be unable through bodily weakness boldly to make confession, Blandina was filled with such power that she was set free from and contrasted with those who tortured her with every kind of torture in turn from morning to evening, and who confessed that they were conquered, since they had nothing left which they could any longer do to her, and that they marvelled at breath remaining in her when her whole body was lacerated and laid open, testifying that one of the tortures by itself was sufficient to end life, let alone so many and such great ones. But the blessed woman, like a noble athlete, gained her strength by her confession, finding refreshment and freedom from pain in saying "I am a Christian," and, "We do nothing vile."

Sanctus also nobly endured with boundless and superhuman courage all the outrages put upon him, the ungodly hoping that from the persistency and magnitude of his tortures something would be heard from his lips of the Christians' unlawful doings; but with such confidence did he array himself against them, that he did not even tell his own name or race or city, nor whether he were a slave or free, but to all their interrogations he returned answer in the Latin tongue, "I am a Christian." This he owned for name, for city, for race, for everything besides, nor did the heathen hear from him any other word. On this account there was kindled a great emulation against him on the part of the governor and the torturers, so that when no other form of torture remained to be inflicted on him, as a last resort they affixed hot brazen plates to the tenderest parts of his body. These were burned, but he remained unmoved and unyielding, steadfast in his confession, refreshed and empowered by the heavenly fountain of the water of life (cf. Rev. xxi. 6; John iv. 14; vii. 38) which proceeds from the heart of Christ. His poor body was a witness to his sufferings, being one entire wound and scar, drawn together and broken out of all human shape. In him Christ suffered and achieved great glory, bringing the adversary to naught, and showing that there is nothing fearful where the Father's love is nor painful where is Christ's glory. For when after some days the wicked men again tortured this witness, thinking that, if they repeated the same punishments upon his limbs, which were so swollen and inflamed that he could not bear the touch of a hand, they would overcome him, or that, dying under his tortures, he would strike fear into the rest, not only did nothing of this sort happen, but contrary to all human expectation he lifted his head and straightened his body under the second tortures, recovering his own former appearance and the use of his limbs, so that by the grace of Christ the second torture became for him no punishment but a means of healing.

Biblias, too, one of those who had denied Christ, the devil thought that he had gulped down, and wishing to condemn her also through (forcing her to utter) slanders, brought her to punishment, to compel her to say impious things about us, as being one already crushed and cowardly. But under the torture she recovered her senses, and, as it were, awoke from a deep sleep, being reminded by the temporal anguish of the eternal punishment in Gehenna; and she determinedly contradicted the slanders, saying, "How could those persons eat children to whom it is not lawful to eat the blood even of irrational animals?" Thereupon she confessed herself a Christian, and was added to the order of the witnesses. The tyrannous punishments being thus brought to naught by Christ through the patient endurance of the witnesses, the devil conceived other contrivances—close confinement in the prison in the dark, and in a most loathsome situation, extending the feet in the stocks, stretching them to the fifth hole, and other cruelties such as enraged underlings who are full of the devil are wont to inflict upon their prisoners. So that very many were suffocated in the prison; those whom the Lord willed thus to depart, showing forth His glory. For those who had suffered such acute tortures, that it seemed impossible for them to continue to live even with every nursing care, remained alive in the prison, destitute indeed of all human care, but strengthened and empowered in body and soul by the Lord, exhorting and encouraging the rest. Whereas the younger ones, and those only just arrested, whose bodies had not been previously ill-treated, could not bear the confinement, and died in the prison.

Now the blessed Pothinus, who had been entrusted with the ministry of the bishopric in Lugdunum, and was more than ninety years of age and quite feeble in body, scarce indeed able to breathe from long bodily weakness, yet strengthened by his eager spirit because of his immediate desire for martyrdom, was himself haled to the judgment-seat, his body broken down with age and disease, his soul preserved within him in order that Christ might triumph through it. And he, being brought to the judgment-seat, and escorted by the police-magistrates and rabble with all kinds of hooting as though he were the Christ, rendered a glorious witness (cp. 1 Tim. vi. 13). Being asked during his examination by the governor who the God of the Christians was, he replied, "If thou art worthy, thou shalt know." Thereupon he was unsparingly pulled about, and was maltreated with all kinds of blows, the nearest ones insulting him in every way with hands and feet, not even respecting his age, while those at a distance hurled at him whatever each could lay hold of, every one thinking it a gross carelessness and impiety if any act of wanton cruelty were omitted; for so they thought to avenge their own gods. Thus, scarcely breathing, he was cast into prison, and after two days yielded up his spirit.

Hereupon a remarkable instance of God's providence

occurred, and the measureless mercy of Jesus was shown—an occurrence seldom happening in the brotherhood, but not beyond the power of Christ. For those who on their first arrest had denied Christ, were imprisoned along with the others and shared their miseries,—for not even in the present time was their denial of any benefit to them—while those who confessed what they were, were imprisoned as "Christians," no other charge being brought against them; the former being detained as guilty of manslaughter and abominable impurity, and being punished two-fold in comparison with the latter. The confessors were comforted by the joy of martyrdom and the hope of the things promised and the Father's Spirit, while the recanters were greatly tormented by their conscience, so that their countenances distinguished them from all the rest when they were led out. The confessors came forth joyously, with glory and much grace on their countenances, so that even their bonds encircled them like a comely decoration, as a bride is decked with fringes of cunningly-worked gold, and they were scented with the sweet savour of Christ (2 Cor. ii. 15), so that some fancied they had actually been anointed with material ointment. But the others were dejected and ashamed and sad-looking, filled to the full with all disgrace, besides being reviled by the heathen as ignoble and cowardly, branded as murderers, and deprived of the all-worthy and glorious and life-giving name. The rest beholding this were strengthened, and when arrested, confessed unhesitatingly, giving no heed to the suggestions of the devil.

* * * * *

Subsequently their martyrdoms embraced every kind of death. For out of different hues and various kinds of flowers they wove one wreath and offered it to the Father. It was indeed right that such noble athletes, who had patiently undergone manifold contests and had greatly conquered, should receive the splendid wreath of incorruption.

Accordingly Maturus and Sanctus and Blandina and Attalus were led forth to the beasts in the public place, and for the popular exhibition of heathen cruelty, a day for beast-fighting being granted directly on our account. Maturus and Sanctus once more went through every form of punishment in the amphitheatre, just as though they had suffered nothing at all before, or rather as having already in many bouts wrested the position from the adversary, and now contending for the wreath itself. They again endured the scourgings in procession which are customary on such occasions, and the halings by the beasts, and all else that the maddened populace yelled for and demanded. Finally they were placed on the iron chair on which their bodies were fried, and the exhalation overwhelmed them. Nor did they even then desist, but became even more maddened against them, wishing to overcome their patience. Yet even so they heard nothing from Sanctus but that word of confession which he had constantly uttered from the first. These two, then, their life having been preserved through all this great and varied agony, were at last sacrificed, having been made a spectacle to the world (1 Cor. iv. 9) throughout that day in place of all the various gladiatorial combats.

Now Blandina, hanging upon a stake, was exposed as food for the wild beasts that were driven in. And because she seemed to be hanging on a cross, and because of her intense prayers, she inspired great courage in the combatants, who saw in this contest, and with their outward eyes in the form of their sister, Him who was crucified for them, that He might persuade those who believe on Him that all who suffer for the glory of Christ have an abiding fellowship with the living God. And when none of the beasts would touch her, she was taken down from the stake and sent back again to the prison, being reserved for another contest, in order that, being victorious in many trials, she might make the condemnation of the crooked serpent (Isa. xxvii. 1) irrevocable, and encourage the brethren; for she, small and weak and despised as she was, put on Christ (Gal. iii. 27), the great and resistless Athlete, and having worsted the adversary in many contests, won through conflicts the wreath of incorruption.

Attalus also was loudly demanded by the people, for he was a man of repute; and he readily entered as a combatant because of his good conscience, since he had been genuinely trained in the Christian rule and had ever been a witness amongst us of the truth. He was led round the amphitheatre, having in front a tablet on which had been written in Latin, THIS IS ATTALUS THE CHRISTIAN. The people indeed were bursting with eagerness for him, but the governor, hearing that he was a Roman, bade him be taken back again with the rest who were in prison, respecting whom he had written to Cæsar, and an answer was awaited from him.

The intervening period was not idle nor fruitless, but through their patient endurance the boundless mercy of Christ was shown forth. For through the living (confessors), the dead (in sins) were quickened: witnesses showed favour to non-witnesses, and there was great joy to the virgin mother as she received back alive those whom she had untimely brought forth as dead. For through their influence most of the lapsed were restored, being both conceived anew and endowed with fresh life; and they learned to confess, and living now and nerved, they went to the tribunal to be again interrogated by the governor, God, who willeth not the death of a sinner (Ezek. xxxiii. 11), but is gracious to penitence, shedding sweetness on them.

Now the rescript of Cæsar was that they should be put to death by torture, but that those who recanted should be released.

At the beginning of the public festival held here, which is thronged with men who attend it from all nations, the governor brought the blessed ones to his tribunal as a spectacle, and displayed them in procession to the crowd. Whereupon he again examined them, and those who appeared to be Roman citizens he beheaded, the rest he sent to the beasts. And Christ was greatly glorified in the case of those who had previously denied Him but now confessed Him, contrary to the expectation of the heathen. Moreover these were examined separately, as certain to be released; but when they confessed, they were added to the order of the witnesses, those only remaining without who had no longer any trace of faith, nor of respect for their wedding garment (Matt. xxii. 11), nor idea of the fear of God, slandering the Way (Acts ix. 2) by their manner of life, being indeed sons of perdition (cf. John xvii. 12; 2 Thess. ii. 3). But all the rest were added to the Church (Acts ii. 47). Amongst those examined was Alexander, a

Phrygian, a physician by profession, who had spent many years in Gaul, and was known to almost every one for his love to God and boldness in the Word, for he was not without a share of apostolic grace. This man, standing by the judgment-seat, and with a nod encouraging the others to their confession, appeared to the bystanders as though in pains of travail. And the populace, exasperated at seeing those who had before recanted once more confessing (their Christianity), hooted at Alexander as the cause of this. Then the governor, turning his attention to him, asked him who he was, and on his replying "A Christian," he fell into a rage and condemned him to the beasts. On the next day he and Attalus entered the arena; for the governor, to please the people, had ordered even Attalus again to the beasts. These men passed through every conceivable device for torture in the amphitheatre, and having endured a magnificent contest, at last were themselves sacrificed. Alexander neither murmured nor groaned at all, but conversed with God in his heart, while Attalus, when placed upon the iron chair and roasted, the hot odour from his poor body being borne aloft, said to the crowd in Latin, "Lo, this it is to eat men, and you are doing it; we neither eat men, nor practise any wickedness." And when asked what name God has, he replied, "God has not a name as a man hath."

Finally, on the last day of the gladiatorial games, Blandina was again brought forward with a lad of about fifteen, named Ponticus. These two had been brought in each day to witness the punishment of the others, and had been pressed to swear by the idols. And because they remained constant and set them at naught, the populace grew furious, so that they respected neither the youth of the boy nor the sex of the woman; but they made them pass through every form of terrible suffering, and through the whole round of punishments, urging them to swear after each one, but they were unable to effect this. For Ponticus, excited to zeal by his sister, so that even the heathen saw that it was she who encouraged and strengthened him, yielded up his spirit after nobly enduring every punishment. And the blessed Blandina, last of all, like a noble mother who had excited her children to zeal, and sent them forward as conquerors to the King, recapitulated in herself all the conflicts of her children and hastened to them, rejoicing and exulting in her death, like one invited to a bridal feast rather than thrown to the beasts. For after the scourging, after the beasts, after the frying, she was at last enclosed in a net and exposed to a bull; and having been many times tossed by the beast, and being no longer sensible of her sufferings on account of her hope and firm hold on the things entrusted to her and her converse with Christ, she also was sacrificed, even the heathen themselves confessing that never yet amongst them had a woman suffered such manifold and great tortures.

Yet not even thus was their madness and cruel hatred towards the saints satiated. For being savage and barbarous tribes, incited by the Wild Beast, they were not easily appeased, their malice taking a fresh and peculiar start in the case of the dead bodies (of their victims). For the persecutors were not ashamed at having been defeated, because they possessed no power of human reasoning; but rather they kindled up their rage like a wild beast, both the governor and people alike displaying unjust hatred against us; that the scripture might be fulfilled, He that is unjust, let him be unjust still, and he that is righteous, let him be righteous still (Rev. xxii. 11). For they cast to dogs those who had been suffocated in the prison, carefully guarding them by night and by day lest any one should be buried by us. Then they gathered together the remains left by the wild beasts and by the fire—how mangled and how charred!—and the heads of the others with their severed bodies, and guarded them likewise from burial with military care for many days. And some snorted and gnashed their teeth at them, seeking to take some further vengeance on them; others sneered and mocked, magnifying their idols and ascribing to them the punishments of the martyrs. The more reasonable, and those who seemed to sympathize most, often rebuked us, saying, "Where is their God? and what did their religion profit them which they preferred before their life?" So various was the behaviour of these men; we ourselves being overwhelmed with sorrow because we could not bury the bodies in the earth. For night did not help us to do this, nor could bribes persuade nor supplication shame our foes; but in every way they guarded them, looking upon it as a great point gained if they prevented them being buried.

*   *   *   *   *

For six days the bodies of the martyrs were publicly exhibited and exposed to the open air, and then they were burnt and reduced to ashes by the godless, and swept away in the river Rhodanus, which flows close by, to prevent any relic of them being seen any longer upon the earth. And this they did, imagining that they could conquer God, and deprive them of their new birth, in order that (in their own words) "they may have no hope of a resurrection, through trusting in which they bring in to us a foreign and strange religion, and despise terrible sufferings, and are willing with joy to die. Now let us see whether they will rise again, and if their God is able to succour them and rescue them out of our hands."—T. H. Bindley, *The Epistle of the Gallican Churches*, pp. 22–44.

No. 58.—The Three Stock Charges against the Christians

From Athenagoras, 177, *Legatio pro Christianis*, cc. i.–iii.

[c. i.] . . . But why is a mere name odious to you? Names are not deserving of hatred: it is the unjust act that calls for penalty and punishment. And accordingly, with admiration of your mildness and gentleness, and your peaceful and benevolent disposition towards every man, individuals live in the possession of equal rights; and the whole empire, under your intelligent sway, enjoys profound peace. But for us who are called Christians you have not in like manner cared; but although we commit no wrong—nay, as will appear in the sequel of this discourse, are of all men most piously and righteously disposed towards the Deity and towards your government—you allow us to be harassed, plundered and persecuted, the multitude making war upon us for our name alone. We venture therefore to lay a statement of our case before you . . . and we beseech you to bestow some consideration upon us also, that we may cease at length to be slaughtered at the instigation of false accusers. For the fine imposed by our persecutors does not aim merely at our property. . . . But when we have surrendered our property, they plot against our very bodies and souls, pouring upon us wholesale charges of crimes of which we are guiltless even in thought. . . .

[c. ii.] . . . It does not comport with your justice, that others when charged with crimes should not be punished till they are convicted, but that in our case the name we bear should have more force than the evidence adduced on the trial, when the judges, instead of enquiring whether the person arraigned have committed any crime, vent their insults on the name, as if that were itself a crime. . . . What therefore is conceded as the common right of all we claim for ourselves, that we shall not be hated and punished because we are called Christians (for what has the name to do with our being bad men?) but be tried on any charges which may be brought against us, and either be released on our disproving them, or punished if convicted of crime —not for the name (for no Christian is a bad man unless he falsely profess our doctrines), but for the wrong which has been done. . . .

[c. iii.] Three things are alleged against us: atheism, Thyestean feasts, Œdipodean intercourse. But if these charges are true, spare no class; proceed at once against our crimes; destroy us root and branch, with our wives and children, if any Christian is found to live like the brutes. . . . But if these things are only idle tales and empty slanders . . . it remains for you to make enquiry concerning our life, our opinions, our loyalty and obedience to you and your house, to government, and thus at length to grant us the same rights (we ask nothing more) as to those who persecute us.—*A.-N.C.L.* ii. 376–9.

No. 59.—Discovery or Revelation?

From Athenagoras, *Legatio pro Christianis*, c. vii.

[c. vii.] Since therefore the unity of the Deity is confessed by almost all, even against their will, when they come to treat of the first principles of the universe, and we in our turn likewise assert that He who arranged this universe is God,—why is it that they can say and write with impunity what they please concerning the Deity, but that against us a law lies in force, though we are able to demonstrate what we apprehend and justly believe, namely that there is one God, with proofs and reasons accordant with truth? For poets and philosophers, as to other subjects so also to this, have applied themselves in the way of conjecture, moved, by reason of their affinity with the afflatus from God, each one by his own soul, to try whether he could find out and apprehend the truth; but they have not been found competent fully to apprehend it, because they thought fit to learn, not from God concerning God, but each one from himself; hence they came each to his own conclusion respecting God, and matter, and forms, and the world. But we have for witnesses of the things we apprehend and believe, prophets, men who have pronounced concerning God and the things of God, guided by the Spirit of God. And you too will admit, excelling all others as you do in intelligence and in piety towards the true God, that it would be irrational for us to cease to believe in the Spirit from God, who moved the mouths of the prophets like musical instruments, and to give heed to mere human opinions.—*A.-N.C.L.* ii. 382 *sq.*

No. 60.—Celsus, *c.* 175, on the Evidence for our Lord's Resurrection

From Origen, *Contra Celsum* [249], ii. § 55 (*Op.* i. 429; *P.G.* xi. 884 *sq.*).

[§ 55] . . . But the question is, Whether any one who was really dead, ever rose with a veritable body? Or do you imagine the statements of others not only to be myths, but to have the appearance of such, while you have discovered a becoming and credible termination to your drama in the voice from the cross, when he breathed his last, and in the earthquake and the darkness? That while alive he was of no assistance to himself, but that when dead he rose again, and showed the marks of his punishment, and how his hands were pierced with nails: who beheld this? A half-frantic woman, as you state, and some other one, perhaps, of those who were engaged in the same system of delusion, who had either dreamed so, owing to a peculiar state of mind, or under the influence of a wandering imagination had formed to himself an appearance according to his own wishes, which has been the case with numberless individuals; or, which is most probable, one who desired to impress others with this portent, and by such a falsehood to furnish an occasion to impostors like himself.—*A.-N.C.L.* xxiii. 58.

No. 61.—Celsus, on the Christian Propaganda

From Origen, *Contra Celsum*, iii. § 55 (*Op.* i. 484; *P.G.* xi. 993 A. B.).

[§ 55] . . . Celsus asserts: "We see, indeed, in private houses workers in wool and leather, and fullers and persons of the most uninstructed and rustic character, not venturing to utter a word in the presence of their elders and wiser masters; but when they get hold of the children privately, and certain women as ignorant as themselves, they pour forth wonderful statements to the effect that they ought not to give heed to their father and to their teachers, but should obey them; that the former are foolish and stupid, and neither know nor can perform anything that is really good, being preoccupied with empty trifles; that they alone know how men ought to live, and that, if the children obey them, they will both be happy themselves, and will make their home happy also. And while thus speaking, if they see one of the instructors of youth approaching, or one of the more intelligent class, or even the father himself, the more timid among them become afraid, while the more forward incite the children to throw off the yoke, whispering that in the presence of father and teachers they neither will nor can explain to them any good thing, seeing they turn away with aversion from the silliness and stupidity of such persons as being altogether corrupt, and far advanced in wickedness, and such as would inflict punishment upon them; but that if they wish [to avail themselves of their aid] they must leave their father and instructors, and go with the women and their playfellows to the women's apartments, or to the leather-shop, or to the fuller's shop, that they may attain to perfection;—and by words like these they gain them over."—*A.-N.C.L.* xxiii. 136 *sq.*

No. 62.—St. James, the Lord's Brother

From Hegesippus [*c.* 160–80], *ap.* Eusebius, *H.E.* II. xxiii. §§ 4–7.

[§ 4] James, the brother of the Lord, succeeded to the government of the Church in conjunction with the apostles. He has been called the Just by all from the time of our Saviour to the present day; for there were many that bore the name of James. [§ 5] He was holy from his mother's womb; and he drank no wine nor strong drink, nor did he eat flesh. No razor came upon his head; he did not anoint himself with oil, and he did not use the bath. [§ 6] He alone was permitted to enter into the holy place; for he wore not woollen, but linen, garments. And he was in the habit of entering alone into the temple, and was frequently found upon his knees begging forgiveness for the people, so that his knees became hard like those of a camel, in consequence of his constantly bending them in his worship of God, and asking forgiveness for the people. [§ 7] Because of his exceeding great justice, he was called the Just and Oblias, which signifies in Greek, "Bulwark of the people" and "Justice," in accordance with what the prophets declare concerning him.—*N. & P.-N.F.* i. 125.

No. 63.—Judaistic Christianity, *c.* 100–35

From Hegesippus [*c.* 160–80], *ap.* Eusebius, *H.E.* (α) III. xx. §§ 1–6 and (β) IV. xxii. §§ 1–4.

(α) [§ 1] Of the family of the Lord there were still living the grandchildren of Jude, who is said to have been the Lord's brother according to the flesh. Information was given that they belonged to the family of David, and they were brought to the Emperor Domitian by the Evocatus. For Domitian feared the coming of Christ as Herod also feared it. [§ 2] And he asked them if they were descendants of David, and they confessed that they were. Then he asked them how much property they had, or how much money they owned. And they both of them answered that they had only nine thousand denarii, half of which belonged to each of them; and this property did not consist of silver, but of a piece of land which contained only thirty nine acres, and from which they raised their taxes and supported themselves by their labour. [§ 3] Then they showed their hands, exhibiting the hardness of their bodies, and the callousness produced upon their hands by continuous toil as evidence of their own labour. [§ 4] And when they were asked concerning Christ and His kingdom, of what sort it was and when and where it was to appear, they answered that it was not a temporal nor an earthly kingdom, but a heavenly and angelic one, which would appear at the end of the world, when He should come in glory to judge the quick and the dead, and to give unto every one according to his works. [§ 5] Upon hearing this, Domitian did not pass judgment against them, but, despising them as of no account, he let them go, and by a decree put a stop to the persecution of the Church. But when they were released, they ruled the churches, because they were witnesses and were also relatives of the Lord. And peace being established, they lived until the time of Trajan.

(β) [§ 1] Hegesippus in the five books of *Memoirs* which have come down to us has left us a most complete record of his own views. In them he states that on a journey to Rome he met a great many bishops, and that he received the same doctrine from all. It is fitting to hear what he says after making some remarks about the epistle of Clement to the Corinthians. His words are as follows: [§ 2] "And the Church of Corinth continued in the true faith until Primus was bishop in Corinth. I conversed with them on my way to Rome, and abode with the Corinthians many days, during which we were mutually refreshed in the true doctrine. [§ 3] And when I had come to Rome I remained there until Anicetus, whose deacon was Eleutherus. And Anicetus was succeeded by Soter, and he by Eleutherus. In every succession and in every city, that is held which is preached by the Law and the Prophets and the Lord." [§ 4] The same author also describes the beginnings of the heresies which arose in his time, in the following words: "And after James the Just had suffered martyrdom, as the Lord had also on the same account, Symeon, the son of the Lord's uncle, Clopas, was appointed the next bishop. All proposed him as second bishop because he was a cousin of the Lord.

Therefore they called the church a virgin, for it was not yet corrupted by vain discourses."—*N. & P.-N.F.* iv. 148 *sq.*, 198 *sq.*

No. 64.—The Epitaph of Abercius Marcellus, Bishop of Hieropolis in Phrygia, *c.* 161-80

The citizen of a notable city I made this [tomb] in my lifetime; that in due season I might have here a resting-place for my body. Abercius by name, I am a disciple of the pure Shepherd, who feedeth His flocks of sheep on mountains and plains, who hath great eyes looking on all sides; for He taught me faithful writings. He also sent me to royal Rome to behold it and to see the golden-robed, golden-slippered Queen. And there I saw a people bearing the splendid seal. And I saw the plain of Syria and all the cities, even Nisibis, crossing over the Euphrates. And everywhere I had associates. In company with Paul, I followed, while everywhere faith led the way, and set before me for food the fish from the fountain, mighty and stainless (whom a pure virgin grasped), and gave this to friends to eat always, having good wine and giving the mixed cup with bread. These words I, Abercius, standing by ordered to be inscribed. In sooth I was in the course of my seventy-second year. Let every friend who observeth this pray for me. But no man shall place another tomb above mine. If otherwise, then he shall pay two thousand pieces of gold to the treasury of the Romans, and a thousand pieces of gold to my good fatherland Hieropolis.—J. B. Lightfoot, *The Apostolic Fathers*,[2] II. i. 496 *sq.*

No. 65.—Conversion of Theophilus, Bishop of Antioch, *c.* 180

From the *Ad Autolycum*, I. c. xiv.

[c. xiv.] Therefore do not be sceptical but believe; for I myself also used to disbelieve that this [*sc.* the general resurrection of all men] would take place; but now, having taken these things into consideration, I believe. At the same time, I met with the sacred Scriptures of the holy prophets, who also by the Spirit of God foretold the things that have already happened, just as they came to pass, and the things now occurring as they are now happening, and things future in the order in which they shall be accomplished. Admitting therefore the proof which events happening as predicted afford, I do not disbelieve, but I believe, obedient to God; whom, if you please, do you also submit to, believing Him, lest if now you continue unbelieving, you be convinced hereafter, when you are tormented with eternal punishments; which punishments, when they had been foretold by the prophets, the later-born poets and philosophers stole from the holy Scriptures, to make their doctrines worthy of credit. . . .—*A.-N.C.L.* iii. 63 *sq.*

No. 66.—Christian Life in the Second Century

From Minucius Felix, *Octavius* [*c.* 180], V. §§ 1–5; XII.

V. Then Cæcilius began as follows: My dear Marcus, you cannot be in doubt as to the matter which we are now to investigate, since, having carefully tested both systems, you have abandoned the one and chosen the other. Nevertheless, for the present occasion your mind should be so trained that you can hold the balance evenly as an upright judge, without inclining to one side more than the other. Otherwise, your verdict will appear to be the expression of your own feelings rather than the result of our arguments. If, then, you will take your seat as an entire stranger, who knows nothing of either party, it will be easy for me to show that everything in human affairs is doubtful, uncertain, undecided, and probable rather than true. For this reason it is the more surprising that some, weary of a thorough search after truth, should blindly give in to any opinion whatever, rather than steadfastly and diligently persevere in their investigations. Surely all must feel grieved and indignant at the thought that certain people—people, too, ignorant of learning, unlettered, and unacquainted even with the meanest arts—should pronounce definitely upon the universe and the supreme power, which, after all these ages, still forms the subject of the deliberations of the philosophers and their numerous schools. And this is only natural, since human insignificance is quite incapable of investigating things divine.

XII. Not even does the experience of the present convince you how deceptive are those empty hopes and useless promises. Miserable wretches, you can guess, from what happens to you during life, what awaits you in death. Look: some of you—the greater, the better part, as you assert—suffer from want, cold, toil, and hunger; and your God permits it, or pretends not to see it; he either will not or cannot help his people; hence he is either powerless or unjust. You, who dream of immortality after death, when unnerved by severe illness, consumed by fever, racked by pain, can you not yet understand your condition? Do you not yet recognize your frailty? Against your will, miserable wretch, you are convicted of weakness, but will not admit it.

But to pass over things common to all, consider again what awaits you—threats, punishment, torture, crosses no longer objects of worship but instruments of suffering, fires which you both anticipate and dread. Where is that God of yours, who is able to help those who come to life again, but not the living? Do not the Romans, without the help of your God, rule, govern, and possess the whole world, and hold sway over yourselves? But you, in the meantime, in your suspense and anxiety abstain from legitimate amusements; you never visit the shows, never join the processions, never attend the public banquets. You express abhorrence of the sacred games, of meat already offered in sacrifice, of libations poured upon the altars. Thus you show your fear of the very gods whom you deny! You never crown your heads with garlands, nor grace your bodies with perfumes; you reserve ungents for funerals, you even refuse to lay wreaths on the grave, pale and trembling wretches, who deserve to be pitied—but by our gods. Therefore, if you have any sense, any feeling of shame, give up prying into the quarters of the sky, the destinies and secrets of the universe; for ignorant, uneducated, rude, uncultivated people, to whom it has not been given to understand human affairs and who are still less qualified to discuss things divine,—for such it is sufficient to look at what is before their eyes.—J. H. Freese, *The "Octavius" of Minucius Felix*, 31–2, 45–7.

No. 67.—The Scillitan Martyrs, July 17, 180

From the *Passio Martyrum Scillitanorum*, 180.

When Præsens for the second time, and Claudianus were the Consuls, on the seventeenth day of July, at Carthage, there were set in the judgment-hall Speratus, Nartzalus, Cittinus, Donata, Secunda, and Vestia.

Saturninus the proconsul said: Ye can win the indulgence of our Lord the Emperor, if ye return to a sound mind.

Speratus said: We have never done ill, we have not lent ourselves to wrong, we have never spoken ill, but when ill-treated we have given thanks; because we pay heed to OUR EMPEROR.

Saturninus the proconsul said: We too are religious, and our religion is simple, and we swear by the genius of our lord the Emperor, and pray for his welfare, as ye also ought to do.

Speratus said: If thou wilt peaceably lend me thine ears, I can tell thee the mystery of simplicity.

Saturninus said: I will not lend mine ears to thee, when thou beginnest to speak evil things of our sacred rites; but rather swear thou by the genius of our lord the Emperor.

Speratus said: The empire of this world I know not; but rather, I serve that God, *whom no man hath seen nor*, with these eyes, *can see.*[1] I have committed no theft; but if I have bought anything I pay the tax; because I know my Lord, the King of kings, and Emperor of all nations.

Saturninus the proconsul said to the rest: Cease to be of this persuasion.

Speratus said: It is an ill persuasion to do murder, to speak false witness.

Saturninus the proconsul said: Be not partakers of this folly.

Cittinus said: We have none other to fear, save only our Lord God, who is in heaven.

Donata said: Honour to Cæsar as Cæsar; but fear to God.[2]

Vestia said: I am a Christian.

Secunda said: What I am, that I wish to be.

Saturninus the proconsul said to Speratus: Dost thou persist in being a Christian?

[1] 1 Tim. vi. 16.

[2] *Cf.* Rom. xiii. 7.

Speratus said: I am a Christian. And with him they all agreed.

Saturninus the proconsul said: Will ye have a space to consider?

Speratus said: In a matter so straightforward there is no considering.

Saturninus the proconsul said: What are the things in your chest?

Speratus said: Books and epistles of Paul, a just man.

Saturninus the proconsul said: Have a delay of thirty days, and bethink yourselves.

Speratus said a second time: I am a Christian. And with him they all agreed.

Saturninus the proconsul read out the decree from the tablet: Speratus, Nartzalus, Cittinus, Donata, Vestia, Secunda, and the rest having confessed that they live according to the Christian rite, since after opportunity offered them of returning to the custom of the Romans they have obstinately persisted, it is determined that they be put to the sword.

Speratus said: We give thanks to God.

Nartzalus said: To-day we are martyrs in heaven; thanks be to God.

Saturninus the proconsul ordered it to be declared by the herald: Speratus, Nartzalus, Cittinus, Veturius, Felix, Aquilinus, Lætantius, Januaria, Generosa, Vestia, Donata, and Secunda, have I ordered to be executed.

They all said: Thanks be to God.

And so they all together were crowned with martyrdom; and they reign with the Father and the Son and the Holy Ghost, for ever and ever. Amen.—tr. J. A. Robinson in *A.-N.C.L.:* additional volume, ed. A. Menzies, 285.

No. 68.—Gnosticism of the Egyptian School: Valentinus, *c.* 135-60

From Irenæus, *Adv. Hæreses* [*c.* 185], I. vi. §§ 1-3.

[§ 1] There being then three principles; the material, first of all, which they call also that on the left hand, necessarily, as they affirm, perishes, as being incapable of receiving any breath of incorruption. But the animal principle, which they denominate likewise that on the right hand, as being midway between the spiritual and [the] material, departs in that direction towards which it makes itself incline. As to the spiritual part, they say it is sent forth, in order that being here joined to the animal, it may be fashioned, sharing the discipline thereof in its conversation here. And this they say is "the salt" and "the light of the world." For the animal principle had need of outward and sensible discipline of various kinds. By such, they say, the world itself was framed, and, what is more, that the Saviour came to the aid of this, the animal part, it having also free-will, that He might save it.

For of those whom He was to save, they affirmed He took on Him the firstfruits: from Achamoth assuming the spiritual principle, from the Demiurgus the animal Christ wherewith He clothed Himself; and by that peculiar dispensation putting on a body which had an animal being, but was constructed by unspeakable art, so as to be both visible and palpable and capable of suffering. They add that He took not on Him anything at all material, matter not being capable of salvation.

As to the end of the world, they say it will be when the whole spiritual creation is formed and perfected in knowledge: meaning those of mankind who are spiritual, who have the perfect knowledge concerning God, and are initiated by Achamoth into her mysteries. And these, they imagine, are themselves.

[§ 2] For mere animal lessons are the discipline of mere animal men, of those who are established by bare faith and works, and possess not the perfect knowledge. And this account they give of us who belong to the Church, which is the reason why they also affirm good conduct to be necessary for us, since otherwise we cannot be saved. As to themselves, they maintain that not by any course of conduct, but because they are by nature spiritual, they shall in any case and by all means be saved. For as the earthly cannot attain salvation (not being, as they say, capable of it), so again the spiritual, which they will have to be themselves, never can admit corruption, whatsoever actions they may be engaged in. For even as gold deposited in mud does not cast off its beauty, but keeps its proper nature, the mud having no power to damage the gold at all: just so they affirm of themselves, that whatever kind of material actions they may be concerned in, they are not at all damaged themselves, nor do they cast away their spiritual subsistence.

[§ 3] For which cause also the most perfect among them do all forbidden things without fear; such things whereof the Scriptures are positive, that they which do them shall not inherit God's kingdom. Thus, in the first place, they eat indifferently of things sacrificed to idols, not esteeming themselves at all stained thereby. And at every holiday amusement of the Gentiles, taking place in honour of the idols, they are the first to assemble; some of them not even abstaining from that murderous spectacle, hated by God and man, of combats with wild beasts, and of single fight. Others again, who are the slaves of all fleshly pleasures, even unto loathing, say that "the carnal things are for the carnal, and the spiritual things for the spiritual, being so assigned." . . .

[§ 4] Yea, and they have many other abominable and godless practices. And while they run down us, who keep ourselves by the fear of God from sinning so much as in thought or word, for being unlearned and knowing nothing; themselves they magnify above measure, under the names of Perfect, and Seeds of Election.—*L.F.* xlii. 18 *sqq.*

No. 69.—The Rule of Faith

From Irenæus, *Adv. Hæreses,* I. x. §§ 1, 2.

[§ 1] The Church, although scattered over the whole world even to its extremities, received from the Apostles and their disciples the faith in one God, the Father Almighty, Maker of heaven and earth, the seas and all that in them is, and in one Christ Jesus, the Son of God, who became incarnate for our salvation, and in the Holy Ghost, who by the prophets proclaimed the dispensations, the advents, the virgin birth, the passion and resurrection from the dead, the bodily ascension of the well-beloved Christ Jesus our Lord into heaven, and his Parousia (Advent) from the heavens in the glory of the Father to gather up all things in Himself and to raise the flesh of all mankind to life, in order that *everything in heaven and in earth and under the earth shall bow the knee* (Phil. ii. 10 f.) to Christ Jesus our Lord and God, our Saviour and our King, according to the will of the invisible Father, and that every tongue should *confess* to him, and that he should pronounce a just judgment upon all, and dismiss the spirits of wickedness and the angels who transgressed and became apostate, and the ungodly, unrighteous, lawless and profane into everlasting fire, but in his graciousness should confer life and the reward of incorruption and eternal glory upon those who have kept his commandments and have abided in his love either from the beginning of their life or since their repentance.

[§ 2] This Kerygma and this faith the Church, although scattered over the whole world, diligently observes, as if it occupied but one house, and believes as if it had but one mind, and preaches and teaches as if it had but one mouth. And although there are many dialects in the world, the meaning of the tradition is one and the same.

For the same faith is held and handed down by the Churches established in the Germanies, the Spains, among the Celtic tribes, in the East, in Libya, and in the central portions of the world. But as the sun, the creation of God, is one and the same in all the world, so is the light of the Kerygma of the truth which shines on all who desire to come to the knowledge of the truth.—F. R. Montgomery Hitchcock, *St. Irenæus Against the Heresies*, 28–30.

No. 70.—Gnosticism of the Syrian School: Satornilus, *c.* 120

From Irenæus, *Adv. Hæreses*, I. xxiv. §§ 1, 2.

[§ 1] . . . Saturninus . . . was of Antioch . . . in Syria [and] like Menander, proclaimed one Father unknown to all, who made Angels, Archangels, Virtues, Powers. And that the world was made by certain Angels, seven in number: and all things therein. And that man was the work of Angels, a bright image from the highest Power appearing from above which they being unable to retain, because it presently hastened back upwards, they exhorted each other (so he affirms) saying, Let us make man in an image and likeness. Who being made, and the frame not admitting of an erect posture, because of the weakness of the Angels, but creeping rather as a vile worm, the Virtue from above pitying it he says, as made in its own likeness, sent forth a spark of life, which set the man upright, and knit his joints, and caused him to live. This spark of life, then, he says, hastens back, after death, to those of the same kind with it: and the other materials of those frames are dissolved.

[§ 2] But the Saviour he declared to be unborn and incorporeal, and without figure, and that in appearance only He was seen as man. And the God of the Jews he said was one of the Angels. And that because all the Princes wished to do away with His Father, Christ came to destroy the God of the Jews, and to save them that believe in Him: and these are they who have a spark of His life. For he first said that two sorts of men were framed by the Angels, one bad and the other good. And because the Demons aid the worst sort, that the Saviour came to do away with evil men and demons, and to save the good. But to marry and to procreate children, they say is of Satan. And many of those who are of him abstain also from [the flesh of] animals, by that sort of pretended continence seducing many. And that of the Prophecies, some were uttered by those Angels who made the world, and some by Satan: whom also he declares to be an angel opposed to the makers of the world, and especially to the God of the Jews. —*L.F.* xlii. 71 *sq*.

No. 71.—Gnosticism of the Egyptian School: Basilides, *c.* 117–38

From Irenæus, *Adv. Hæreses*, I. xxiv. §§ 3–6.

[§ 3] Basilides [in Alexandria, xxiv. § 1], that he may seem to have invented somewhat higher and more like the truth, draws out to a very great length the tenor of his doctrine, declaring that Mind first is born of the unborn Father, that from it again Reason is born, then from Reason Prudence, and from Prudence Wisdom and Power, and from Wisdom and Power the Virtues and Princes and Angels, these whom they call "the first"; and that by them the first heaven was made. That afterwards by derivation from these others also were made, and that they made another Heaven like the former; and that in like manner others, being made by derivation from these, Anti-types of those which are above them, formed out another, a third Heaven; and a fourth of these coming downward from the third and so on by the same rule were made, as they say, one Prince and Angel after another, and three hundred and sixty-five heavens. And that this is why the year has so many days, according to the number of the heavens.

[§ 4] And that those Angels by whom subsist the later Heaven which we also behold, ordered all things which are in the world, and divided among them the earth and those nations which are upon it. And that their chief is He who is accounted to be the God of the Jews. And because He wanted to subjugate the other nations to His own people, *i.e.* the Jews, therefore (they say) all the other Princes stood and acted against Him. And this is why the other nations started aside from His nation. But that the unborn and unnamed Father, seeing their destruction, sent His firstborn, Mind (and this is He who is called Christ), to free such as believe in Him from the power of those who framed the world. Yea, and that He appeared to the nations of them as a man on earth, and wrought mighty works. Accordingly, that He did not suffer, but that one Simon, a Cyrenian, being compelled, bare His cross for Him; and that while he was crucified in error and ignorance, his form being changed by Him, that men should suppose him to be Jesus, Jesus Himself took the form of Simon, and stood and derided them. For being an incorporeal Power, and the Mind of the unborn Father, His form was changed according to His own will: and so (they say) He ascended to Him that sent Him, mocking them, since He could not be held, and was invisible to all. And that such as know this are accordingly delivered from the Princes who made the world. And that we ought not to confess him that was crucified, but Him that came in man's form and was thought to be crucified, and was called Jesus, and sent by the Father, that by His arrangement He might do away with the works of the makers of the world. If any man therefore, saith he, confess the Crucified, that man is yet a slave, and under the power of those who made our bodies; while he who denies Him is free from them, and knows the ordinance of the unborn Father.

[§ 5] Further, that salvation is of the soul only, for the body is by nature corruptible. And that the very Prophecies, too, were from the Princes who made the world, and the Law especially from their Prince, who brought the people out of the land of Egypt. That he despises also things offered to idols, and accounts them nothing, but uses them without any scruple; and accounts also the practice of all other deeds, and of all sorts of lust, a thing indifferent. Moreover, these also make use of magic, and images, and incantations, and invocations, and all other kinds of curious art. . . .

[§ 6] . . . Their word is, Do thou know all men, but thee let no man know. Wherefore also they who are such are ready for denial: nay rather, it is impossible that they should suffer for the Name's sake, being just what all are. . . .—*L.F.* xlii. 72 *sqq.*

No. 72.—Cerinthus and the Ebionites

From Irenæus, *Adv. Hæreses*, (α) I. xxvi. §§ 1, 2, and (β) V. i. § 3.

(α) [§ 1] And a certain Cerinthus, too, in Asia, taught that the world was not made by the First God, but by a certain power far separated and distant from the Royalty which is above all, and which knows not the God over all. And he added that Jesus was not born of a virgin (for that seemed to him impossible), but was the son of Joseph and Mary, like all other men, and had more power than men in justice, prudence and wisdom. And that after his Baptism there descended on him from that Royalty which is above all, Christ in the figure of a Dove, and that he then declared the unknown Father, and did mighty works, but that in the end Christ again soared back from Jesus, and that Jesus suffered and rose again, but Christ remained impassible, as being spiritual.

[§ 2] But those who are called Ebionites agree, indeed, that the world was made by God, but in the opinions which relate to the Lord they do not hold with Cerinthus and

Carpocrates. But the only Gospel they use is that according to Matthew; and they reject the Apostle Paul, calling him an Apostate from the Law. And the prophetic writings they try to explain with peculiar accuracy: and they are circumcised, and persevere in the customs which belong to the Law, and in a Jewish mode of life: even to the worshipping of Jerusalem, as though it were the House of God.

(β) [§ 3] Again the Ebionites, too, are vain, not receiving by faith into their soul the union of God and Man, but abide in the old leaven of their [natural] generation: and will not understand that "the Holy Ghost" came "upon" Mary, and "the power of the Highest overshadowed" her; "wherefore also that which is born" is holy, even the Son of the Most High God, the Father of all, Who wrought His Incarnation, and exhibited a new sort of generation; that as by the former generation we inherited death, so by this generation we might inherit life. These, therefore, reject the infusion of the Heavenly Wine, and will have it to be earthly water alone, not receiving God into that which they mingle, but abiding in him who was overcome, and cast out of Paradise, even in Adam. . . .—*L.F.* xlii. 77 *sq.*, 451.

No. 73.—Gnosticism of the Pontic School: Marcion, *c.* 160

From Irenæus, *Adv. Hæreses*, I. xxvii. §§ 1–3.

[§ 1] One Cerdon, too, taking his beginning from Simon and his set, sojourned in Rome under Hyginus, who occupied the ninth place in the episcopal succession from the Apostles, and taught that the God proclaimed by the Law and the Prophets is not the Father of our Lord Jesus Christ, the one being revealed, the other unknown; the one again being Just, the other Good.

[§ 2] And Marcion of Pontus came in his place, and extended his school, shamelessly blaspheming Him who is called God by the Law and the Prophets; affirming Him to be an evil-doer, and fond of wars, and inconstant also in His judgment, and contrary to Himself: and as for Jesus, that he came from that Father who is above the God who made the world, into Judæa in the time of Pontius Pilate the Governor, who was Tiberius Cæsar's Procurator, and was manifest in human form to the inhabitants of Judæa, to do away the Prophets and the Law and all the works of that God who made the world, whom he also calls Ruler of the world. And, moreover, mutilating the Gospel according to St. Luke, and taking away all that is written of our Lord's birth, and much also from the doctrine of our Lord's discourses, wherein it is most plainly written how our Lord confessed the maker of this world to be His Father: he persuaded his disciples that he was himself more trustworthy than the Apostles who delivered the Gospel: while he was putting into their hands not the Gospel but a small portion of it. And in likewise the Epistles of the Apostle Paul too were mutilated by him, by taking out whatever is plainly spoken by the Apostle of the God who made the world, how that He is the Father of our Lord Jesus Christ; and whatsoever out of the prophetic writings the Apostle hath quoted in his teaching, as predictive of the coming of the Lord.

[§ 3] And salvation, he says, will be of our souls only, those souls which have learned his doctrine: but the body, because forsooth it is taken from the earth, cannot possibly partake of Salvation.—*L.F.* xlii. 78 *sq.*

No. 74.—The Argument from Tradition

From Irenæus, *Adv. Hæreses*, III. iii. §§ 1–4: iv. § 1.

iii. [§ 1] Any one who wishes to discern the truth may see in every Church in the whole world the Apostolic tradition clear and manifest. We can enumerate those who were appointed as bishops in the Churches by the Apostles and their successors to our own day, who never knew and never taught anything resembling their foolish doctrine. Had the Apostles known any secret mysteries which they taught privately and *sub rosa* to the perfect, they would surely have entrusted this teaching to the men in whose charge they placed the Churches. For they wished them to be without blame and reproach to whom they handed over their own position of authority. But as it would be very long in a book of this kind, to enumerate the Episcopal lists in all the Churches, by pointing out the Apostolic tradition and creed, which has been brought down to us by a succession of bishops, in the greatest, most ancient, and well-known Church, founded by two most glorious Apostles, Peter and Paul at Rome, we can confute all those who in any other way, either for self-pleasing, or vainglory, or blindness, or badness, hold unauthorized meetings. For unto this Church, which holds a leading position among the Churches, must needs resort every Church—that is, the faithful who are everywhere—inasmuch as the Apostolic tradition is always preserved by the faithful who are everywhere.

[§ 2] The blessed Apostles after founding and building up the Church entrusted the office of bishop to Linus. Paul speaks of this Linus in his Epistles to Timothy. Anencletus followed him. After him, in the third place after the Apostles, Clement was appointed bishop. He not only saw the blessed Apostles, but also had intercourse with them, and had their preaching ringing in his ears and before his eyes. He was not alone in this, for there were still many left at the time who had been instructed by the Apostles. When Clement was bishop a great dissension arose in Corinth among the brethren, and the Church in Rome sent a powerful letter to the Corinthians, urging them to have peace, renewing their faith and announcing to them the tradition they had lately received from the Apostles. This was to the effect that there is one God Almighty, Maker of heaven and earth, Creator of man, who brought in the deluge, called Abraham, led forth the people from the land of Egypt, spoke to Moses, appointed the Law, sent the prophets, and has prepared fire for the devil and his angels. That He, the Father of our Lord Jesus Christ, was proclaimed by the Churches any one who chooses may see from this writing, which was before the time of these false teachers, who speak of another God above the Demiurge (Creator).

[§ 3] Euarestos succeeded this Clement, and Alexander Euarestos, and then Sixtus, the sixth after the Apostles, was appointed. After him came Telesphorus, who had a glorious martyrdom. Then came Hyginus, Pius, Anicetus, Soter, and Eleutherus, the twelfth from the Apostles, now occupies the see. In the same order and in the same succession the tradition of the Apostles in the Church and *the preaching of the truth* has come down to us.

[§ 4] And Polycarp was not only instructed in the faith by the Apostles, and personally acquainted with many who had seen the Lord, but he was also appointed by the Apostles for Asia as bishop in the Church at Smyrna. Him even I saw in my early youth. For he remained a long time with us and was exceedingly old. And after a glorious and conspicuous martyrdom he passed away, having always taught these things which he learnt from the Apostles, which also the Church hands down and which alone are true. All the Churches throughout Asia, and the successors of Polycarp, a much more reliable and trustworthy witness of the truth than Valentinus and Marcion and other ill-disposed persons, add similar testimony.

In the time of Anicetus, when staying in Rome, Polycarp converted many of these heretics to the Church of God, declaring that this was the one and only truth he had received from the Apostles, and this had been handed down to us by the Church. Some also heard him say that John, the disciple of our Lord, went into the baths in Ephesus, but, seeing Cerinthus inside, he rushed away from the baths, without bathing, and said, "Let us fly lest the baths fall, for Cerinthus the foe of the truth is within." And Polycarp himself on one occasion, when he met Marcion and he said, "Do you recognize me?" answered, "I recognize you as the firstborn of Satan." So careful were the Apostles and their pupils to avoid even conversation with any of those who misrepresent the truth, as Paul also said, "A heretic after the first and second admonition avoid" (Titus iii. 10). There is also an excellent letter from Polycarp to the Philippians, from which they may learn the quality of his faith and *the preaching of the truth*, who are willing and who care for their salvation.

The Church in Ephesus, founded by Paul, and where John lived unto the days of Trajan, is also a true witness of the tradition of the Apostles.

iv. [§ 1] Seeing that we have so many proofs, there is no need to seek among others for the truth which we can easily obtain from the Church. For the Apostles have brought fully and completely all the truth to her, lodging it with her as with a rich bank, so that any one who wishes may draw from her the draught of life.—F. R. Montgomery Hitchcock, *St. Irenæus Against the Heresies*, 84 *sq*. (slightly altered, iii. § 1).

No. 75.—The Four Gospels

From Irenæus, *Adv. Hæreses,* II. xi. 8.

For it is impossible that the Gospels should be in number either more or fewer than these. For since there are four regions of the world wherein we are, and four principal winds, and the Church is as seed sown in the whole earth, and the Gospel is the Church's pillar and ground, and the breath of life: it is natural that it should have four pillars, from all quarters breathing incorruption, and kindling men into life. Wherefore it is evident that the Artificer of all things, the Word, who sitteth upon the Cherubims, and keepeth all together, when He was made manifest unto men, gave us His Gospel in four forms, kept together by one Spirit. As David, imploring His presence, saith, "Thou that sitteth upon the Cherubims, show Thyself." For indeed, the Cherubim had four faces, and their faces are images of the dispensation of the Son of God. For "the first living creature," it saith, was "like a lion" [St. John], denoting His real efficiency, His guiding power, His royalty; "and the second like a calf" [St. Luke], signifying His station as a Sacrificer and Priest; "and the third having the face of a man" [St. Matthew], most evidently depicting His presence as man; "and the fourth like an eagle in flight" [St. Mark], declaring the gift of the Spirit flying down upon the Church. —*L.F.* xlii. 235.

No. 76.—The translation of *Isaiah* vii. 14

From Irenæus, *Adv. Hæreses*, III. xxi. § 1.

[§ 1] God therefore became Man, and the Lord Himself saved us, giving the sign of the Virgin. Untrue therefore is the interpretation of certain who venture thus to interpret the Scripture: "Behold the *damsel* shall be with child, and shall bear a son"; as Theodotion of Ephesus translated it and Aquila of Pontus, both of them Jewish proselytes: whom the Ebionites following, say that he was born of Joseph: whereby to the best of their power they undo this so great economy of God: making void the witness of the prophets, which is God's work. For the prophecy was given in the first place before the removal of the people to Babylon took place, *i.e.* before the Medes and Persians received the dominion; and next it was translated in Greek by the Jews themselves, long before the times of our Lord's Advent; that no suspicion may be left whether haply it was in deference to us that the Jews so translated the words. Whereas, had they foreknown our existence, and our use of these testimonies out of the Scriptures, they would never have hesitated themselves to throw their own Scriptures into the fire; as proving both that all other nations partake of life, and demonstrating that those who boast to be the house of Jacob and the people of Israel, are even disinherited from the grace of God.—*L.F.* xlii. 287 *sq.*

No. 77.—The Christian Sacrifice

From Irenæus, *Adv. Hæreses*, IV. xviii. §§ 4–6.

[§ 4] . . . And this offering the Church alone offers pure unto the Creator, presenting it unto Him with thanksgiving from the things which He has made. But the Jews offer it not, for their hands are full of blood: for they have not received the Word, which is offered to God. No, nor yet any of the congregations of the heretics. For some of them, who say that there is another Father besides the Creator, in offering unto Him things which appertain to our creation, make Him out desirous of that which is another's, and covetous of others' goods. And those who say that the things which pertain to us were made through decay and ignorance and passion, sin against their own Father, in offering to Him the fruits of ignorance, passion and decay: rather insulting than giving Him thanks.

And how can they be assured that the bread whereon thanks have been given is the Body of their Lord, and the Cup that of His Blood, if they do not acknowledge Him the Son of the Creator of the world; *i.e.* His Word, whereby the tree bears fruit, and the fountains flow down, and the earth yields first the blade, then afterwards the ear, then the full corn in the ear?

[§ 5] And how say they that the flesh passes into corruption and partakes not of life, which is nourished by the Lord's Body and by His Blood. Either let them change their opinion, or decline to make the offerings which I have mentioned. But our opinion is in harmony with the Eucharist, and the Eucharist again confirms our opinion. And we offer to Him the things which are His own, showing forth accordingly our communion and union, and professing a resurrection of flesh and spirit: viz. that as bread from the earth, receiving the summons of God, is no longer common bread but an Eucharist, composed of two things, both an earthly and an heavenly one, so also our bodies, partaking of the Eucharist, are no longer corruptible, having the hope of eternal resurrection.

[§ 6] For we offer unto Him, not as though He had need, but as giving thanks to His Sovereignty, and sanctifying His creation. . . . Accordingly, He will have us also to offer our gift at the altar very often, without ceasing. The altar then is in heaven; for thither our prayers and oblations are directed. . . .—*L.F.* xlii. 360 *sq.*

No. 78.—Succession from the Apostles

From Irenæus, *Adv. Hæreses*, IV. xxvi. § 2.

Wherefore we should hearken to those presbyters who are in the Church; those who have their succession from the Apostles, as we have pointed out; who with their succession in the episcopate received a sure gift of the truth, at the good pleasure of the Father; but the rest, who withdraw from the primitive succession, and gather in any place whatever, we must hold in suspicion; either as heretics and evil-minded: or as making division. . . . All these have fallen from the truth.—*L.F.* xlii. 385.

No. 79.—The Argument from the Eucharist to the Incarnation

From Irenæus, *Adv. Hæreses*, V. ii. §§ 2, 3.

[§ 2] And vain altogether are they who despise God's entire plan, and deny the salvation of the flesh, and scorn its new Birth, saying that it cannot receive incorruption. But if the flesh may not be saved, of course neither did the Lord redeem us by His own Blood, nor is the Cup of the Eucharist the Communion of His Blood, nor the Bread which we break the Communion of His Body. . . . That chalice which is of the creature, He professed to be His own Blood, wherewith He imbueth our blood; and the bread which is of the creature, He affirmed to be His own Body, from which He nourisheth our bodies.

[§ 3] Since therefore both the cup, which is mingled, and the bread, which is made, receiveth the Word of God, and the Eucharist becometh the Body of Christ, and of these the substance of our flesh groweth and subsisteth, how say they that the flesh is not capable of the gift of God, which is eternal life?—that flesh which is nourished by the Body and Blood of the Lord, and is a member of Him? . . . And even as the wood of the vine, arched down into the ground, beareth fruit in its due time, and the corn of wheat falling into the earth and mouldering, is raised up manifold by the Spirit of God, Who upholdeth all things: and afterwards by the Wisdom of God cometh to be used by men, and having received to itself the Word of God, becometh an Eucharist, *i.e.* the Body and Blood of Christ: so also our bodies, nourished thereby and put into the ground, and dissolved therein, shall rise again in their own time, the Word of God giving them resurrection to the glory of God and His Father.—*L. F.* xlii. 452–4.

No. 80.—The Letter of Irenæus to Florinus

From Eusebius, *H.E.* V. xx. §§ 4–8.

[§ 4] These doctrines, O Florinus, to speak mildly, are not of sound judgment. These doctrines disagree with the Church, and drive into the greatest impiety those who accept them. These doctrines, not even the heretics outside of the Church, have ever dared to publish. These doctrines the presbyters, who were before us, and who were companions of the Apostles, did not deliver to thee.

[§ 5] For when I was a boy I saw thee in lower Asia with

Polycarp, moving in splendour in the royal court, and endeavouring to gain his approbation.

[§ 6] I remember the events of that time more clearly than those of recent years. For what boys learn, growing with their mind, becomes joined with it; so that I am able to describe the very place in which the blessed Polycarp sat as he discoursed, and his goings out and his comings in, and the manner of his life, and his physical appearance, and his discourses to the people, and the accounts which he gave of his intercourse with John and with the others who had seen the Lord. And as he remembered their words, and what he heard from them concerning the Lord, and concerning His miracles and His teaching, having received them from "eye-witnesses of the Word of life," Polycarp related all things in harmony with the Scriptures.

[§ 7] These things being told me by the mercy of God, I listened to them attentively, noting them down, not on paper but in my heart. And continually, through God's grace, I recall them faithfully. And I am able to bear witness before God that if that blessed and apostolic presbyter had heard any such thing, he would have cried out and stopped his ears, as was his custom, would have exclaimed, "O good God, unto what times hast thou spared me that I should endure these things?" And he would have fled from the place where, sitting or standing, he had heard such words.

[§ 8] And this can be shown plainly from the letters which he sent, either to the neighbouring churches for their confirmation, or to some of the brethren, admonishing and exhorting them.—*N. & P.-N.F.* i. 238 *sq.*

No. 81.—The Apology and Martyrdom of Apollonius, *c.* 180–5

From *The Acta S. Apollonii.*

Christ, who giveth all things, prepareth a crown of righteousness for those who are well-minded and stand firm by the faith in God; for the chosen ones of God are called to this righteousness, in order that, having fought the good fight with fortitude, they may attain the promises which God, who lies not, hath promised to those who love

Him with their whole soul. One of these also was the blessed martyr and goodly champion of Christ, Apollonius. He had lived a good and ascetic life in the great Rome, and, desirous of the earnest of his heavenly call, he was numbered among the holy martyrs of Christ. The blessed one bore witness before the Senate and Terentius [= Perennis] the Prefect, and gave his answers with great boldness, whose memorials are as follows:—

[1] Terentius, the Prefect, commanded that he should be brought before the Senate, and said to him, O Apollonius, wherefore dost thou resist the invincible laws and decree of the Emperors, and dost refuse to sacrifice to the gods?" [2] Apollonius said, "Because I am a Christian; therefore I fear God who made heaven and earth, and sacrifice not to empty idols."

[3] The Prefect said, "But thou oughtest to repent of this mind of thine because of the edicts of the Emperors, and take oath by the good fortune of the autocrat Commodus." [4] Apollonius replied, "Hear with understanding this my answer. He who repents of just and good works, in truth such a man is godless and without hope; but he who repents of lawless deeds and of evil thoughts, and returns not again to them, such a one is a lover of God, and hath regard to the hope. [5] And now I am finally resolved in this my mind to keep the beautiful and glorious command of God, which He taught by my Lord Christ, who knoweth the thoughts of men, and beholdeth whatsoever is done in secret or in the open. [6] It is best to swear not at all but in all things to live in peace and truth; for a great oath is the truth, and for this reason it is a bad and an ill thing to swear by Christ; but because of falsehood there is disbelief, and because of disbelief there is swearing. I am willing to swear in truth by the true God that we too love the Emperor, and offer up prayers for His Majesty."

[7] The Prefect said, "Come, then, and sacrifice to Apollo, and to the other gods, and to the Emperor's image." [8] Apollonius said, "As to my change of mind, and as to the oath I have given thee an answer; but as to sacrifices I and all Christians offer a bloodless sacrifice to God, Lord of heaven and earth, and of the sea, and of every living

being, in behalf of the spiritual and rational images who have been appointed by the Providence of God to rule over the earth. [9] Wherefore, according to the command of the God-given precept, we make our prayers to Him who dwells in heaven, who is the only God, that they may justly rule upon this earth, knowing for certain that he (*i.e.* Commodus) also is established Emperor, through none other but only through the one King, God, who holds every one in His hand." [10] The Prefect said, "Surely thou wast not summoned hither to talk philosophy. I will give thee one day's respite that thou mayest consider thine interest and advise thyself concerning thy life." And he ordered him to be taken to prison.

[11] And after three days he commanded him to be brought forward, and said to him, "What counsel hast thou formed for thyself?" [12] Apollonius answered, "To remain firm in my religion, as I told thee before." [13] The Prefect said, "Because of the decree of the Senate I advise thee to repent and to sacrifice to the gods to whom all the earth gives homage and sacrifices; for it is far better for thee to live among us than to die a miserable death. Methinks thou art not unacquainted with the decree of the Senate. [14] Apollonius said, "I know the command of the Omnipotent God, and I remain firm in my religion; and I do no homage to idols made with hands, which have been fashioned of gold and silver and wood, and which neither see nor hear; because they are the work of men's hands, and they know not the true service of God. [15] But I have learnt to adore the heavenly God, and to do homage to Him alone, who breathed the breath of life into all men and continually dispenses life unto all. [16] And I will not again debase myself and cast myself down into the pit. For it is a great shame to do homage to vile things, and it is a servile action to adore what is vain. And men sin in adoring such things. Foolish were those who invented them, and yet more senseless they that adore them and honour them. [17] The Egyptians do homage to an onion in their folly. [18] The Athenians unto this very day make and adore the head of an ox in copper, which they call the good fortune of Athens. And this they have even set up in a conspicuous place near to

the statue of Zeus and Herakles, in order that they may pray to them. [19] And yet what more is this than dried clay or a baked potsherd? Eyes have they, and see not; ears have they, and hear not; hands have they, but draw not things to themselves; feet have they, and walk not; for the mere form bestoweth not real substance; and I think that Socrates also was making ridicule of the Athenians when he swore by the poplar tree, and by the dog and by dry wood. [20] In the first place, men sin against themselves by worshipping them. [21] In the second place, they are guilty of impiety towards God, because they do not know the truth. The Egyptians, again, have given the name of God to the onion, and to a wooden mortar, and to the fruits of the field, which we feed upon, and which enter the belly, and pass out into the sweepings; these things have they adored; aye, and they do homage to a fish and to the dove, and to the dog, and to a stone, and a wolf; and they worship every one of them, the fictions of their own minds. [22] In the third place, men sin whenever they pay homage to men and to angels and to demons, naming them gods."

[23] The Prefect answered, "You have philosophized enough, and have filled us with admiration; but dost thou not know this, O Apollonius, that it is the decree of the Senate that no one shall be named a Christian anywhere at all?" [24] Apollonius answered, "Aye, but it is not possible for a human decree of the Senate to prevail over the decree of God. For so far as men frivolously hate those who benefit them and slay them, just in this wise in many ways men stand aloof from God. [25] But know this, that God has appointed death, and after death judgment upon all, over kings and poor men, rulers and slaves and freemen, and philosophers and ignorant men. [26] But there is a distinction of death (from death); for this reason the disciples of Christ do daily die, torturing their desires, and mortifying them according to the Divine Scriptures. For we have no part at all in dissolute desires, nor do we allow impure sights, nor a lewd glance, nor an ear that listens to evil, lest our souls be wounded thereby. [27] But since we live such a fair life, and exercise such good resolutions, we think it no hardship to die for the true God; for what-

soever we are, we are because of God, and for Him we endure tortures, that we may not die miserably the everlasting death. [28] And moreover we do not resent having our goods taken from us, because we know that, whether we live or whether we die, we are the Lord's. Fever, or jaundice, or any other disease can slay a man. I may expect to die from one or the other of these."

[29] The Prefect said, "Art thou bent upon death?" [30] Apollonius answered, "It is my desire to live in Christ, but I have no fear of death because of any love of life; for there is not anything that is more estimable than the life eternal, which is the source of deathlessness for the soul that hath lived here a noble life." [31] The Prefect said, "I do not understand thy meaning." [32] Apollonius said, "And what can I do for thee? for the Word of God illumines the heart, as the light gives sight to our eyes."

[33] A certain philosopher who was at hand said, "O Apollonius, thou dost insult thyself, for thou art gone exceedingly astray, although thou dost even think to speak profound truths." [34] Apollonius said, "I have learnt to pray and not to insult; but thy dissembling bears witness to the blindness of thy heart, for the truth appears to be an insult only to the senseless." [35] The magistrate said, "Tell me plainly what thou dost mean." [36] Apollonius answered, "The Word of God, the Saviour of souls and of bodies, became man in Judæa and fulfilled all righteousness, and was filled gloriously with Divine wisdom, and taught a pure religion, such as beseemed the son of men, and to put to silence the beginning of sins. [37] For He taught us to pacify anger, to moderate desire, to abate and diminish appetite, to put away sorrow, to take part in pity, to increase love, to cast away vain-glory, to abstain from taking vengeance, not to be vindictive, to despise death, not indeed from lawlessness but as bearing with the lawless; to obey the laws of God, to reverence rulers, to worship God, to entrust the spirit to immortal God, to look forward to judgment after death, to expect rewards after the resurrection to be given by God to those who have lived in piety. [38] Teaching all this, by word and deed, along with great firmness, and glorified by all for the benefits which He conferred on them, He was slain at last, as were also before Him philosophers

and just men. For the just are seen to be a cause of offence to the unjust. [39] As also the Divine Scripture saith: We will bind the just man because he was a cause of offence to us; [40] but also one of the Greek philosophers said: The just man shall be tortured, he shall be spat upon, and last of all he shall be crucified. [41] Just as the Athenians passed an unjust sentence of death, and charged him falsely, because they yielded to the mob, so also our Saviour was at last sentenced to death by the lawless: by the lawless who were filled with envy and malice against Him, [42] as also against the prophets who were before Him, who spake beforehand concerning Him thus: He shall come and shall do good unto all and shall persuade all men by His goodness even to worship God the Father and Maker of all, in whom also we believe, rendering homage, because we learned from Him pure commandments, which we knew not, and, therefore, we are no longer in error, but, having lived a good life, we await the hope to come."

[43] The magistrate said, "I thought that thou wast changed in the night from that mind of thine." [44] Apollonius said, "And I expected that thy thoughts would be changed in the night, and the eyes of thy spirit be opened by my answer; and that thy heart would bear fruit, and that thou wouldst worship God, the Creator of all, and unto Him continually offer thy prayers by means of compassion; for compassion shown to men by men is a bloodless sacrifice and holy unto God."

[45] The magistrate said, "I would fain let thee go; but I cannot because of the decree of the Senate; yet with benevolence I pronounce sentence on thee"—and he ordered him to be beheaded with a sword. [46] Apollonius said, "I thank God for thy sentence." [47] And the executioners straightway led him away and beheaded him, while he continued to glorify the Father and Son and Holy Spirit; to whom be glory for ever. Amen.—F. C. Conybeare, *Monuments of Early Christianity*, pp. 35-48.

No. 82.—Polycrates, Bishop of Ephesus, to Victor, Bishop of Rome, 189–†98

From Eusebius, *H.E.* V. xxiv. §§ 2–7.

[§ 2] We observe the exact day, neither adding nor taking away. For in Asia also great lights have fallen asleep, which shall rise again on the day of the Lord's coming, when He shall come with glory from heaven, and shall seek out all the saints. Among these are Philip, one of the twelve Apostles, who fell asleep in Hierapolis; and his two aged virgin daughters, and another daughter who lived in the Holy Spirit and now rests at Ephesus; [§ 3] and moreover John who was both a witness and a teacher, who reclined upon the bosom of the Lord, and, being a priest wore the sacerdotal plate. He fell asleep at Ephesus. [§ 4] And Polycarp in Smyrna, who was a bishop and martyr; and Thraseas, bishop and martyr from Eumenia, who fell asleep in Smyrna. [§ 5] Why need I mention the bishop and martyr Sagaris who fell asleep in Laodicea, or the blessed Papirius, or Melito the eunuch who lived altogether in the Holy Spirit and who lies in Sardis, awaiting the episcopate from heaven, when he shall rise from the dead? [§ 6] All these observed the fourteenth day of the passover according to the Gospel, deviating in no respect, but following the rule of faith. And I also, Polycrates, the least of you all, do according to the tradition of my relatives, some of whom I have closely followed. For seven of my relatives were bishops, and I am the eighth. And my relatives always observed the day when the people put away the leaven. [§ 7] I therefore, brethren, who have lived sixty-five years in the Lord, and have met with the brethren throughout the world, and have gone through every Holy Scripture, am not affrighted by terrifying words. For those greater than I have said: "We ought to obey God rather than man."—*N. & P.-N.F.* i. 242.

No. 83.—Montanism

From the Anonymous, *c.* 192–3, *ap.* Eus., *H.E.* V. xvi. §§ 6–10.

[§ 6] . . . Their opposition and their recent heresy which has separated them from the Church arose on the following account: [7] There is said to be a certain village called Ardabau in that part of Mysia, which borders upon Phrygia. There first, they say, when Gratus was proconsul of Asia, a recent convert, Montanus by name, through his unquenchable desire for leadership, gave the adversary opportunity against him. And he became beside himself, and being suddenly in a sort of frenzy and ecstasy, he raved, and began to babble and utter strange things, prophesying in a manner contrary to the constant custom of the Church handed down by tradition from the beginning. [§ 8] Some of those who heard his spurious utterances at that time were indignant and they rebuked him as one that was possessed, and that was under the control of a demon, and was led by a deceitful spirit, and was distracting the multitude; and they forbade him to talk, remembering the distinction drawn by the Lord and His warning to guard watchfully against the coming of false prophets. But others, imagining themselves possessed of the Holy Spirit and of a prophetic gift, were elated and not a little puffed up; and forgetting the distinction of the Lord, they challenged the mad and insidious and seducing spirit, and were cheated and deceived by him. In consequence of this, he could no longer be held in check so as to keep silence. [§ 9] Thus by artifice, or rather by such a system of wicked craft, the devil, devising destruction for the disobedient, and being unworthily endured by them, secretly excited and inflamed their understandings which had already become estranged from the true faith. And he stirred up, besides, two women, and filled them with the false spirit, so that they talked wildly and unreasonably and strangely, like the person already mentioned. And the spirit pronounced him blessed as they rejoiced and gloried in him, and puffed them up by the magnitude of his promises. But sometimes he rebuked them openly in a wise and faithful manner, that he might seem to be a reprover. But those of the Phrygians that were deceived were few in number. And the arrogant spirit taught them to revile the entire universal Church under heaven, because the spirit of false prophecy received neither honour from it nor entrance into it. [§ 10] For the faithful in Asia met often in many places throughout Asia to consider this matter, and examined the novel utterances and pronounced them profane, and rejected the heresy, and thus these persons were expelled from the Church and debarred from communion.—*N. & P.-N.F.* i. 231 *sq.*

No. 84.—Montanism

From Apollonius, *c.* 197, *ap.* Eus., *H.E.* V. xviii. §§ 2-4.

[§ 2] His actions and his teaching show who this new teacher [Montanus] is. This is he who taught the dissolution of marriage; who made laws for fasting; who named Pepuza and Tymion, small towns in Phrygia, Jerusalem, wishing to gather people to them from all directions; who appointed collectors of money, who contrived the receiving of gifts under the name of offerings; who provided salaries for those who preached his doctrine, that its teaching might prevail through gluttony. [§ 3] . . . We show that these first prophetesses themselves, as soon as they were filled with the Spirit abandoned their husbands. How falsely, therefore, they speak who call Prisca a virgin. [§ 4] . . . Does not all Scripture seem to you to forbid a prophet to receive gifts and money? When therefore I see the prophetess receiving gold and silver and costly garments, how can I avoid reproving her? . . .—*N. & P.-N.F.* i. 235.

No. 85.—The Gospel of Peter

From the letter of Serapion, Bishop of Antioch, 192–†209, to the Church of Rhossus *ap.* Eusebius, *H.E.* VI. xii. §§ 3–6.

[§ 3] For we, brethren, receive both Peter and the other apostles as Christ: but we reject intelligently the writings falsely ascribed to them, knowing that such were not handed down to us. [§ 4] When I visited you, I supposed that all of you held the true faith, and as I had not read the Gospel which they put forward under the name of Peter, I said, "If this is the only thing which occasions dispute among you, let it be read." But now having learned, from what has been told me, that their mind was involved in some heresy, I will hasten to come to you again. Therefore, brethren, expect me shortly. [§ 5] But you will learn, brethren, from what has been written to you, that we perceived the nature of the heresy of Marcianus, and that, not understanding what he was saying, he contradicted himself. [§ 6] For having obtained this Gospel from others who had studied it diligently, namely, from the successors of those who first used it, whom we call Docetæ (for most of their opinions are connected with the teaching of that school), we have been able to read it through, and we find many things in accordance with the true doctrine of the Saviour, but some things added to that doctrine, which we have pointed out for you farther on.—*N. & P.-N.F.* i. 258.

No. 86.—The alleged consecration of Clement by St. Peter

From the *Epistle of Clement to James*, *c.* 200.

Clement to James, the Lord ['s brother] and the bishop of bishops, who rules Jerusalem, the holy church of the Hebrews, and the churches everywhere excellently founded by the providence of God, with the elders and deacons, and the rest of the brethren, peace be always.

[c. i] Be it known unto you, my lord, that Simon, who for the sake of the true faith and the most sure foundation of his doctrine, was set apart to be the foundation of the Church and, for this end, was by Jesus Himself, with His truthful mouth, named Peter, the firstfruits of our Lord, the first of the Apostles . . . having come as far as Rome . . . himself by violence, exchanged this present existence for life.

[c. ii] But about that time when he was about to die, the brethren being assembled together, he suddenly seized my hand, and rose up, and said, in presence of the church: "Hear me, brethren and fellow-servants. Since, as I have been taught by the Lord and Teacher Jesus Christ, whose apostle I am, the day of my death is approaching, I lay hands upon this Clement as your bishop, and to him I entrust my chair of discourse, even to him who has journeyed with me from the beginning to the end and has heard all my homilies." . . .

[c. xix] Having thus spoken, he laid his hands upon me in the presence of all, and compelled me to sit in his own chair. And when I was seated, he immediately said to me: "I entreat you . . . that . . . you send to James, the brother of the Lord, a brief account of . . . the discourses preached by me in every city." . . .

[c. xx] Whence I, my lord James, having promised as I was ordered . . . despatch them to you, inscribing them, *Clement's Epitome of the popular sermons of Peter.*—*A.-N. C.L.* xvii. 6–16.

No. 87.—Bad Emperors the worst Persecutors

From Tertullian, *Apology* [197], c. v.

To treat somewhat of the origin of the kind of laws, there was an ancient decree, that no god should be consecrated by the Emperor, unless approved by the Senate. Witness Marcus Aurelius in the case of his own god Alburnus. This also maketh for our cause, that with you deity is measured according to the judgment of man. A god, unless he please man, shall not be a god. Man will now be obliged to be propitious to a god. Tiberius, therefore, in whose time the name of Christ entered into the world, laid before the Senate, with his own vote to begin with, things announced to him from Palestine in Syria, which had there manifested the truth of the Divinity of that Person. The Senate, because they had not themselves approved it, rejected it. Cæsar held by his sentence, threatening peril to the accusers of the Christians. Consult your Annals: there ye will find that Nero was the first to wreak the fury of the sword of the Cæsars upon this sect, now springing up especially at Rome. But in such a first founder of our condemnation we even glory. For whoever knoweth him can understand that nothing save some great good was condemned by Nero. Domitian, too, who was somewhat of a Nero in cruelty, had tried it, but forasmuch as he was also a human being, he speedily stopped the undertaking, even restoring those whom he had banished. Such have ever been our persecutors; unjust, impious, infamous, whom even yourselves have been wont to condemn, by whom whosoever were condemned ye have been wont to restore. But out of so many princes thenceforward to him of the present day, who had any savour of religion and humanity, show us any destroyer of the Christians. But we on the other hand have one to show who protected them, if the letters of that most august Emperor Marcus Aurelius be enquired of, wherein he testifieth of that drought in Germany removed by the shower obtained by the prayers of the Christians who chanced to serve in his army. As he did not openly take off the penalty from the men of that sect, so in another way he openly made away with it by adding a sentence, and that a more horrid one, against the accusers also. What sort of laws then be those which only the impious, the unjust, the infamous, the cruel, the foolish, the insane, execute against us, which Trajan in part foiled by forbidding that the Christians should be enquired after; which no Hadrian, though a clear searcher into all things curious, no Vespasian, though the vanquisher of the Jews, no Pius, no Verus, hath pressed against us?—*L.F.* x. 12 *sqq.*

No. 88.—The Testimony of the Soul

From Tertullian, *Apology*, c. xvii.

Will ye that we prove Him to be, from His own works, so many and such as they are, by which we are maintained, by which we are supported, by which we are delighted, by which also we are made afraid? Will ye that we prove it by the witness of the soul itself, which although confined by the prison of the body, although straitened by evil training, although unnerved by lust and desires, although made the servant of false gods, yet when it recovereth itself as from a surfeit, as from a slumber, as from some infirmity, and is in its proper condition of soundness, it nameth God, by this name only, because the proper name of the true God, "Great God," "Good God," and "which God grant," are words in every mouth. It witnesseth also that He is its Judge: "God seeth," "I commend to God," "God shall recompense me." O testimony of a soul, by nature Christian! Finally, in pronouncing these words, it looketh not to the Capitol, but to Heaven; for it knoweth the dwelling-place of the true God: from Him and from thence it descended. —tr. *L.F.* x. 40.

No. 89.—The Logos

From Tertullian, *Apology*, c. xxi.

We have already set forth that God formed this universal world by His Word, and His Reason and His Power. Among your own wise men also it is agreed that *Logos*, that is, Word and Reason, should be accounted the maker of all things. For Zeno determineth that this maker, who hath formed all things and ordered them, should also be called Fate, and God, and the Mind of Jupiter, and the Necessity of all things. These titles doth Cleanthes confer upon the Spirit which, he affirmeth, pervadeth the universe. And we also ascribe, as its proper substance, to the Word, and the Reason, and the Power also, through which we have said that God hath formed all things, a Spirit in which is the Word when it declareth, and with which is the Reason when it ordereth, and over which is the Power when it executeth. This, we have learned, was brought forth from God, and by this forth-bringing was begotten, and therefore is called the Son of God, and God, from being "of one substance" with Him; for that God also is a Spirit. Even when a ray is put forth from the sun, it is part of a whole; but the sun will be in the ray because it is a ray of the sun, and the substance is not divided but extended. So cometh Spirit of Spirit and "God of God," as "light" is kindled "of light," the parent-matter remaineth entire and without loss, although thou shouldest borrow from it many channels of its qualities. So likewise that which hath come forth from God is God, and the Son of God, and both are one. And so this Spirit of Spirit, and God of God, hath become the second in mode, not in number, in order, not in condition, and hath gone forth, not gone out of the original source. Therefore this ray of God, as was ever foretold before, entering into a certain virgin, and in her womb endued with the form of flesh, is born Man joined together with God. The flesh stored with the Spirit is nourished, groweth to manhood, speaketh, teacheth, worketh, and is Christ.—*L.F.* x. 46 *sqq*.

No. 90.—Christians are Loyal Subjects

From Tertullian, *Apology*, c. xxxii.

We have also another and a greater need to pray for the Emperors, and, moreover for the whole estate of the Empire, and the fortunes of Rome, knowing as we do, that the mighty shock which hangeth over the whole world, and the end of time itself, threatening terrible and grievous things, is delayed because of the time allowed to the Roman Empire. We would not, therefore, experience these things, and while we pray that they may be put off, we favour the long continuance of Rome. But, moreover, as we swear not by the Genii of the Cæsars, so we do swear by their health, which is of greater dignity than all Genii. Ye know not that Genii are called "Dæmons," and hence by a diminutive title "dæmonia." We in the Emperors reverence the judgment of God, Who hath set them over the nations.—*L.F.* x. 72 *sq.*

No. 91.—The Numbers of the Christians

From Tertullian, *Apology*, c. xxxvii.

We are a people of yesterday, and yet we have filled every place belonging to you, cities, islands, castles, towns, assemblies, your very camp, your tribes, companies, palace, senate, forum! We leave you your temples only! We can count your armies: our numbers in a single province will be greater. For what war should we not be sufficient and ready, even though unequal in numbers, who so willingly are put to death, if it were not in this religion of ours more lawful to be slain than to slay? We could fight against you even unarmed and without rebelling, but only disagreeing with you, by the mere odium of separation. For if so large a body of men as we were to break away from you into some remote corner of the globe, surely the loss of so many citizens, of whatsoever sort they might be, would cover your kingdom with shame, yea, and would punish you by their very desertion of you.—*L.F.* x. 78 *sq.*

No. 92.—Christian Worship

From Tertullian, *Apology*, c. xxxix.

We are a body formed by our joint cognizance of Religion, by the unity of discipline, by the bond of hope. We come together in a meeting and a congregation as before God, as though we would in one body sue Him by our prayers. This violence is pleasing to God. We pray also for Emperors, for their ministers and the powers, for the condition of the world, for the quiet of all things, for the delaying of the end. We come together to call the sacred writings to remembrance, if so be that the character of the present times compel us either to use admonition or recollection in anything. In any case, by these holy words we feed our faith, raise our hopes, establish our confidence, nor do we the less strengthen our discipline by inculcating precepts. Here, too, are exercised exhortations, corrections and godly censure. For our judgment also cometh with great weight, as of men well assured that they are under the eye of God; and it is a very grave forestalling of the judgment to come, if any shall have so offended as to be put out of the communion of prayer, of the solemn assembly, and of all holy fellowship. The most approved elders preside over us, having obtained this honour not by money, but by character; for with money is nothing pertaining unto God purchased. Even if there be with us a sort of treasury, no sum is therein collected, discreditable to Religion as though she were bought. Every man placeth there a small gift on one day in each month, or whensoever he will, so he do but will, and so he be but able; for no man is constrained, but contributeth willingly. These are as it were the deposits of piety; for afterwards they are not disbursed in feasting and in drinking, and in disgusting haunts of gluttony, but for feeding and burying the poor, for boys and girls without money and without parents, and for old men now house-ridden, for the shipwrecked also, and for any who in the mines, or in the islands, or in the prisons, become their Creed's pensioners, so that it be only for the sake of the way of God. But it is the exercise of this sort of love which doth, with some, chiefly brand us with a mark of evil. "See," say they, "how they love each other"; for they themselves hate each other: and "see how ready they are to die for each other"; for they themselves are more ready to slay each other.—*L.F.* x. 80 *sq.*

No. 93.—Philosophy the Mother of Heresy

From Tertullian, *De præscriptione hæreticorum* [*c.* 200], c. vii.

Philosophy is the theme of worldly wisdom, that rash interpreter of the Divine Nature and Order. And in fact, heresies are themselves equipped by philosophy. Thence come Valentinus' "æons" and I know not what infinite "ideas" and "trinity of man." He was a Platonist. Thence, too, the "better God" of Marcion, so called because of his tranquillity. He came from the Stoics. And when the soul is affirmed to perish, that is a tenet taken from the Epicureans. And when the restoration of the flesh is denied, that is assumed from the uniform teaching of all the philosophers. And when matter is identified with God, that is the doctrine of Zeno. And when any statement is made about a fiery God, Heracleitus comes in. The same themes are pondered by heretics and philosophers: the same subjects of consideration are involved—Whence came evil, and why? and Whence came man, and how? and—a question lately propounded by Valentinus—Whence came God? From Desire, forsooth, and an Abortion. Wretched Aristotle! who established for them the dialectic art, so ingenious in the construction and refutation of propositions, so crafty in statements, so forced in hypotheses, so inflexible in arguments, so laborious in disputes, so damaging even to itself, always reconsidering everything, so that it never treats thoroughly of anything at all.—T. H. Bindley: Tertullian, *On the Prescription of Heretics*, 43-5.

No. 94.—The Rule of Faith

From Tertullian, *De præscriptione hæreticorum*, c. xiii.

Now the Rule of Faith—that we may here at this point make our profession of what we maintain—is unquestionably that wherein our belief is affirmed that there is but One God, the Selfsame with the Creator of the world, Who produced all things out of nothing through His Word sent down in the beginning of all things; that this Word is called His Son, Who in the Name of God was seen under divers forms by the patriarchs, was ever heard in the prophets, and lastly was brought down by the Spirit and Power of God the Father into the Virgin Mary, became Flesh in her womb, and being born of her lived as Jesus Christ; that thereafter He proclaimed a new law and a new promise of the Kingdom of Heaven, wrought miracles, was crucified, and on the third day rose again, was caught up into the heavens, and sat down at the right hand of the Father; that He sent the Vicarious Power of the Holy Spirit to lead believers; that He will come with glory to take the saints into the enjoyment of life eternal and of the heavenly promises, and to adjudge the wicked to fire perpetual, after the resurrection of both good and bad has taken place together with the restoration of their flesh.

This Rule, taught (as it will be proved) by Christ, admits no questionings amongst us, save those which heresies introduce and which make heretics.—*Ibid.* 53, *sq.*

No. 95.—The Argument from Tradition

From Tertullian, *De præscriptione hæreticorum*, cc. xx., xxi.

[c. xx.] Out of the number of His disciples He attached to Himself twelve special ones who were destined to be the teachers of the nations. Consequently, when one of them was struck off, He bade the eleven remaining ones to go and teach all nations, who were to be baptized into the Father and into the Son and into the Holy Spirit. Immediately, therefore, the Apostles (whose title denotes their being sent), having added to their number by lot a twelfth, Matthias, in the place of Judas, on the authority of a prophecy in a Psalm of David, and having obtained the promised power of the Holy Spirit for miracles and for utterance, first throughout Judæa bore witness to the faith in Christ Jesus; and, having founded Churches, then went forth into the world and spread abroad the same doctrine of the same Faith to the nations. In like manner, too, they founded Churches in every city, from which the rest of the Churches hereafter have derived the transmission of their faith and the seeds of their doctrine, and are daily deriving them in order to become Churches. Thus these Churches themselves are also reckoned as Apostolic because they are the offspring of Apostolic Churches. Every kind of thing must necessarily be classed according to its origin. Consequently these Churches, numerous and important as they are, form but the one Primitive Church founded by the Apostles, from which source they all derive. So that all are primitive and all are Apostolic; whilst that all are in one Unity is proved by the fellowship of peace and title of brotherhood and common pledge of amity—privileges which nothing governs but the one tradition of the selfsame Bond of Faith.

[c. xxi.] On this ground, therefore, we rule our limitation that if the Lord Jesus Christ sent the Apostles to preach, no others ought to be received as preachers save those whom Christ appointed; since no other knoweth the Father save the Son, and he to whom the Son hath revealed Him. Nor does the Son appear to have revealed Him to any but the Apostles whom He sent to preach—surely only what He revealed to them.

Now what they preached—that is, what Christ revealed to them—I rule ought to be proved by no other means than through the same Churches which the Apostles themselves founded by preaching to them *viva voce,* as men say, and afterwards by Epistles. If this is so, it follows accordingly that all doctrine which agrees with those Apostolic Churches and original founts of Faith must be reckoned for Truth, as preserving unquestionably that which the Churches received from the Apostles, and the Apostles from Christ, and Christ from God; and, on the other hand, that all doctrine which savours contrary to the Truth of the Churches and of the Apostles of Christ and of God, must be condemned at once as having its origin in falsehood. It remains therefore for us to show whether this our doctrine—the Rule of which we have set forth above—is derived from the tradition of the Apostles; and, as a deduction from this, whether the other doctrines come of falsehood.—*Ibid.* 60–2.

No. 96.—The Disorders of Heretics

From Tertullian, *De præscriptione hæreticorum*, c. xli.

I must not omit a description, too, of the heretics' actual manner of life, how foolish it is, how earthly, how materialistic, without seriousness, without authority, without discipline—as beseems their peculiar faith.

In the first place, it is uncertain who is a catechumen and who a baptized believer; they all alike reproach, they all alike hear, and all alike pray—even heathens, if any should have chanced to enter. They will "throw that which is holy to dogs, and pearls" (albeit false ones) "to swine." They will have it that their subversion of discipline is simplicity, and call our care for discipline affectation. They unite in communion also with every one from every quarter. For it is of no importance to them, although they are teaching different doctrines, so long as they agree in an attack upon the One Truth. They are all puffed up; they all promise knowledge. Their catechumens are perfected before they are instructed. The very women amongst the heretics, how precocious they are! They presume to teach, to dispute, to practise exorcism, to promise cures, perchance also to baptize! Their ordinations are heedless, capricious, fickle. Now they appoint novices, now men hampered by worldly ties, now apostates from us, so as to bind them by ambition since they cannot by truth. Nowhere is preferment readier than in the camp of rebels, where the simple fact of being there is itself a merit. Consequently one man is bishop to-day, another to-morrow. To-day he is a deacon who to-morrow will be a reader; to-day he is a presbyter who will to-morrow be a laic. For even on laics do they impose sacerdotal functions!—*Ibid.* 91–2.

No. 97.—Unwritten Traditions

From Tertullian, *De Corona Mil.* [201], cc. iii., iv.

[c. iii.] But thou sayest, even where tradition is pleaded, written authority ought to be required. Wherefore let us enquire whether none, save a written tradition, ought to be received. Certainly we shall deny that it ought to be received, if there be no precedents to determine the contrary in other observances which, without any Scripture document, we defend on the ground of tradition alone, and by the supports of consequent custom. In fact, to begin with Baptism, when we are about to come to the water, in the same place, but at a somewhat earlier time, we do in the Church testify, under the hand of a chief minister, that we renounce the devil and his pomp and his angels. Then we are thrice dipped, pledging ourselves to something more than the Lord hath prescribed in the Gospel; then, some undertaking the charge of us, we first taste a mixture of honey and milk, and from that day we abstain for a whole week from our daily washing. The Sacrament of the Eucharist commanded by the Lord at the time of supper and to all, we receive even at our meetings before daybreak, and from the hands of no others than the heads of the Church. We offer on one day every year oblations for the dead as birthday honours. On the Lord's Day we account it unlawful to fast, or to worship upon the knees. We enjoy the same freedom from Easter Day even to Pentecost. We feel pained if any of the wine, or even of our bread, be spilled on the ground. In all our travels and movements, in all our coming in and going out, in putting on our shoes, at the bath, at the table, in lighting our candles, in lying down, in sitting down, whatever employment occupieth us, we mark our forehead with the sign of the cross. [c. iv.] For these, and such-like rules, if thou requirest a law in the Scriptures, thou shalt find none. Tradition will be pleaded to thee as originating them, custom as confirming them, and faith as observing them.—*L.F.* x. 161 *sqq.*

No. 98.—Infant Baptism

From Tertullian, *De baptismo* [*c.* 200–6], c. xviii.

Consequently in view of the circumstances and will, even the age of each person, a postponement of Baptism is most advantageous, particularly, however, in the case of children. For what need is there, if it is not so urgent, that the sponsors also should be brought into danger, being as they are themselves also by reason of their mortality capable of falling short of their promises and being deceived by the development of an evil disposition? The Lord indeed says: "Forbid them not to come unto Me." Let them come, then, while they are growing up; let them come while they are learning, while they are being taught whither to come; let them become Christians, when they have been able to know Christ. Why hurries the age of innocence to the remission of sins? Shall we act more cautiously in worldly matters? Shall one to whom earthly substance is not entrusted, be entrusted with heavenly?—A. Souter, *Tertullian's Treatises on Prayer and on Baptism*, 69 *sq.*

No. 99.—Exomologesis

From Tertullian, *De penitentia* [*c.* 200–6], c. ix.

[c. ix.] The more straitened then the work of this second and only remaining repentance, the more laborious its proof, so that it may not be only borne upon the conscience within, but may be also exhibited by some outward act. This act which is better and more commonly expressed by a Greek word, Ἐξομολόγησις, is Confession whereby we acknowledge our sin to the Lord, not because He knoweth it not, but inasmuch as by confession satisfaction is ordered, from confession repentance springeth, by repentance God is appeased. Wherefore Confession is a discipline for the abasement and humiliation of man, enjoining such conversation as inviteth mercy; it directeth also even in the matter of dress and food, to lie in sackcloth and ashes, to hide his body in filthy garments, to cast down his spirit with mourning, to exchange for severe treatment the sins which he hath committed; for the rest, to use simple things for meat and drink, to wit, not for the belly's sake but for the soul's sake; for the most part also, to cherish prayer by fasts, to groan, to weep and to moan day and night unto the Lord his God; to throw himself upon the ground before the presbyters, and to fall on his knees before the beloved of God; to enjoin all the brethren to bear the message of his prayer for mercy. All these things doeth Confession, that it may commend repentance; that by fearing danger it may honour God; that by judging of itself the sinner, it may act in the stead of God's wrath, and that, by means of temporal affliction, it may—I will not say frustrate, but—discharge the eternal penalties.—*L.F.* x. 364 *sq.*

No. 100.—The Visions of a Montanist Woman

From Tertullian, *De anima* [*c.* 208–11], c. ix.

. . . For seeing that we acknowledge spiritual *charismata*, or gifts, we too have merited the attainment of the prophetic gift, although coming after John [the Baptist]. We have now amongst us a sister whose lot it has been to be favoured with sundry gifts of revelation, which she experiences in the Spirit by ecstatic vision amidst the sacred rites of the Lord's Day in the church; she converses with angels, and sometimes even with the Lord; she both sees and hears mysterious communications; some men's hearts she understands, and to them who are in need she distributes remedies. Whether it be in the reading of the Scriptures, or in the chanting of psalms, or in the preaching of sermons, or in the offering up of prayers, in all these religious services matter and opportunity are afforded her of seeing visions. It may possibly have happened to us, whilst this sister of ours was rapt in the Spirit, that we had discoursed in some ineffable way about the soul. After the people are dismissed at the conclusion of the sacred services, she is in the regular habit of reporting to us whatever things she may have seen in vision; for all her communications are examined with the most scrupulous care, in order that their truth may be probed. "Amongst other things," says she, "there has been shown to me a soul in bodily shape, and a spirit has been in the habit of appearing to me; not, however, a void and empty illusion, but such as would offer itself to be even grasped by the hand, soft and transparent and of an ethereal colour, and in form resembling that of a human being in every respect." This was her vision, and for her witness there was God; and the apostle most assuredly foretold [1 Cor. xii. 1–11] that there were to be Spiritual gifts in the Church.—*A.-N.C.L.* xv. 427.

No. 101.—The Fall

From Tertullian, *De anima*, c. xli.

There is, then, besides the evil which supervenes on the soul from the intervention of the evil spirit an antecedent and, in a certain sense, natural evil which arises from its corrupt origin. For, as we have said before, the corruption of our nature is another nature having a god and father of its own, namely the author of [that] corruption. Still there is a portion of good in the soul, of that original, divine and genuine good, which is its proper nature. For that which is derived from God is rather obscured than extinguished. It can be obscured, indeed, because it is not God; extinguished, however, it cannot be, because it comes from God. As therefore light, when intercepted by an opaque body, still remains, although it is not apparent, by reason of the interposition of so dense a body; so likewise the good in the soul, being weighed down by the evil, is, owing to the obscuring character thereof, either not seen at all, its light being wholly hidden, or else only a stray beam is there visible where it struggles through by an accidental outlet. Thus some men are very bad, and some very good; but yet the souls of all form but one genus: even in the worst there is something good, and in the best there is something bad. For God alone is without sin: and the only man without sin is Christ, since Christ is also God. Thus the divinity of the soul bursts forth in prophetic forecasts in consequence of its primeval good; and being conscious of its origin it bears testimony to God [its author] in exclamations such as: *Good God! God knows!* and *Good-bye!* Just as no soul is without sin, so neither is any soul without seeds of good. Therefore, when the soul embraces the faith, being renewed in its second birth by water and the power from above, then the veil of its former corruption being taken away, it beholds the light in all its brightness. It is also taken up [in its second birth] by the Holy Spirit, just as in its first birth it is embraced by the unholy spirit. The flesh follows the soul now wedded to the Spirit, as a part of the bridal portion—no longer the servant of the soul, but of the Spirit. Oh! happy marriage, if in it there is committed no violation of the nuptial vow!—*A.-N.C.L.* xv. 505 *sq*.

No. 102.—Modalist Monarchianism

From Tertullian, *Adv. Praxean* [after 213], c. i.

Manifold are the ways in which the devil has shown his enmity to the truth. He has at length striven to shatter [it] by defending it. He claims that there is but one God, the all-powerful creator of the universe, in order to make a heresy even out of that one. He says that the Father Himself descended into the virgin, [that He likewise] was born of her and [Himself] suffered; even that He Himself is Jesus Christ. The Serpent forgot himself; for when trying Jesus Christ after he had been baptized by John, he approached him as Son of God, knowing full well that God had a Son, even from the very Scriptures out of which he was then building up the temptation. "If thou art the Son of God, speak that these stones become loaves"; again, "If thou art the Son of God, cast thyself down hence; for it is written that He"—that is the Father—"hath given His messengers charge over thee to uphold thee by their hands lest anywhere thou shouldst strike thy foot against a stone." Or shall he upbraid the Gospels with falsehood, and say: "It is Matthew's and Luke's concern, not mine? It was God Himself that I approached, the all-powerful Himself whom I assayed hand to hand; it was for this reason that I attacked. But if he had been merely the Son of God, I should never have delayed to tempt him." In truth, however, it is rather "he himself" who "has been a liar from the beginning," he and any man he has privily sent of his own accord such as Praxeas. For it was Praxeas who first, from Asia, imported this kind of perversity from Roman soil, a restless being in other respects, and puffed up besides with boasting about his martyrdom, which consisted merely in an ordinary brief, if irksome, period in prison; whereas, even if he had "surrendered his body to be burnt up," it would have "profited him nothing" as he had not "the love" of God, whose "gifts" he even violated. For when the then bishop of Rome was now recognizing the prophecies of Montanus, Prisca and Maximilla, and as the result of that recognition was seeking to introduce peace to the churches of Asia and Phrygia, it was he who did by making false statements about these very prophets and their churches, and by defending the authoritative acts of his predecessors, compel him both to recall the letters of peace that had already been despatched and to give up his project of welcoming their gifts. So Praxeas managed two pieces of the devil's business at Rome; he drove out prophecy and brought in heresy, he put the Paraclete to flight and crucified the Father. Praxeas' "tares" have borne fruit here too, having been "sown above" the pure teaching "while" many "slept"; thereafter through him whom God willed, they seemed to have been revealed, and even pulled up by the roots. Furthermore, the presbyter who taught them had given sureties for his reform, and his signed promise remains in the possession of the carnal men in whose presence the transaction took place at the time. Ever since there has been silence. As for ourselves, the recognition and defence of the Paraclete afterwards separated us from these carnal men. Those tares had, however, at that time everywhere "choked the seed." For some time that fact lay hidden through hypocrisy, such was its cunning vitality, and now it has burst forth again.—A. Souter, *Tertullian Against Praxeas*, 29 *sq*.

No. 103.—The Abstinences of Montanism

From Tertullian, *De jejunio* [after 213], cc. i., ii., x., xiii., xv.

[c. i.] . . . It is these [the Psychics] which raise controversy with the Paraclete; it is on this account that the New Prophecies are rejected: not that Montanus and Priscilla and Maximilla preach another God, nor that they disjoin Jesus Christ [from God], nor that they overturn any particular rule of faith or hope, but that they plainly teach more frequent fasting than marrying. Concerning the limit of marrying, we have already published a defence of monogamy. Now our battle is the battle of the secondary, or rather the primary, continence, in regard of the chastisement of diet. They charge us with keeping fasts of our own; with prolonging our Stations generally into the evening; with observing xerophagies likewise, keeping our food unmoistened by any flesh, and by any juiciness, and by any kind of specially succulent fruit; and with not eating or drinking anything with a winey flavour; also with abstaining from the bath, congruent with our dry diet. They are therefore constantly reproaching us with novelty. . . .

[c. ii.] . . . In the Gospel, they think that those days were definitely appointed for fasts in which "the bridegroom was taken away" [Mark ii. 18–20]; and that these are now the only legitimate days for Christian fasts. . . . Accordingly [they think] that, with regard to the future, fasting was to be indifferently observed by the New Discipline, of choice not of command, according to the times and needs of each individual: that this withal had been the observance of the Apostles, imposing [as they did] no other yoke of definite fasts to be observed by all generally, nor similarly of Stations either, which [they think] have withal days of their own (the fourth and sixth days of the week), but yet take a wide range according to individual judgment, neither subject to the law of a given precept nor [to be protracted] beyond the last hour of the day, since even prayers the ninth hour generally concludes, after Peter's example which is recorded in the Acts. Xerophagies, however, [they consider] the novel name of a studied duty, and very much akin to heathenish superstition. . . .

[c. x.] In like manner they censure, on the count of novelty, our Stations as being enjoined; some, moreover, [censure them] as being prolonged habitually too late, saying that this duty ought also to be observed of free choice, and not continued beyond the ninth hour—[deriving their rule], of course, from their own practice. . . . [The practice] comes from the death of the Lord. . . . I am equally able . . . to fix the condition of late protraction of the Station; [namely] that we are to fast till a late hour, awaiting the time of the Lord's sepulture, when Joseph took down and entombed the body which he had requested. Thence [it follows] that it is even irreligious for the flesh of the servants to take refreshment before their Lord did.

[c. xiii.] . . . But it is enough for me that it is a customary practice for the bishops withal to issue mandates for fasts to the universal commonalty of the church: I do not mean for the special purpose of collecting contributions of alms, as your beggarly fashion has it, but sometimes too from some particular cause of ecclesiastical solicitude.

[c. xv.] . . . Two weeks of xerophagies in the year [and

not the whole of these, the Sabbaths, to wit, and the Lord's Days, being excepted] we offer to God, abstaining from things which we do not reject but defer. . . .—*A.-N.C.L.* xviii. 124–5; 139 *sqq.;* 148.

No. 104.—The Rigorous Discipline of Montanism

From Tertullian, *De pudicitia* [*c.* 217–22], c. i.

[c. i.] Christian modesty is being shaken to its foundations. . . . I hear that there has even been an edict set forth, and a peremptory one, too. The Sovereign Pontiff[1]—that is, the bishop of bishops—issues an edict: "I remit, to such as have discharged [the requirements of] repentance, the sins both of adultery and of fornication." Oh! edict, on which cannot be inscribed "Good deed!" And where shall this liberality be posted up? On the very spot, I suppose, on the very gates of the sensual appetites, beneath the very titles of the sensual appetites. There is the place for promulgating such repentance, where the delinquency itself shall haunt. There is the place to read the pardon, where entrance shall be made under the hope thereof. But it is in the Church that this [edict] is read, and in the Church that it is pronounced: and [the Church] is a virgin! Far, far from Christ's betrothed be such a profanation! . . . This too, therefore, shall be a count in my indictment against the Psychics; against the fellowship of sentiment also which I myself formerly maintained with them.—*A.-N. C.L.* xviii. 57, 112.

No. 105.—A Plea for Christianity under Dionysiac Phraseology

From Clement of Alexandria [*c.* 200], *Protrepticus*, c. xii.

Come, O madman, not leaning on the thyrsus, not crowned with ivy; throw away the mitre; throw away the fawn-skin; come to thy senses. I will show thee the Word, and the mysteries of the Word, expounding them after thine own fashion. This is the mountain beloved of God, not the subject of tragedies like Cithæron, but consecrated to dramas of the truth—a mountain of sobriety, shaded with forests of purity. . . .

[1] Pope Callistus, *c.* 217–†22.

Come thou also, O aged man, leaving Thebes, and casting away from thee both divination and Bacchic frenzy, allow thyself to be led to the truth. I give thee the staff [of the Cross] on which to lean. Haste, Tiresias; believe, and thou shalt see . . . O truly sacred mysteries! O stainless light! My way is lighted with torches, and I survey the heavens and God; I become holy whilst I am initiated. The Lord is the hierophant, and seals while illuminating him who is initiated, and presents to the Father him who believes, to be kept safe for ever. Such are the revelries of my mysteries. If it is thy wish, be thou also initiated; and thou shalt join the choir along with angels around the unbegotten and indestructible and only true God, the Word of God, raising the hymn with us.—*A.-N.C.L.* iv. 107 *sq.*

No. 106.—On Laughter

From Clement of Alexandria [*c.* 200], *Pæd.* II. v. §§ 45–7.

[§ 45] Pleasantry is allowable, not waggery. [§ 46] Besides, even laughter must be kept in check; for when given vent to in the right manner, it indicates orderliness, but when it issues differently it shows a want of restraint.

For, in a word, whatever things are natural to men we must not eradicate from them, but rather impose on them limits and suitable times. For man is not to laugh on all occasions because he is a laughing animal, any more than the horse neighs on all occasions because he is a neighing animal. But as rational beings we are to regulate ourselves suitably, harmoniously relaxing the austerity and over-tension of our serious pursuits, not inharmoniously breaking them up altogether.

For the seemly relaxation of the countenance in a harmonious manner—as of a musical instrument—is called a smile. So also is laughter on the face of well-regulated men termed. But the discordant relaxation of countenance in the case of women is called a giggle, and is meretricious laughter; in the case of men, a guffaw, and is savage and insulting laughter. "A fool raises his voice in laughter," says the Scripture; "but a clever man smiles almost imperceptibly.'[1] The clever man, in this case, he calls wise, inasmuch as he is differently affected from the fool.

[§ 47] But, on the other hand, one needs not be gloomy, only grave. For I certainly prefer a man to smile who has a stern countenance than the reverse; for so his laughter will be less apt to become the object of ridicule.

Smiling even requires to be made the subject of discipline. If it is at what is disgraceful, we ought to blush rather than smile, lest we seem to take pleasure in it by sympathy; if at what is painful, it is fitting to look sad rather than to seem pleased. For to do the former is a sign of rational human thought; the other infers suspicion of cruelty.—*A.-N.C.L.* iv. 219 *sq.*

No. 107.—Clement of Alexandria: His Conversion and his Teachers

From Clement of Alexandria, *Strom.* I. i. § 11.

[§ 11] Now this work of mine in writing is not artfully constructed for display; but my memoranda are stored up against old age, as a remedy against forgetfulness, truly an image and an outline of those vigorous and animated discourses, which I was privileged to hear, and of blessed and truly remarkable men.

Of these the one in Greece, an Ionian; the other in Magna Græcia; the first of these from Cœle-Syria, the second from Egypt, and others in the East. The one was born in the land of Assyria, and the other, a Hebrew, in Palestine.

When I came upon the last [*sc.* Pantænus]—he was the first in power—having tracked him out concealed in Egypt, I found rest. He the true, the Sicilian bee, gathering the spoil of the flowers of the prophetic and apostolic meadow, engendered in the souls of his hearers a deathless element of knowledge.

Well, they preserving the tradition of the blessed doctrine derived directly from the holy apostles, Peter, James, John and Paul, the son receiving it from the father (but few were like the fathers), came by God's will to us also to deposit these ancestral and apostolic seeds.—*A.-N.C.L.* iv. 355.

[1] Ecclus. xxi. 20.

No. 108.—Philosophy a Preparation for the Gospel

From Clement of Alexandria, *Strom.* I. v. § 28.

[§ 28] Accordingly, before the Advent of the Lord, philosophy was necessary to the Greeks for righteousness, And now it becomes conducive to piety; being a kind of preparatory training to those who attain to faith through demonstration. "For thy foot," it is said, "will not stumble,"[1] if thou refer what is good, whether belonging to the Greeks or to us, to Providence. For God is the cause of all good things; but of some primarily, as of the Old and the New Testament; and of others by consequence, as philosophy. Perchance, too, philosophy was given to the Greeks directly and primarily, till the Lord should call the Greeks. For this was "a schoolmaster to bring" the Hellenic mind, as the Law the Hebrews, "to Christ."[2] Philosophy, therefore, was a preparation, paving the way for him who is perfect in Christ.—*A.-N.C.L.* iv. 366.

No. 109.—On Flight in Persecution

From Clement of Alexandria, *Strom.* IV. x. §§ 76–7.

[§ 76] When again He says, "When they persecute you in this city, flee ye to the other,"[3] He does not advise flight as if persecution were an evil thing; nor does He enjoin them, by flight, to avoid death, as if in dread of it, but wishes us neither to be the authors nor abettors of any evil to any one, either to ourselves or the persecutor and murderer. For He, in a way, bids us take care of ourselves. But he who disobeys is rash and foolhardy.

[§ 77] And if he who kills a man of God sins against God, he also who presents himself before the judgment-seat becomes guilty of his death. And such is also the case with him who does not avoid persecution, but out of daring presents himself for capture. Such a one, as far as in him lies, becomes an accomplice in the crime of the persecutor. And if he also uses provocation, he is wholly guilty, challenging the wild beast. And similarly, if he afford any cause for conflict or punishment, or retribution

[1] Prov. iii. 23. [2] Gal. iii. 24. [3] Matt. x. 23.

or enmity, he gives occasion for persecution. Wherefore, then, we are enjoined not to cling to anything that belongs to this life; but "to him that takes our cloak to give our coat," not only that we may continue destitute of inordinate affection, but that we may not by retaliating make our persecutors savage against ourselves, and stir them "up to blaspheme the Name."—*A.-N.C.L.* xii. 173 *sq.*

No. 110.—The True Gnostic

From Clement of Alexandria, *Strom.* VI. xiii. § 105.

[§ 105] He, then, who first moderated his passions and trained himself for impassibility, and developed to the beneficence of Gnostic perfection, is here equal to the angels. Luminous already, and like the sun shining in the exercise of beneficence, he speeds by righteous knowledge through the love of God to the sacred abode, like as the apostles. . . .—*A.-N.C.L.* xii. 365.

No. 111.—Faith and Knowledge

From Clement of Alexandria, *Strom.* VII. x. § 57.

[§ 57] Faith, then, is a compendious knowledge of the essentials, but knowledge is a sure and firm demonstration of the things received through faith, being itself built up by the Lord's teaching on the foundation of faith, and carrying us on to unshaken conviction and scientific certainty. As I mentioned before, there seems to me to be a first kind of saving change from heathenism to faith, a second from faith to knowledge; and this latter, as it passes on into love, begins at once to establish a mutual friendship between that which knows and that which is known. And, perhaps, he who has arrived at this stage has already "attained equality with the angels."[1] At any rate, after he has reached the final ascent in the flesh, he still continues to advance, as is fit, and presses on through the holy Hebdomad into the Father's house, to that which is indeed the Lord's abode,[2] being destined there to be, as it were, a light standing and abiding for ever, absolutely secure

[1] Lk. xx. 36. [2] Jn. xiv. 2.

from all vicissitude.—F. J. A. Hort & J. B. Mayor, *Miscellanies*, Bk. VII. p. 101.

No. 112.—The Divisions of Christendom

From Clement of Alexandria, *Strom.* VII. xv. §§ 89–91.

[§ 89] The next thing is to reply to the charges brought against us by Greeks and Jews. . . . The first charge they allege is this very point that the diversity of sects shows belief to be wrong, for the voice of truth is drowned amid the din of conflicting assertions. To whom we reply that both among you Jews and among the most approved of the Greek philosophers, there have been multitudes of sects, yet of course you do not say that one should hesitate to be a philosopher or a follower of the Jews on account of the internal discord of your sects. In the next place it was prophesied by the Lord that the seed of heresy would be sown upon the truth like "tares upon wheat" (and what was prophesied cannot but come to pass), the cause of this being that the beautiful is always shadowed by its caricature.

[§ 90] . . . We ought in no way to transgress the rule of the Church. Above all, the confession which deals with the essential articles of the faith is observed by us, but disregarded by the heretics. Those then are to be believed who hold firmly to the truth. Using this defence broadly, we are now entitled to reply to them that physicians also, though holding different opinions in accordance with their particular schools, are still equally engaged in the practice of healing. Does then any one who is suffering in body and needs medical treatment refuse to call in a physician owing to the diversity of medical schools? So neither should he who is diseased in soul and full of idols plead the heresies as his excuse in regard to the recovery of health and conversion to God. Aye, and we are told that "heresies are for the sake of those who are approved"; and by "approved" is meant either those who are coming to the faith, if they show unusual discrimination in approaching the teaching of the Lord (like "the approved money-changers" who distinguish the spurious from the legal coin by the false stamp), or those who are in the faith itself, and have already approved themselves therein, both by their life and their knowledge.

[§ 91] It is for this reason, therefore, that we need more attention and consideration to determine how we should live with strictness and what is true piety. For it is evident that the trouble and difficulty of ascertaining the truth have given rise to questionings, from whence spring vain and self-willed heresies, when men have not learnt nor really received knowledge, but have merely got a conceit of it. We must therefore spend more thought in searching for the very truth, which alone has for its subject the very God. And sweet are the discovery and the remembrance which attend on toil.—F. J. A. Hort & J. B. Mayor, *Miscellanies*, Bk. VII. pp. 157–61.

No. 113.—The Misuse of Scripture by Heretics

From Clement of Alexandria, *Strom.* VII. xvi. § 96.

[§ 96] So we too, obtaining from the Scriptures themselves a perfect demonstration concerning the Scriptures, derive from faith a conviction which has the force of demonstration. And though it be true that the heretics also have the audacity to make use of the prophetic Scriptures, yet in the first place they do not use them all, and in the second place they do not use them in their entirety, nor as the general frame and tissue of the prophecy suggest; but picking out ambiguous phrases, they turn them to their own opinions, plucking a few scattered utterances, without considering what is intended by them, but perverting the bare letter as it stands. For in almost all the passages they employ, you will find how they attend to the words alone, while they change the meaning, neither understanding them as they are spoken, nor even using in their natural sense such extracts as they adduce. But truth is discovered not by altering the meanings of words (for by so doing they will subvert all true teaching) but by considering what is perfectly fitting and appropriate to the Lord and the Almighty God, and by conforming each thing that is proved according to the Scriptures from similar passages of the Scriptures themselves.—*Ibid.* 169 *sq.*

No. 114.—Redemption

From Clement of Alexandria, *Quis dives salvetur?* [*c.* 203], c. xxxvii.

[§ 37] What is still wanting? Look at the mysteries of love, and then thou shalt be admitted to see the bosom of the Father, Whom the only begotten God alone hath declared (John i. 18). God Himself also is love (1 John iv. 8, 16), and because of love He was seen by us. And the ineffable part of His nature became Father, but that part which has sympathy for us became Mother. The Father by loving became woman-like, and the great sign of this is the Son Whom He begat of Himself, and the fruit produced from love is love. For this cause He Himself came down, for this cause He put on man, for this cause He willingly suffered man's lot, that having been brought to the measure of the weakness of us, whom He loved, He might bring us in return to the measure of His power. And being about to be offered, and giving Himself as a ransom, He leaves us a new covenant: "My love I give unto you." What means this, and how great is this love? For the sake of each of us He laid down His life—worth no less than the universe. He demands of us in return our lives for the sake of each other.—P. M. Barnard, *Who is the rich man that is being saved?* 63–5.

No. 115.—St. John and the Robber

From Clement of Alexandria, *Quis dives salvetur?* c. xlii.

[§ 42] But that thou mayest have confidence, if thou thus truly repent, that there remains for thee a sufficient hope of salvation, hear a legend that is no legend, but a true story concerning John the Apostle, that has been handed down and preserved in memory. For when, on the death of the tyrant, he removed from the island of Patmos to Ephesus, on being invited, he went also to the neighbouring districts of the Gentiles; in one place appointing Bishops, in another setting in order whole Churches, in another ordaining a ministry, or individuals of those indicated by the Spirit. Being come then to one of the cities not far off (some people also tell its name), and having set the brethren at rest on other matters, at last he fixed his eyes on the presiding Bishop, and seeing a young man of considerable bodily strength, and fair in appearance, and fervent in soul, he said, "This man I give into thy keeping with all earnestness before the Church and Christ as witnesses." On the Bishop's accepting and promising everything, he again repeated the same earnest charge and invocation of witnesses. Then the Apostle went away to Ephesus, and the elder taking with him to his home the young man entrusted to him, nourished him, made a friend of him, cherished him, at last enlightened him; and after this he ceased to take further care of him or to watch over him, as having set over him the perfect defence, the seal of the Lord. But he had received his freedom too soon: certain idle and dissolute companions, men accustomed to evil doings, join in mischievous association with him; at first they lead him on with expensive banquets; then on occasion, when going out at night to rob, they take him with them; then they require him to join them in some greater deed. Little by little he grew accustomed to it, and through the greatness of his nature, like a hard-mouthed and strong horse, swerving from the straight course, and taking the bit between his teeth, he was carried on deeper into the gulf. Despairing altogether of salvation in God, without the least further consideration, as being once and for all lost, he claimed by doing some great wrong to share the same fate as the others. Taking with him these same men, he levied a robber band, and was himself ready as a robber-chief, most violent, most bloodthirsty, most cruel. Time passed, and on some necessity arising they sent for John. He, after arranging the affairs for which he had come, said, "Come now, O Bishop, give back the deposit which I and Christ entrusted to thee in the presence of the Church, over which thou presidest as witness." He was at first astonished, thinking that money which he had not received was being fraudulently claimed from him, and could neither believe concerning what he had not got nor disbelieve John. But when he said, "I demand back the young man, and the soul of thy brother," the elder, with deep groans and even with tears, said, "That man is dead." "How, and when, and by what death?" "He is dead to God," he said, "for he has turned out evil, and reprobate, and to crown all, a robber; and now, instead of the Church, he has chosen the mountain with a band of men like himself." The Apostle tore his garment, and beat his head, with great groaning. "A fine guardian," he said, "art thou, whom I left in charge of thy brother's soul; but let a horse now be brought me, and let some one be my guide on the way." Just as he was he rode straight away from the church itself; and coming to the place, he is seized by the outpost of the robbers; he neither flees, nor asks to be freed, but shouts, "For this purpose am I come; take me away to your leader." The leader armed as he was, waited for a while, but, when he recognized John on his approach, he was ashamed and turned to flight. But the Apostle, forgetful of his own age, pursued him with all his might, crying out, "Why dost thou fly from me, my child, thine own father, unarmed, and old? Pity me, my child, fear not; thou hast yet hope of life; I will be surety to Christ for thee; if it be needful, I will willingly suffer the death thou deservest, as the Lord suffered death for us; on thy behalf will I give my own life. Stand, believe Christ has sent me." He, when he heard, at first stood with downcast eyes, then threw away his weapons, then trembled and wept bitterly. As the old man came towards him he embraced him, excusing himself with his groans as best he could, baptized a second time with his tears, hiding only his right hand. Then the Apostle pledged himself, and vowed that he had found pardon for him from the Saviour, prayed on his knees, kissed his very right hand as cleansed by his repentance, and brought him back to the Church; then he prayed for him with abundant prayers, and joined with him in wrestling in continuous fasts, and soothed his mind with varied exhortations, and did not go away, as they say, till he had restored him to the Church, thus affording a great example of real repentance, and a great proof of new birth, a monument of a visible resurrection.—*Ibid.* 71–6.

No. 116.—The Persecution of Domitian, *c.* 96

From Dio Cassius [*fl.* 180–229], *Epitome* LXVII. xiv. §§ 1–3 [Excerpta per Xiphilinum, xi. cent.], ed. L. Dindorf iv. 119 *sq.* (Teubner, Lipsiæ, 1864).

[§ 1] . . . And in the same year Domitian slew amongst many others Flavius Clemens in his consulship, though he was his cousin and had to wife his own kinswoman, Flavia Domitilla.

[§ 2] Against them both was brought a charge of atheism; and on this many others who made shipwreck on Jewish customs were condemned, of whom some were put to death, while others were at the least deprived of their property; but Domitilla was only banished to Pandateria.

[§ 3] Glabrio, however, who had been consul with Trajan he also slew, partly on the same charges as the rest, and partly because he fought with beasts.—H. M. Gwatkin, *Selections from Early Christian Writers*, 11.

No. 117.—The Scriptures Acknowledged by the Roman Church

From [? Hippolytus †236], the Muratorian Canon, *c.* 175–200.

[§ 1] . . . But at some he (? St. Mark) was present, and he set them down thus.

The third book of the Gospel, that according to Luke, the well-known physician Luke wrote in his own name in order, after the ascension of Christ, and when Paul had associated him with himself as one studious of right. Nor did he himself see the Lord in the flesh; and he, according as he was able to accomplish it, began[1] his narrative with the nativity of John.

The fourth Gospel is that of John, one of the disciples. When his fellow-disciples and bishops entreated him he said, "Fast ye now with me for the space of three days, and let us recount to each other whatever may be revealed to each of us." On the same night it was revealed to Andrew, one of the apostles, that John should narrate all

[1] Or "and he, too, as he was able to ascertain [events, so set them down]. So he began," etc. (Gwatkin, *Selections* No. xxii.).

things in his own name as they called them to mind.[1] And hence although different points are taught us in several books of the Gospels, there is no difference as regards the faith of believers, inasmuch as in all of them all things are related under one sovereign Spirit which concern the [Lord's] nativity, His passion, His resurrection, His conversation with His disciples, and His twofold advent—the first in the humiliation of rejection, which is now past, and the second in the glory of royal power, which is yet in the future. What marvel is it then that John brings forward these several things so constantly in his epistles also, saying in his own person, "What we have seen with our eyes, and heard with our ears, and our hands have handled, that have we written." For thus he professes himself to be not only the eyewitness, but also the hearer; and, besides that, the historian of all the wondrous facts concerning the Lord in their order.

[§ 2] Moreover, the Acts of all the Apostles are comprised by Luke in one book, and addressed to the most excellent Theophilus, because these different events took place when he was present himself; and he shows this clearly [*i.e.* that the principle on which he wrote was to give only what fell under his own notice] by the omission of the passion of Peter, and also of the journey of Paul when he went from the city [Rome] to Spain.

[§ 3] As to the Epistles of Paul, again, to those who will understand the matter, they indicate of themselves that they are, and from what place or with what object they were directed. He wrote, first of all, and at considerable length to the Corinthians, to check the schism of heresy; and then to the Galatians, to forbid circumcision; and then to the Romans on the rule of the [Old Testament] Scriptures, and also to show them that Christ is the first object in these: which it is [not] needful for us to discuss severally, as the blessed Apostle Paul, following the rule of his predecessor John, writes to no more than seven churches by name in this order: the first to the Corinthians, the second to the Ephesians, the third to the Philippians, the fourth to the Colossians, the fifth to the Galatians, the sixth to the Thessalonians, the seventh to the Romans. Moreover,

[1] Or "and they were all to certify."—*Ibid.*

though he writes twice to the Corinthians and the Thessalonians for their correction, it is yet shown [*i.e.* by this sevenfold writing] that there is but one Church spread abroad through the whole world. And John too, indeed, in the Apocalypse, although he writes only to seven churches, yet addresses all. He wrote besides these, one to Philemon, and one to Titus, and two to Timothy, in simple personal affection and love indeed; and yet these are hallowed in the esteem of the Catholic Church, [and] in the regulation of ecclesiastical discipline. There are also in circulation one to the Laodiceans, and another to the Alexandrians, forged under the name of Paul, ⌜[and] addressed against⌝[1] the heresy of Marcion; and there are also several others which cannot be received into the Catholic Church, for it is not suitable for gall to be mingled with honey.

[§ 4] The Epistle of Jude indeed, and two bearing the name of John, are accepted in the Catholic [Church]. And the [book of] Wisdom, written by the friends of Solomon in his honour [is admitted]. ⌜We receive also the Apocalypse of John and [that of] Peter⌝;[2] though some amongst us will not have this latter read in the Church. But the *Shepherd* did Hermas write very recently in our times in the City of Rome, while his brother, Bishop Pius, sat in the chair of the Church of Rome. And therefore it ought also to be read; but it cannot be publicly read in the Church to the people, either among the prophets as their number is complete, or among the Apostles, to the end of time.

⌜Of [the writings of] Arsinous, called also Valentinus, or of Miltiades⌝,[3] we receive nothing at all. ⌜Those, too, who wrote the new Book of Psalms for Marcion⌝,[4] together with Basilides and the founder of the Asian Cataphrygians [are rejected].—*A.-N.C.L.* Vol. IX. pt. ii. 159 *sqq.*

[1] Or "to suit" (Gwatkin, *Selections* No. xxii.), *i.e.* in the interest of.

[2] Or from an amended text, "The Apocalypse also of John, and of Peter [one Epistle, which] only we receive; there is also a second." —*Ibid.*

[3] Or from an amended text, "of V. the Arsinoite and his friends." —*Ibid.*

[4] Or from an amended text, "Who have also composed a long new Book of Psalms."—*Ibid.*

No. 118.—Adoptionist Monarchianism

From Hippolytus, *Refutatio omnium hæresium* [*c.* 235], vii. § 35.

But there was a certain Theodotus, a native of Byzantium, who introduced a novel heresy. He announces tenets concerning the originating cause of the universe, which are partly in keeping with the doctrines of the true Church, in so far as he acknowledges that all things were created by God. Forcibly appropriating, however, [his notions of] Christ from the school of the Gnostics, and of Cerinthus and Ebion, he alleges that [our Lord] appeared in some such manner as I shall now describe. [According to this, Theodotus maintains] that Jesus was a [mere] man, born of a Virgin, according to the counsel of the Father, and that after he had lived promiscuously with all men, and had become pre-eminently religious, he subsequently at his baptism in Jordan received Christ, Who came from above and descended [upon him] in the form of a dove. And this was the reason [according to Theodotus] why [miraculous] powers did not operate within him prior to the manifestation in him of that Spirit which descended [and] which proclaims Him to be the Christ. But [among the followers of Theodotus] some are disposed [to think] that never was this man made God, [even] at the descent of the Spirit; whereas [others maintain that He was made God] after the resurrection from the dead.—*A.-N.C.L.* vi. 303 *sq.*

119.—An Account of Montanism

From Hippolytus, *Refutatio omnium hæresium,* viii. § 19.

But there are others who themselves are even more heretical in nature [than the Quartodecimans], and are Phrygians by birth. These have been rendered victims of error from being previously captivated by [two] wretched women, called a certain Priscilla and Maximilla, whom they supposed [to be] prophetesses. And they assert that into these the Paraclete Spirit had departed; and antecedently to them, they in like manner consider Montanus as a prophet. And being in possession of an infinite number of their books, [the Phrygians] are overrun with delusion; and they do not judge whatever statements are made by them, according to [the criterion of reason]; nor do they give heed unto those who are competent to decide; but they are heedlessly swept onwards, by the reliance which they place on these [impostors]. And they allege that they have learned something more through these than from Law and prophets and the Gospels. But they magnify these wretched women above the Apostles and every gift of Grace, so that some of them presume to assert that there is in them a something superior to Christ. These acknowledge God to be the Father of the Universe, and Creator of all things, similarly with the Church, and [receive] as many things as the Gospel testify concerning Christ. They introduce, however, the novelties of fasts, and feasts, and meals of parched food, and repasts of radishes, alleging that they have been instructed by the women. And some of these assent to the heresy of the Noëtians, and affirm that the Father Himself is the Son, and that this [One] came under generation, and suffering, and death.—*A.-N.C.L.* Vol. VI. 325 *sq.*

No. 120.—The Misdeeds of Callistus, Bishop of Rome, *c.* 217–†22

From Hippolytus, *Refutatio omnium hæresium*, ix. § 12.

. . . . . . The impostor [Callistus], having ventured on such [outrageous] opinions, established a school [of theology] in antagonism to the Church, adopting the foregoing system of instruction. And he first invented the device of conniving with men in regard of their indulgence in [sensual] pleasures, saying that all had their sins forgiven by himself. . . . This [heretic] propounded the opinion, that, if a bishop was guilty of any sin, even if [a sin] unto death,[1] he ought not to be deposed. About the time of this man, bishops, priests and deacons who had been twice married and thrice married began [to be allowed] to retain their place among the clergy. If also, however, any one who is in Holy Orders should get married, [Callistus per-

[1] 1 *John* v. 16, *i.e.* the sins of *Acts* xv. 28; idolatry, murder, sensuality.

mitted] such a one to continue in Holy Orders, as if he had not sinned. . . . He permitted females, if they were unwedded, and burned with passion at an age at all events unbecoming, or if they were not disposed to overturn their own dignity through a legal marriage, that they might have whomsoever they would choose as a bedfellow, whether a slave or free, and that a [woman], though not legally married, might consider such [a companion] as a husband. Whence women, reputed believers, began to resort to . . . scandalous conduct . . . on account of their not wishing to have a child by a slave or by any paltry fellow, for the sake of their family and excessive wealth. . . . And, withal, after such audacious acts, they, lost to all shame, attempt to call themselves a Catholic Church.[1] And some under the supposition that they will attain prosperity, concur with them. During the [pontificate of] this [Callistus] for the first time, second baptism was presumptuously attempted by them.—*A.-N.C.L.* vi. 343 *sqq.*

No. 121.—The Invocation, *c.* 225

From Hippolytus, †236, *The so-called Egyptian Church Order,* ed. R. H. Connolly (*Texts and Studies,* VIII. No. 4, p. 176), or *The Apostolic Tradition.*

Let [the bishop] give thanks and say: "The Lord be with you," and let all say: "And with thy spirit." "Lift up your hearts." "We lift them up unto the Lord." "Let us give thanks unto the Lord." "It is meet and right." And then let him proceed thus:—

"We give Thee thanks, O God, through Thy beloved Son Jesus Christ, Whom in the last days Thou didst send to us, a Saviour and Redeemer, and Angel of Thy counsel; Who is Thy inseparable Word, through Whom Thou didst make all things, and He was well pleasing unto Thee: Thou didst send Him from heaven into the womb of a Virgin; He was conceived and became incarnate, and was shown to be Thy Son, being born of the Holy Spirit and a Virgin; Who, fulfilling Thy will and acquiring a holy people for Thee, stretched out His hands for suffering, that He might free from suffering those

[1] Hippolytus having withdrawn into a schism of his own.

who believed in Thee. And when He was betrayed to His voluntary passion, that He might loose (the pains of) death and break the chains of the devil, might tread underfoot (the powers of) Hell, and lead forth the righteous, fix the boundary thereof and make known His Resurrection, taking bread and giving thanks to Thee, He said: TAKE, EAT: THIS IS MY BODY, WHICH IS BROKEN FOR YOU. Likewise also the cup saying: THIS IS MY BLOOD, WHICH IS SHED FOR YOU: AS OFTEN AS YE DO THIS YE SHALL DO IT FOR MY MEMORIAL.

"Mindful, therefore, of His death and resurrection, we offer to Thee this bread, and this cup, giving thanks to Thee because Thou hast deemed us worthy to stand before Thee and minister unto Thee: and we beseech Thee that Thou wouldst send Thy Holy Spirit upon this oblation of Thy Holy Church; and that joining them together Thou wouldest grant it to all Thy holy ones who partake, for fulfilment with the Holy Spirit and for the confirmation of faith in truth; that we may praise Thee and glorify Thee through Thy Son Jesus Christ; through Whom to Thee be glory and honour, to Father and Son with the Holy Spirit, in Thy Holy Church, both now and to the ages of the ages. Amen."—A. Linton, *Twenty-five Consecration Prayers*, 30 *sq*.

No. 122.—The History of Susanna

From Julius Africanus, ?170–?†250, *Ep. ad Origenem*, § 1.

[§ 1] Greeting, my lord and son, most worthy Origen: from Africanus. In your sacred discussion with Agnomon, you referred to that prophecy of Daniel which is related of his youth. This at that time, as was meet, I accepted as genuine. Now, however, I cannot understand how it escaped you that this part of the book is spurious. For, in sooth, this section, although apart from this it is elegantly written, is plainly a more modern forgery. There are many proofs of this. When Susanna is condemned to die, the prophet is seized by the Spirit, and cries out that the sentence is unjust. Now, in the first place, it is always in some other way that Daniel prophesies—by visions, and dreams, and an angel appearing to him, never by prophetic inspiration. Then, after crying out in this extraordinary fashion, he detects them in a way no less incredible, which not even Philistion the play-writer would have resorted to. For, not satisfied with rebuking them through the Spirit, he placed them apart, and asked them severally where they saw her committing adultery. And when the one said "Under a holm-tree" (πρῖνον), he answered that the angel would saw him asunder (πρίσειν): and in a similar fashion menaced the other who said "Under a mastich-tree" (σχῖνον), with being rent asunder (σχισθῆναι). Now in Greek it happens that "holm-tree" and "saw asunder" and "rend" and "mastich-tree" sound alike: but in Hebrew they are quite distinct. But all the books of the Old Testament have been translated from Hebrew into Greek.—*A.-N.C.L.* x. 369.

No. 123.—The LXX Departures from the Hebrew

From Origen, 185–†254, *Ep. ad Africanum*, §§ 4, 5.

[§ 4] . . . And, forsooth, when we notice such things [*sc.* the LXX departures from the Hebrew], we are forthwith to reject as spurious the copies in use in our churches, and to enjoin the brotherhood to put away the sacred books current among them, and to coax the Jews, and persuade them to give us copies which shall be untampered with, and free from forgery! Are we to suppose that that Providence which in the sacred Scriptures has ministered to the edification of all the Churches of Christ, had no thought for those bought with a price, for whom Christ died; whom, although His Son, God, who is love, spared not, but gave Him up for us all, that with Him He might freely give us all things?

[§ 5] In all these cases, consider whether it would not be well to remember the words "Thou shalt not remove the ancient landmarks which thy fathers have set."[1] Nor do I say this because I shun the labour of investigating the Jewish Scriptures, and comparing them with ours, and noticing their various readings. Thus, if it be not arrogant to say it, I have already to a great extent done to the best of my ability, labouring hard to get at the meaning in all

[1] Prov. xxii. 28.

the editions and various readings; while I paid particular attention to the interpretation of the Seventy, lest I might be found to accredit any forgery to the churches which are under heaven, and give occasion to those who seek such a starting-point for gratifying their desire to slander the common brethren, and to bring some accusation against those who shine forth in our community. And I make it my endeavour not to be ignorant of their various readings, lest in my controversies with the Jews, I should quote to them what is not found in their copies, and that I may make some use of what is found there, even although it should not be in our Scriptures. For if we are so prepared for them in our discussions, they will not, as is their manner, scornfully laugh at Gentile believers for their ignorance of the true reading as they have them. So far as to the *History of Susanna* not being found in the Hebrew.—*A.-N.C.L.* x. 374 *sq*.

No. 124.—The Authorship of the Epistle to the Hebrews

From Origen, *ap*. Eusebius, *H.E.* VI. xxv. §§ 11–14.

[§ 11] In addition he makes the following statements in regard to the Epistle to the Hebrews in his Homilies upon it:—

"That the verbal style of the Epistle entitled 'To the Hebrews' is not rude like the language of the Apostle who acknowledged himself 'rude in speech,' that is, in expression; but that its diction is purer Greek, any one who has the power to discern differences of phraseology will acknowledge. [§ 12] Moreover, that the thoughts of the Epistle are admirable, and not inferior to the acknowledged Apostolic writings, any one who carefully examines the Apostolic text will admit." [§ 13] Farther on he adds:—

"If I gave my opinion, I should say that the thoughts are those of the Apostle, but the diction and phraseology are those of some one who remembered the Apostolic teachings, and wrote down at his leisure what had been said by his teacher. Therefore if any church holds that this Epistle is by Paul, let it be commended for this. For not without reason have the ancients handed it down as Paul's. [§ 14]

But who wrote the Epistle, in truth God knows. The statement of some who have gone before us is that Clement, bishop of the Romans, wrote the Epistle, and of others that Luke, the author of the Gospel and the Acts, wrote it."—*N. & P.-N.F.* i. 273.

No. 125.—The Parabolic Element in Scripture

From Origen, *Philocalia*, i. §§ 11, 17, 30.

[§ 11] The right way then to read the Scriptures and extract their meaning, so far as we have been able to discover from examining the oracles themselves, appears to be as follows:—Solomon in the Proverbs gives a rule respecting the divine doctrines of Scripture to this effect: "Do thou thrice record them with counsel and knowledge that thou mayst answer with words of truth to those who try thee with hard questions."[1] A man ought then in three ways to record in his own soul the purposes of the Holy Scriptures: that the simple may be edified by, as it were, the *flesh* of Scripture (for thus we designate the primary sense), the more advanced by its *soul*, and the perfect by the spiritual law, which has a shadow of the good things to come.[2] . . . As man consists of body, soul and spirit,[3] so, too, does Scripture which has been granted by God for the salvation of men. And thus we explain that passage in the *Shepherd*—a book which some treat with contempt—in which Hermas is commanded to write two books, and then read to the elders of the Church what he has learned from the Spirit. "Thou shalt write two books, and give one to Clement and one to Grapte; and Grapte shall admonish the widows and orphans, Clement shall send to the cities abroad, and thou shalt read to the elders of the Church."[4] Grapte who admonishes the widows and orphans is the bare *letter* of Scripture: it admonishes those readers whose souls are in the stage of childhood, and who cannot yet call God their Father, and are therefore styled "orphans"; it moreover admonishes souls, no longer consorting with the unlawful bridegroom, but remaining in a widowed state because not yet worthy of the true Bridegroom. Clement,

[1] Prov. xxii. 20 *sq.*
[2] Heb. x. i.
[3] 1 Thess. v. 23.
[4] *Shepherd:* Vis. II. iv. § 3.

the reader who has got beyond the *letter*, is said to send what is said to the cities abroad, that is to say, the souls which have escaped from the bodily desires and lower aims. And next the writing is forsaken, and the disciple himself of the Spirit is bidden "read" to the wise and hoary-headed elders of the whole Church of God with the living voice. . . .

[§ 17] Anyway, will any man of sense suppose that there was a first day, a second and a third, evening and morning, without sun and moon and stars? and the first, as it were, even without a heaven? And who is so silly as to imagine that God, like a husbandman, planted a garden in Eden eastward, and put in it a tree of life, which could be seen and felt, so that whoever tasted of the fruit with his bodily teeth received the gift of life, and further that any one as he masticated the fruits of this tree partook of good and evil? And if God is also said to walk in the garden in the evening, and Adam to hide himself under the tree, I do not suppose that any one will doubt that these passages by means of seeming history, though the incidents never occurred, figuratively reveal certain mysteries. . . . Why, even the Gospels abound in incidents of the same kind. We read of the devil taking Jesus into a lofty mountain, that from thence he might show Him the kingdoms of the whole world and their glory. Who but a careless reader of these things would not condemn the supposition that with the bodily eye, which required a lofty height if the parts down below at the foot were to be seen, Jesus beheld the kingdoms of Persia, Scythia, India, and Parthia, and the glory of their rulers among men? And, similarly, the careful student may observe countless other instances in the Gospels, and may thus be convinced that with the historical events, literally true, different ones are interwoven which never occurred.

[§ 30] . . . Seeing then that the Scripture itself consists as it were of a *body* which is seen, and a *soul* therein apprehended by the reason, and a *spirit*, that which corresponds to the copies and shadow of heavenly things, let us call upon Him who created Scripture with a body, soul and spirit, the body for those who were before us, the soul for us, and the spirit for those who in the coming age shall inherit eternal life, and are destined to reach the heavenly, archetypal things contained in the Law; and then let us search not for the letter, but for the soul of what we are considering. Then, if we are able, we will ascend also to the spirit, corresponding to the principles involved in the sacrifices of which we read. —G. Lewis, *The Philocalia of Origen*, 12 *sq*., 17 *sq*., 30.

No. 126.—The Tradition of the Church

From Origen, *De principiis* [*c*. 230]: Præfatio, §§ 2–10.

[§ 2] Since many, however, of those who profess to believe in Christ differ from each other not only in small and trifling matters, but also on subjects of the highest importance . . . it seems on that account necessary first of all to fix a definite limit and to lay down an unmistakable rule regarding each one of these, and then to pass to the investigation of other points. . . . As the teaching of the Church, transmitted in orderly succession from the Apostles and remaining in the churches to the present day, is still preserved, that alone is to be accepted as truth which differs in no respect from ecclesiastical and apostolical tradition.

[§ 3] Now it ought to be known that the holy Apostles, in preaching the faith of Christ, delivered themselves with the utmost clearness on certain points which they believed to be necessary to every one, even to those who seemed somewhat dull in the investigation of divine knowledge; leaving, however, the grounds of their statements to be examined into by those who should deserve the excellent gifts of the Spirit, and who, especially by means of the Holy Spirit Himself, should obtain the gift of language, of wisdom and of knowledge; while on other subjects they merely stated the fact that things were so, keeping silence as to the manner or origin of their existence; clearly in order that the more zealous of their successors, who should be lovers of wisdom, might have a subject of exercise on which to display the fruit of their talents—those persons, I mean, who should prepare themselves to be fit and worthy receivers of wisdom.

[§ 4] The particular points clearly delivered in the teaching of the Apostles are as follow:—

First, That there is one God, who created and arranged

all things, and who, when nothing existed, called all things into being—God from the first creation and foundation of the world—the God of all just men, of Adam, Abel, etc. . . . and that this God, in the last days, as He had announced beforehand by His prophets, sent our Lord Jesus Christ to call in the first place, Israel to Himself, and in the second place the Gentiles, after the unfaithfulness of the people of Israel. This just and good God, the Father of our Lord Jesus Christ, Himself gave the law, and the prophets, and the gospels, being also the God of the Apostles and of the Old and New Testaments.

Secondly, That Jesus Christ Himself, who came [into the world], was born of the Father before all creatures; that after He had been the servant of the Father in the creation of all things—"For by Him all things were made"—He in the last times, divesting Himself [of His glory], became man and was incarnate although God, and while made man remained the God which He was; that He assumed a body like to our own, differing in this respect only, that it was born of a virgin and of the Holy Spirit; that this Jesus Christ was truly born, and did truly suffer, and did not endure this death common [to man] in appearance only, but did truly die; that He did truly rise from the dead; and that after His resurrection He conversed with His disciples, and was taken up [into heaven].

Then, *thirdly*, the Apostles related that the Holy Spirit was associated in honour and dignity with the Father and the Son. But in His case it is not clearly distinguished whether He is to be regarded as born or innate, or also as a Son of God or not: for these are points which have to be enquired into out of Sacred Scriptures according to the best of our ability, and which demand careful investigation. And that this Spirit inspired each one of the Saints, whether prophets or Apostles: and that there was not one Spirit in the men of the old dispensation, and another in those who were inspired at the advent of Christ, is most clearly taught throughout the churches.

[§ 5] After these points, also, the apostolic teaching is that the soul, having a substance and life of its own, shall, after its departure from the world, be rewarded according to its deserts, being destined to obtain either an eternal life of blessedness, if its action shall have procured this for it, or to be delivered up to eternal fire and punishments, if the guilt of its crimes shall have brought it down to this; and also that there is to be a time of resurrection from the dead, when this body which now "is sown in corruption, shall rise in incorruption," and that which "is sown in dishonour, will rise in glory." This also is clearly defined in the teaching of the Church, that every rational soul is possessed of free-will and volition; that it has a struggle to maintain with the devil and his angels, and opposing influences, because they strive to burden it with sins; but if we live rightly and wisely, we shall endeavour to shake ourselves free of a burden of that kind. From which it follows also that we understand ourselves not to be subject to necessity, so as to be compelled, by all means, even against our will, to do either good or evil. For if we are our own masters, some influences perhaps may impel us to sin, and others help us to salvation: we are not forced, however, by any necessity, either to act rightly or wrongly, which those persons think is the case who say that the courses and movements of the stars are the cause of human actions, not only of those which take place beyond the influence of the freedom of the will, but also of those which are within our power. But with respect to the soul, whether it is derived from the seed by a process of traducianism, so that the reason or substance of it may be considered as placed in the seminal particles of the body themselves, or whether it has any other beginning; and this beginning itself, whether it be by birth or not, or whether bestowed upon the body from without or no, is not distinguished with sufficient clearness in the teaching of the Church.

[§ 6] Regarding the devil and his angels, and the opposing influences, the teaching of the Church has laid down that these beings exist indeed; but what they are, or how they exist, it has not explained with sufficient clearness. This opinion, however, is held by most, that the devil was an angel, and that, having become an apostate, he induced as many of the angels as possible to fall away with himself, and these up to the present time are called his angels.

[§ 7] This also is a part of the Church's teaching, that the world was made and took its beginning at a certain time, and is to be destroyed on account of its wickedness. But what existed before this world, or what will exist after it, has not become certainly known to the many, for there is no clear statement regarding it in the teaching of the Church.

[§ 8] Then, finally, that the Scriptures were written by the Spirit of God, and have a meaning, not only such as is apparent at first sight, but also another, which escapes the notice of most. For those [words] which are written are the forms of certain mysteries, and the images of divine things. Respecting which there is one opinion throughout the whole Church, that the whole law is indeed spiritual; but that the spiritual meaning which the law conveys is not known to all, but to those only on whom the grace of the Holy Spirit is bestowed in the word of wisdom and knowledge.

. . . . . .

[§ 10] This also is part of the teaching of the Church, that there are certain angels of God, and certain good influences, which are His servants in accomplishing the salvation of men. When these, however, were created, or of what nature they are, or how they exist, is not clearly stated. . . .—*A.-N.C.L.* Vol. X. 1 *sqq*.

No. 127.—Origen on the Treatment by Celsus of Our Lord's Miracles

From Origen, *Contra Celsum* [*c*. 249], i. § 68 (*Op*. i. 382 *sq*.: *P.G.* xi. 788 A., B.).

[§ 68] But after this, Celsus, having a suspicion that the great works performed by Jesus, of which we have named a few out of a great number, would be brought forward to view, affects to grant that these statements may be true which are made regarding His cures, or His resurrection, or the feeding of a multitude with a few loaves, from which many fragments remained over, or those other stories which Celsus thinks the disciples have recorded as of a marvellous nature; and he adds: "Well, let us believe that these were actually wrought by you." But he then immediately compares them to the tricks of jugglers, who profess to do more wonderful things, and to the feats performed by those who have been taught by Egyptians, who in the middle of the market-place, in return for a few obols, will impart the knowledge of their most venerated arts, and will expel demons from men, and dispel diseases, and invoke the souls of heroes, and exhibit expensive banquets, and tables and dishes, and dainties having no real existence, and who will put in motion, as if alive, what are not really living animals, but which have only the appearance of life. And he asks, "Since then these persons can perform such feats, shall we of necessity conclude that they are 'Sons of God,' or must we admit that they are the proceedings of wicked men under the influence of an evil spirit?"—*A.-N.C.L.* x. 474 *sq.*

No. 128.—The Gospel not Specially Meant for Fools

From Origen, *Contra Celsum*, iii. § 49 (*Op.* i. 479 *sq.*: *P.G.* xi. 984 B.).

[§ 49] This statement also is untrue that it is "only foolish and low individuals, and persons devoid of perception, and slaves, and women, and children, of whom the teachers of the divine word wish to make converts." Such indeed does the Gospel invite, in order to make them better; but it invites also others who are very different from these, since Christ is the Saviour of all men, and especially of them that believe, whether they be intelligent or simple."—*A.-N.C.L.* xxiii. 130.

No. 129.—On Prayer to the Most High God

From Origen, *Contra Celsum*, viii. § 26 (*Op.* i. 761: *P.G.* xi. 1556 B., C.).

[§ 26] . . . Away, then, with this counsel which Celsus gives us, to offer prayer to demons; it is not to be listened to for a moment: for our duty is to pray to the Most High God alone, and to the only begotten, the first-born of the whole creation, and to ask Him as our High Priest to present the prayers which ascend to Him from us, to His God and our God, to His Father and the Father of those who direct their lives according to His word.—*A.-N.C.L.* xxiii. 513.

No. 130.—Philosophy and Christianity

From Origen, *In Gen. Hom.*, xiv. § 3 (*Op.* ii. 98: *P.G.* xii. 237 *sq.*)

[§ 3] Philosophy is neither at variance with the law of God at all points, nor in harmony with it in all. Many philosophers write of the one God as having created all things. On this point they are at one with the law of God. Some go so far as to add that God made and rules all things by His Word, and that it is the Word of God by whom all things are ordered. In this they write what is agreeable not only to the law but to the Gospel as well. Moral and, as it is called, physical, philosophy take the same view as we do, at most points. They differ, however, from us in saying that matter is co-eternal with God. They differ when they affirm that God takes no interest in the affairs of mortal men, and that His providence is confined to the regions above the orb of the moon. They differ from us in making the lives of men, as they are born, dependent upon the stars in their courses. They differ in asserting that this world is eternal, *i.e.* that it will not be brought to an end.—K.

No. 131.—The Proceedings under the Edict of Decius, 250

From Cyprian, Bishop of Carthage, 248–†58, *De lapsis* [25], § 2 (*C.S.E.L.* III. i. 237 *sq.*).

[§ 2] Confessors, bright in the honours of an unsullied name, and glorious in the praise of virtue and faith, we with joyful countenances behold; we salute, with an holy kiss; we embrace, after many longings, with infinite delight. Soldiers of Christ are before us, a white-robed army, whose firm encounter broke the fierce assault of the persecution which was upon them, men prepared to endure a prison, and armed to undergo death. Manfully have ye fought against the world; a glorious spectacle you have been in the sight of God, and an example to brethren who shall follow in your track. That conscientious voice hath said the name of Christ, which had already made confession of His Creed; those honoured hands used to no Service but that of God, would nought of the sacrifices of the sacrilegious; those mouths sanctified by heavenly food, after the Body and Blood of the Lord, loathed the profane contagion and the relics of idol-feasts; from the impious and sinful veil, which covered the heads of those who were led to sacrifice, your heads have continued free; the forehead which, purified by the mark divine, was unable to suffer the devil's crown, has reserved itself for the crown of the Lord. How joyfully does Mother Church receive you into her bosom, returning from the battle!—*L.F.* iii. 153 *sq.*

No. 132.—The Worldliness of Christians, during the Long Peace, c. 210–50

From Cyprian, *De lapsis*, §§ 5, 6 (*C.S.E.L.* III. i. 240 *sq.*).

[§ 5] . . . If we apprehend the cause of our losses, we have then a remedy for the blow. It has pleased the Lord to prove His family; and as long repose had corrupted the discipline which had come down to us from Him, the divine judgment awakened our faith from a declining, and, should I so speak, an almost slumbering state; and whereas we deserved yet more for our sins, the most merciful Lord hath so moderated all, that what has passed has seemed rather a trial of what we were, than an actual infliction.

[§ 6] Every one was applying himself to the increase of wealth; and forgetting both what was the conduct of believers under the Apostles, and what ought to be their conduct in every age, they with insatiable eagerness for gain devoted themselves to the multiplying of possessions. The priests were wanting in religious devotedness, the ministers in entireness of faith; there was no mercy in works, no discipline in manners. Men wore their beards disfigured, and women distained their complexion with a dye. The eyes were changed from what God made them, and a lying colour was passed upon the hair. The hearts of the simple were misled by treacherous artifices, and brethren became entangled in seductive snares; ties of marriage were formed with unbelievers; members of Christ abandoned to the heathen. Not only rash swearing was heard, but even false; persons in high place were swollen with contemptuousness, poisoned reproaches fell from their mouths, and men were sundered by unabating quarrels.

Numerous bishops, who ought to be an encouragement and example to others, despising their sacred calling, engaged themselves in secular vocations, relinquished their Chair, deserted their people, strayed among foreign provinces, hunted the markets for mercantile profits; tried to amass large sums of money, while they had brethren starving within the church, took possession of estates by fraudulent proceedings, and multiplied their gains by accumulated usuries.—*L.F.* iii. 156 *sq.*

No. 133.—The Undoing of Baptism and Communion, by Apostasy

From Cyprian, *De lapsis*, §§ 8, 9 (*C.S.E.L.* III. i. 242 *sq.*).

[§ 8] Alas! there are, from whom all this is fallen and passed out of memory. They did not even wait to be arrested before they went up, or questioned before they made their denial. Many were they that fell before the fight, laid low without meeting the foe, and not even leaving it to themselves to seem unwilling in sacrificing to the idols. They ran to the market-place of their own accord, of their own will they hasted to their death; as if they had always wished it, as if embracing an opportunity, to which they had all along been looking. How many, whom the magistrates put off at the time, through press of nightfall, and how many who even entreated that their undoing might not be delayed! How can any one make violence an excuse for his guilt, when the violence was rather on his own part, and to his own destruction? When they came, thus willingly, to the Capitol, when they spontaneously submitted themselves to the commission of that dreadful deed, was there no tottering in the limbs, no blackness upon the face, no sickness of the heart and collapsing of the arms? Did not the senses die, the tongue cleave, and speech fail? Could the servant of God stand there, and speak and renounce Christ, he who before had renounced the Devil and the world? The altar where he went to perish, was it not a funeral pile? From an altar of the Devil which he witnessed in the smoke and redolence of its vile odour, ought he not to shudder at it and flee off, as from the death and sepulchre of his existence? Why bring an offering, wretched man, why present a victim, for slaughter? You are yourself an offering for the altar, you are yourself come as a victim; you have slaughtered there your own salvation, your hope; your faith was burnt in those funeral flames.

[§ 9] Many, however, were unsatisfied with doing destruction upon themselves; men were urged to their ruin by mutual encouragements, and the fatal cup of death was offered from mouth to mouth. That nothing might be wanting to their load of guilt, even infants in their parents' arms, carried or led, were deprived, while yet tender, of what was granted them in the commencement of life. Will not these children in the day of judgment say: "We did no sin; it was not our will to hasten from the Bread and Cup of the Lord, to an unhallowed pollution. We perish through unfaithfulness not our own, and our parents on earth have robbed us of the parentage in heaven: they forfeited for us the Church as a Mother, and God as a Father, and thus, while young and unaware, and ignorant of that grievous act, we are included in a league of sin by others, and perish through their deceit."—*L.F.* iii. 158 *sq.*

No. 134.—The Appointment of Bishops

From Cyprian, *Ep.* lxvii. §§ 3–5
(*C.S.E.L.* III. ii.737–9).

[§ 3] . . . Wherefore [1] a people, which obeyeth the precepts of the Lord, feareth God, ought to separate itself from a prelate who is a sinner, nor mingle itself up with the sacrifices of a sacrilegious priest; [2] especially since it has itself the power either of choosing worthy priests or rejecting the unworthy.

[§ 4] This, too, we see to be derived from divine authority, that a priest should be chosen in presence of the people, in sight of all, and be approved worthy and fit by public sentence and testimony as in Numbers [xx. 25, 26] the Lord commanded Moses. God commanded a priest to be appointed before all the congregation; that is, He instructs and shows us that the ordinations of priests ought only to be solemnized with the knowledge of the people standing

[1] Num. xvi. 26. [2] *i.e.* bishop: as nearly always in Cyprian.

by, that so by their presence either the crimes of the wicked may be detected or the merits of the good proclaimed, and so the ordination be right and lawful, as having been examined with the suffrage and judgment of all. . . .

[§ 5] Wherefore the practice received from divine tradition and apostolic observance must be diligently upheld and kept, which is also by us and by almost all the provinces, namely that to the due solemnization of ordinations, all the neighbouring bishops of the same province should meet together among the people for whom a prelate is ordained, and the bishop should be chosen in the presence of the people, who know most fully the lives of each, and are thoroughly acquainted with the character of every one from his conversation.—*L.F.* xvii. 211 *sq.*

No. 135.—A *Libellus* of the Decian Persecution

From Egypt [Fayoum, 1893].

To those who have been elected to preside over the sacrifices in the village of Alexander's Island [comes this petition] from Aurelius Diogenes, son of Satabus, of the village of Alexander's Island, aged seventy-two, with a scar on his right eyebrow. I have always sacrificed to the gods; and now, in your presence, and according to the terms of the edict, I have sacrificed and [poured libations ?] and [tasted] the sacrificial victims, and I ask you to append your signature. Farewell. Presented by Aurelius Diogenes.—I, Mys [. . . the son of . . .] non, [saw him] sacrificing, and have subscribed. In the first year of Imperator Cæsar Gaius Messius Quintus Trajanus Decius Pius Felix Augustus, on Epiphi 2 (= June 26, 250).—J. A. F. Gregg, *The Decian Persecution*, 155.

No. 136.—The Martyrdom of St. Pionius, March 12, 250

From the *Martyrium Pionii*, cc. xix, xx. (O. von Gebhardt, *Acta Martyrum selecta*, 111–3; or R. Knopf, *Ausgewählte Märtyrerakten*, 72 *sq.*).

[c. xix] [§ 1] After some time, the Proconsul came to Smyrna. Pionius was brought before him and bare his testimony, minutes being taken by the appointed officials, on March 12. [§ 2] Taking his seat upon the tribunal, Quintilianus the Proconsul asked: "What is your name?" "Pionius." [§ 3] "Will you sacrifice?" "No." [§ 4] "What form of worship, or persuasion, do you belong to?" "That of the Catholics." [§ 5] "What do you mean by 'Catholics'?" "I am a presbyter of the Catholic Church." [§ 6] "Are you their teacher?" "Yes, I used to teach." [§ 7] "Were you a teacher of folly?" "Of religion, sir." [§ 8] "Religion, indeed! What sort?" "The religion of God the Father, Who made all things." [§ 9] "Well, sacrifice." "No: I can only pray to God." [§ 10] "Why, we all worship the gods, and heaven, and the gods that are in heaven. Why do you lift up your eyes to the sky? Sacrifice to it." [§ 11] "I lift up my eyes, not to the sky; but to Him that made the sky, and the heaven, and all that in them is." [§ 12] "Tell me, who was it that made it?" "I cannot tell you." [§ 13] "To be sure, it was God, that is, Zeus, who is in heaven; he is the king of all the gods."

[c. xx] [§ 1] Pionius was silent, and was strung up. Then said [the officers of the court] to him: "Sacrifice." He answered: "No." [§ 2] They tortured him again with iron talons, and said, "Change your mind; what madness is this?" "It is no madness: it is the fear of the living God." [§ 3] The Proconsul [then intervened]: "Many others have sacrificed, and they are alive and in their right mind." "I cannot sacrifice." [§ 4] "But now that you have been to the question, consider a little with yourself, and change your mind." "Not I, sir." [§ 5] One of the bystanders interposed with: "Why are you so bent upon death?" "Not upon death," replied Pionius, "but upon life." [§ 6] Then said Quintilianus the Proconsul, "You are so bent upon death that you make nothing of it. Sometimes when men are prosecuted for quite a small sum of money, they will brave death with the wild beasts. You are one of those men. Since you are bent upon death, you shall be burnt alive." [§ 7] He wrote the sentence upon [the tablet] and therefrom [the Clerk of the Court] read it aloud in Latin: "We have ordered Pionius, who has confessed himself a Christian, to be burned alive.". . .—K. & A. J. Mason, *Historic Martyrs of the Primitive Church*, 132 *sq.*

No. 137.—The *Libelli pacis*, 250–1

From Cyprian, *Epistle* xxvii. §§ 1, 2 (*C.S.E.L.* III. ii. 540 *sqq.*).

[§ 1] Since my former epistle to you, dearest brethren, in which my conduct was explained, and some slight account given of my discipline and diligence, there hath occurred another matter, of which also you ought not to be uninformed. For our brother Lucianus, himself also one of the Confessors, glowing indeed in faith and strong in courage, but insufficiently grounded in the reading of the word of the Lord, has attempted certain things, making himself for some while past an authority to the ignorant populace, in that letters written in his hand have been given to many persons indiscriminately, in the name of Paulus. Whereas Mappalicus the martyr, being cautious and modest, regardful of the law and discipline, gave letters contrary to the Gospel, but, moved by domestic piety, recommended only that peace should be granted to his mother [and sister], who had lapsed; Saturninus also, being still in prison, after the torture, issued no letters of that sort. But Lucianus, not only while Paulus was still in prison, gave letters in his name indiscriminately written with his own hand; but even after his decease, continued to do the same in his name, saying that he had been ordered to do so by Paulus; not knowing that the Lord must rather be obeyed than the fellow-servant. In the name of Aurelius too, a youth who has endured the torture, many letters have been given, written with the hand of the same Lucianus, because Aurelius did not know how to write.

[§ 2] To check this practice in some degree, I wrote a letter which I sent to you under cover of my last Epistle; wherein I failed not to beg and persuade them, that they would have regard to the law of the Lord and to the Gospel. But after I had sent this letter to them, in the hope that something might be done, as it were more moderately and temperately, the same Lucianus wrote a letter in the name of all the Confessors, whereby the whole bond of faith, and the fear of God, and the Commandment of the Lord, and the sanctity and strength of the Gospel, were well-nigh dissolved. For he wrote in the name of all, that they had granted peace to all, and that they wished this sentence to be notified through me to other Bishops, a copy of which letter I have transmitted to you.—*L.F.* xvii. 56 *sq.*

No. 138.—The Request of the Confessors at Carthage to their Bishop, Cyprian

From Cyprian, *Epistle* xxiii. (*C.S.E.L.* III. ii. 536).

Know that we have granted peace to all of whose behaviour, since the commission of their crime, you are satisfied; and we desire, through you, to make this known to other Bishops also. We wish you to maintain peace with the holy martyrs. Lucianus wrote this; there being present of the clergy an Exorcist and a Reader.—*L.F.* xvii. 53 *sq.*

No. 139.—Cyprian's Proposals to the Laity of Carthage, 250

(*a*) From Cyprian, *Epistle* xvii. §§ 1–3 (*C.S.E.L.* III. ii. 521 *sqq.*).

[§ 1] . . . The blessed martyrs have written to me about certain persons, requesting that their desires may be considered. When peace is first given to us all by the Lord, and we have begun to return to the Church, each case shall be examined in your presence and with the aid of your judgment.

[§ 2] I hear, however, that some of the presbyters, neither mindful of the Gospel nor considering what the martyrs have written to me, nor reserving to the Bishop the honour due to his priesthood and chair, have already begun to communicate with the lapsed and to offer to Oblation for them, and to give them the Holy Eucharist; whereas they ought by a due course to attain hereto. For since, in lesser offences, which are not committed against God, penance is done for an appointed time, and confession made, with enquiry into the life of him who is doing penance, nor may any come to communion, except hands shall first have been laid on him by the Bishop and clergy, how much more in these most grievous and extremest sins, ought all things to be observed with caution and reserve, according to the discipline of the Lord! This our presbyters and deacons ought indeed to have advised you, that so they might tend the sheep committed to them, and instruct them in the way of attaining salvation according to the divine appointment. I know both the meekness and the fear of our people, that they would have been watchful in appeasing and deprecating the wrath of God, had not certain of the presbyters, in order to please, deceived them.

[§ 3] Do then even ye guide them individually, and by your advice and restraint temper the minds of the lapsed in accordance with the divine precepts. Let no one gather prematurely a bitter fruit. Let no one before he have carefully repaired it, again entrust to the deep his ship shattered and broken by the waves. Let no one hasten to recover and clad himself in a tattered garment until he have seen it mended by a skilful workman, and have received it dressed from the hands of the fuller. I pray they may listen patiently to our advice, await our return, that when, by the mercy of God, we shall come unto you, having summoned several of my colleagues, we may, after the discipline of the Lord, and in the presence of the Confessors, and your judgments also had, examine the letters and requests of the blessed Martyrs. On this subject I have written to the Clergy and to the Martyrs and Confessors, both which epistles I have desired to be read to you.—*L.F.* xvii. 43 *sq.*

No. 140.—Cyprian's Proposals to the Clergy of Carthage

From Cyprian, *Epistle* xviii. § 1 (*C.S.E.L.* III. ii. 523 *sq.*).

[§ 1] . . . Since I see that there is as yet no opening for my coming to you, and summer has already begun, a season troubled with continual and severe sicknesses, I think that the cases of our brethren should be met; so that they, who have received letters from the martyrs, and may be helped by their privilege with God, if they are seized with any ailment or danger of sickness, may, without waiting for my presence, make confession of their sin before any presbyter at hand, or if a presbyter shall not be found, and death approaches, then even before a deacon; that so, receiving imposition of hands unto repentance, they may go to the Lord with that peace which the martyrs in their letters to me have requested for them.—*L.F.* xvii. 44 *sq.*

No. 141.—Cyprian's Proposals to the Presbyters and Deacons

From Cyprian, *Epistle* xix. § 2 (*C.S.E.L.* III. ii. 525 *sq.*)

[§ 2] Since you inform me that some are too forward, and urgently press to receive communion; and you desire me to give you some regulation in this matter; I think that I wrote fully enough on this subject in my last epistle, that they who had received letters from the martyrs, and may, by their aid, be holpen with the Lord amid their sins, if they begin to be sore pressed by any sickness or peril, may (after they have confessed and received imposition of hands from you) be remitted unto the Lord with the peace promised them by the martyrs. But for the rest who, not having obtained letters from the martyrs, complain invidiously; since this is a case that concerns not a few, nor one church nor one province, but the whole world, let them await from the protection of the Lord, the public peace of the Church itself. For this is becoming to the modesty and discipline and character of us all; that the bishops meeting with the clergy, and in the presence of the laity who stand fast, to whom also for their faith and fear honour is to be shown, may settle all things with the due reverence of a common consultation.—*L.F.* xvii. 45 *sq.*

No. 142.—Cyprian's Proposals to the Roman Clergy

From Cyprian, *Epistle* xx. § 3 (*C.S.E.L.* III. ii. 528).

[§ 3] . . . But whereas it seemed right that both honour should be shown to the martyrs, and yet the violence of those who desired to throw everything into confusion be checked; and, moreover, having read your letter, lately sent to my clergy through Crementius the subdeacon, to the effect that those should be holpen who, having lapsed, were seized with sickness, and who repenting, desired communion—I thought it right to abide by what was your opinion also, lest our conduct in the Ministry, which ought to be united and to agree in all things, should in some respect differ. As to the cases of the rest, notwithstanding they have received letters from the martyrs, I ordered them to be entirely deferred, and to be reserved until my return; that so, when the Lord shall have vouchsafed us peace, and several bishops shall have met together, we may, with the assistance of your counsel also, set in order and restore everything.—*L F.* xvii. 48.

No. 143.—Novatus

From Cyprian, *Epistle* lii. § 2 (*C.S.E.L.* III. ii. 617 *sq.*).

[§ 2] For of Novatus no news need have been sent from you [*sc.* Cornelius, bishop of Rome, 251–†3] to us, but rather he should have been made known by us to you, as one ever eager for innovation . . . an enemy to peace. Lastly, when Novatus departed from among you, that is, when the storm and whirlwind departed, a calm in part succeeded there, and glorious and good confessors who had left the Church at his incitation, after he had left the city, returned to the Church. It is the same Novatus, who amongst us scattered the first flames of discord and schism, who separated some of the brethren here from their bishop, who, amid the very persecution, was to ours as another persecution in overthowing the minds of the brethren. He it is who, without my permission or knowledge, of his own factiousness and ambition made Felicissimus his follower deacon; and in company with his own storm, sailing to Rome also to overthrow the Church, he there contrived similar and like plots, rending a portion of the laity from the clergy, cleaving asunder the concord of the brotherhood who were closely knit together and mutually loved each other. In short, as Rome from her greatness ought to have precedency of Carthage, there he committed greater and more grievous crimes. He who here made a deacon against the Church, there made a bishop [*sc.* Novatian].—*L.F.* xvii. 112 *sq.*

No. 144.—Pope Cornelius, 251–†3; and the Roman Hierarchy

From Cyprian, *Epistle* lv. § 8 (*C.S.E.L.* III. ii. 629).

[§ 8] I come now, dearest brother, to the character of Cornelius our colleague; that you, with us, may more truly know Cornelius, not from the lies of malignants and detractors, but from the judgment of the Lord God, Who made him a bishop, and from the testimony of his fellow-bishops, the whole number of whom throughout the world have unanimously agreed. For—which with praise and honour commends our beloved Cornelius to God and Christ and His Church, and also to all his fellow-prelates—he did not on a sudden arrive at the episcopate, but promoted through all ecclesiastical offices, and having often deserved well of the Lord in divine services, he mounted to the lofty summit of the priesthood, along all the steps of holy duty. Moreover, he neither himself asked nor wished for the episcopate, nor as others [*sc.* Novatian] whom the swelling of their own arrogance and pride inflates, seized it; but quiet in all respects and meek, and such as they are wont to be, who are chosen of God to this office, agreeably to the retirement of his virgin-continency, and to the humility of his innate and guarded modesty, he does not, as some, use violence to be made a bishop; but himself suffered violence so as to receive the episcopate by compulsion. And he was made bishop by very many of our colleagues then present in the city of Rome, who sent to us letters touching his ordination, remarkable for their high and honourable testimony and praise. Cornelius, moreover, was made bishop by the judgment of God and His Christ, by the testimony of almost all the clergy, by the suffrages of the people who were then present, and by the college of ancient priests and good men; at a time when no one had been made before him, when the place of Fabian, *i.e.* when the place of Peter, and the rank of the sacerdotal chair was vacant. This, therefore, being filled by the will of God, and ratified by the consent of all of us, whosoever would thenceforth be made bishop [*sc.* of Rome, *i.e.* Novatian], must necessarily be made without; nor can he have ordination of the Church, who does not maintain the unity of the Church.—*L.F.* xvii. 120 *sq.*

No. 145.—Letter of Cornelius to Fabius, Bishop of Antioch, ? 251–†2

From Eusebius, *H.E.* VI. xliii. § 11.

[§ 11] This avenger of the Gospel [*sc.* Novatian] then, did not know that there should be but one bishop in a Catholic church; yet he was not ignorant (for how could he be?) that in it there were forty-six presbyters, seven deacons, seven sub-deacons, forty-two acolytes, fifty-two exorcists, readers and janitors, and over fifteen hundred widows and persons in distress, all of whom the grace and kindness of the Master nourish.—*N. & P.-N.F.* i. 288.

No. 146.—The Decisions of the Council of Carthage, June 251

From Cyprian, *Epp.*, lv. §§ 6, 17, 23; lxvii. § 6 (*C.S.E.L.* III. ii. 627 *sq.;* 635 *sq.;* 641; 741).

[lv. § 6] However, according to what had been before determined, when the persecution was lulled, and opportunity given for meeting together, a large number of bishops whom their own faith and the protection of the Lord had preserved uninjured and safe, met together and, the divine Scriptures being adduced on both sides, we balanced our resolution with wholesome moderation; so that neither should hope of communion and peace be altogether denied to the lapsed, lest through desperation they should fall away still further, and because the Church was shut against them, following the world, should live as heathens; nor yet on the other hand should evangelical strictness be relaxed, so that they might rush in haste to communion; but that penance should be long protracted, and the Fatherly clemency entreated with mourning, and the cases and purposes and exigencies of each be examined; as is expressed in a tract [*sc.* the *De lapsis*] which I trust has reached you, where the several heads of our determinations are collected together. And lest the number of bishops in Africa should seem insufficient, we wrote to Rome also on this subject to our colleague Cornelius, who himself likewise in a Council held with very many of our co-prelates, agreed in the same opinion with us, with like solemnity and wholesome moderation.

[§ 17] But since there is in them what by subsequent penitence may revive . . . it was determined . . . that the cases of each being examined, takers of certificates [*libellatici*] be for the time admitted; that to those who have sacrificed [*sacrificati*] relief should be given in their last moments because "in the grave there is no confession" [Ps. vi. 5], nor can any one be urged by us to penitence, if the fruit of penitence is withdrawn. Should the battle first come, strengthened by us he will be found armed for the battle; but should sickness press upon him before the battle, he departs with the consolation of peace and communion.

[§ 23] . . . The Lord in the Gospel pronounces "them that mourn blessed" [Matt. v. 4], because he who mourns invites mercy; he who is froward and proud, heaps up wrath against himself and punishment in the judgment to come. Wherefore . . . we have determined, that they who do not repent nor testify sorrow for their sins with all their heart and with open profession of their grief, are to be altogether forbidden the hope of communion and peace, if in sickness and peril they begin to entreat for it; because not repentance for sin, but the warning of impending death, compels them to ask, nor does he deserve to receive solace in death, who has not thought that he should die.

[lxvii. § 6] Wherefore since . . . Basilides [bishop of Leon] and Martial [bishop of Merida] have been defiled with the profane certificate of idolatry . . . in vain do such attempt to usurp the episcopate, it being evident that men of that mind can neither preside over the Church of Christ, nor ought to offer sacrifices to God: especially since our colleague Cornelius, a peaceable and righteous priest, and by the favour of the Lord honoured also with martyrdom, long since decreed in conjunction with us and with all the bishops constituted throughout the whole world, that such men might indeed be admitted to do penance, but must be kept back from the orders of the clergy and the honour of the priesthood.—*L.F.* xvii. 119 *sq.*, 126, 131, 213.

No. 147.—The Unity of the Church

From Cyprian, the *De Catholicæ Ecclesiæ Unitate* [251], §§ 4–6 (*C.S.E.L.* III. i. 212–5).

[§ 4] If any one consider and weigh this, he will not need length of comment or argument. It is easy to offer proofs to a faithful mind, because in that case the truth may be quickly stated. The Lord said unto Peter, "I say unto thee," saith He, "that thou art Peter, and upon this rock I will build my Church, and the gates of hell shall not prevail against it. And I will give unto thee the Keys of the Kingdom of heaven, and whatsoever thou shalt bind on earth, shall be bound also in heaven, and whatsoever thou shalt loose on earth shall be loosed in heaven." [To him again, after His resurrection, He says, "Feed my sheep."] Upon him, being one, He builds His Church; and though He gives to all the Apostles an equal power, and says, "As my Father sent me, even so send I you; receive ye the Holy Ghost: whosesoever sins ye remit, they shall be remitted to him, and whosesoever sins ye retain, they shall be retained": —yet in order to manifest unity, He has by His own authority so placed the source of the same unity, as to begin from one. Certainly, the other Apostles also were what Peter was, endued with an equal fellowship both of honour and power; but a commencement is made from unity, that the Church may be set before us as one: which one Church in the Song of Songs, doth the Holy Spirit design and name in the person of our Lord: "My dove, my spotless one, is but one; she is the only one of her mother, elect of her that bare her." He who holds not this unity of the Church, does he think that he holds the faith? He who strives against and resists the Church, is he assured that he is in the Church? For the blessed Apostle Paul teaches this same thing, and manifests the sacrament of unity, thus speaking: "There is one body, and one Spirit, even as ye are called in one hope of your calling; one Lord, one faith, one baptism, one God."

[§ 5] This unity firmly should we hold and maintain, especially we bishops, presiding in the Church, in order that we may approve the episcopate itself to be one and undivided. Let no one deceive the brotherhood by falsehood; no one corrupt the truth of our faith by a faithless treachery. The episcopate is one; it is a whole in which each enjoys full possession. The Church is likewise one, though she be spread abroad, and multiplies with the increase of her progeny: even as the sun has rays many, yet one light; and the tree, boughs many, yet its strength is one, seated in the deep-lodged root; and as when many streams flow down from one source, though a multiplicity of waters seems to be diffused from the bountifulness of the overflowing abundance, unity is preserved in the source itself. Part a ray of the sun from its orb, and its unity forbids this division of light; break a branch from the tree, once broken it can bud no more; cut the stream from its fountain, the remnant will be dried up. Thus the Church, flooded with the light of the Lord, puts forth her rays through the whole world, with yet one light which is spread upon all places, where its unity of body is not infringed. She stretches forth her branches over the universal earth, in her riches of plenty, and pours abroad her bountiful and onward streams; yet is there one head, one source, one Mother, abundant in the results of her fruitfulness. It is of her womb that we are born; our nourishing is from her milk; our quickening from her breath.

[§ 6] The spouse of Christ cannot become adulterate. She is undefiled and chaste; owning but one home, and guarding with virtuous modesty the sanctity of one chamber. She it is who keeps us for God, and appoints unto the Kingdom the sons she has borne. Whosoever parts company with the Church, and joins himself to an adulteress, is estranged from the promises of the Church. He who leaves the Church of Christ, attains not to Christ's rewards. He is an alien, an outcast, an enemy. He can no longer have God for a Father, who has not the Church for a mother. If any man was able to escape who remained without the ark of Noah, then will that man escape who is out of doors beyond the Church.—*L.F.* iii. 133 *sqq*.

No. 148.—The African Custom of Re-baptism, 255–6

From Cyprian, *Ep.* lxxiii. § 3 (*C.S.E.L.* III. ii. 780).

[§ 3] But with us it is no new or sudden thing to decide that they are to be baptized, who come from heretics to the Church, in that now many years and a length of time have passed away, since, under Agrippinus of honoured memory, very many prelates being convened, determined this: and thenceforward until this day, so many thousand heretics in our provinces have been converted to the Church who despised not or hesitated, nay with full consent of reason and will, have been glad to attain the grace of the life-giving laver and saving baptism.—*L.F.* xvii. 244 *sq.*

No. 149.—The Roman Maxim against Re-baptism

From Cyprian, *Ep.* lxxiv. § 1 (*C.S.E.L.* III. ii. 799).

[§ 1] Although in the letters of which I sent you copies, dearest brother, I have fully expressed all which is to be said upon baptizing heretics; yet since you have desired to be informed what answer our brother Stephen returned to my letter, I have sent you a copy of that answer; on reading which, you will more and more discover his error, in that he endeavours to uphold the cause of heretics against Christians and against the Church of God. For among other things arrogant or extraneous or self-contradictory, which he wrote without due instruction and caution, he moreover added this: "If then any shall come to you from any heresy whatsoever, be there no innovations beyond what has been handed down, namely that hands be laid on such to repentance, since those who are properly heretics do not baptize such as come to them from one another, but only admit them to communion." He has forbidden one coming from any heresy whatsoever to be baptized in the Church; *i.e.* he has adjudged the baptisms of all heretics to be right and lawful.—*L.F.* xvii. 260 *sq.*

No. 150.—Schismatical Baptism Invalid

From Cyprian, *Ep.* lxix. § 7 (*C.S.E.L.* III. ii. 756).

[§ 7] But if any here object and say that Novatian holds the same rule that the Catholic Church holds, baptizes with the same Creed wherewith we also baptize, acknowledges the same God the Father, the same Son Christ, the same Holy Ghost, and therefore can claim the power of baptizing, because he seems not to differ from us in the baptismal interrogatory—whoso thinks that this may be objected, let him know in the first place that we and schismatics have not one rule of the Creed, nor the same interrogatories. For when they say, "Dost thou believe remission of sins and eternal life by the holy Church?" they lie in their interrogatory, since they have no Church. Then, moreover, they themselves confess with their own mouths that remission of sins can only be given by the holy Church; and, not having this, they shew that sins cannot be remitted with them.—*L.F.* xvii. 225.

No. 151.—Heretical Baptism Invalid

From Cyprian, *Ep.* lxxi. § 1 (*C.S.E.L.* III. ii. 771).

[§ 1] . . . I know not on what presumption some of our Colleagues are led to think that such as have been washed among the heretics ought not to be baptized when they come to us; because, they say, there is "one baptism." For baptism is therefore one because the Church is one, and baptism cannot be out of the Church. For seeing there cannot be two baptisms, if heretics truly baptize, then they have the baptism. And whoso by his own authority allows this privilege to them, yields and allows to them that the enemy and adversary of Christ seem to have the power of washing, purifying and sanctifying man. But we say that such as come thence are not re-baptized but baptized by us. For neither do they receive anything there, where there is nothing; but they come to us that here they may receive where is all grace and truth; for both grace and truth are one.—*L.F.* xvii. 237.

No. 152.—The Essentials of Valid Baptism

From Cyprian, *Ep.* lxxiii. §§ 4, 5 (*C.S.E.L.* III. ii. 781 *sq.*). "Right 'form' only" [Rome]. "No: right faith as well" [Africa].

[§ 4] But since I found it written in an Epistle, of which you sent me a copy, that "no enquiry is to be made who baptized, since the baptized may receive remission of sins according to his own faith," I thought this topic not to be passed over, especially when, in the same Epistle, I observed some mention to be made of Marcion also, saying that not even such as came from him were to be baptized in the name of Jesus Christ. We ought, therefore, to consider the Faith of those who believe without: whether, on the ground of having the same Faith, they can obtain any grace. For if heretics and we have one Faith, we may also have one grace. If the Patripassians, Anthropians, Valentinians, Apelletians, Ophites, Marcionites and others, pests, swords and poisons, for the destruction of the truth, confess the same Father, the same Son, the same Church with us, then, too, they may have the "one baptism," if they have also the "one Faith."

[§ 5] And not to weary you by going through all heresies, and reviewing the follies or phrenzies of each, since, too, it is painful to utter what one shudders or is ashamed to know, let us for the time enquire as to Marcion only, who is mentioned in the Epistle you transmitted me, whether the ground of his baptism can stand. For the Lord, after His resurrection, sending His disciples, instructed and taught them how they ought to baptize, saying, "All power," etc. [Matt. xxviii. 18, 19]. He intimates the Trinity in whose sacrament the nations were to be baptized. Does Marcion then hold this Trinity? Does he maintain the same Father, the Creator, as we? Knoweth he the same Son Christ, born of the Virgin Mary; who, being "the Word, was made flesh"; who "bore our sins"; who by dying overcame death; who first, by Himself, consecrated "the resurrection of the flesh," and showed to His disciples that He had risen in the same flesh? Far other is the Faith with Marcion; yea, and with the other heretics. Rather there is nothing with them but faithlessness and blasphemy and contention, at enmity with holiness and truth. How then can he who is baptized among them be thought to have obtained "remission of sins," and the grace of the Divine mercy, who hath not the truth of the Faith itself? For if, as some think, a man could receive anything out of the Church according to his faith, assuredly he hath received what he believed. But believing what is false, he could not receive the true; but rather things adulterous and profane, like his belief.—*L.F.* xvii. 245 *sqq.*

No. 153. — The Synodal Letter of the Fifth Council of Carthage (first on Baptism), 255

From Cyprian, *Ep.* lxx. §§ 1, 2 (*C.S.E.L.* III. ii. 767 *sq.*).

[§ 1] When we were together in Council, dearest brethren, we read the letter which you addressed to us respecting those who are brought to be baptized by heretics and schismatics, whether, when they come to the one true Catholic Church, they ought to be baptized. . . . No one can be baptized without the Church, in that there is one baptism appointed in the holy Church. . . . The water then must be first cleansed and sanctified by the bishop; that it may be able, by baptism therein, to wash away the sins of the baptized. . . .

[§ 2] Moreover, the very interrogatory which is put in baptism, is a witness of the truth. For when we say "Dost thou believe in eternal life, and remission of sins through the holy Church?" we mean that remission of sins is not given except in the Church; but that, with heretics, where the Church is not, sins cannot be remitted. They, therefore, who claim that heretics can baptize, let them either change the interrogatory or maintain the truth; unless indeed they ascribe a Church also to those who they contend have baptism.—*L.F.* xvii. 233 *sq.*

No. 154.—The Decision of the Sixth Council of Carthage (second on Baptism), 256

From Cyprian, *Ep.* lxxiii. § 1 (*C.S.E.L.* III. ii. 778 *sq.*).

[§ 1] You have written to me, dearest brother, desiring to know the bearings of my mind concerning the baptism of heretics, who being placed without, and set down out of the Church, claim to themselves a matter over which they have neither right nor power. This baptism we cannot account valid or lawful, since plainly among them it is unlawful. And whereas we have already expressed in our letters what we decreed in Council when very many of us were met together, what also I afterwards replied to Quintus, our colleague, enquiring of the same matter. And now, too, when we had met together, bishops of the provinces both of Africa and Numidia, to the number of seventy-one, we again confirmed this same by our sentence, ruling that there is one baptism, that appointed in the Catholic Church; and that accordingly whosoever come from the adulterous and profane water, to be cleansed and sanctified by the truth of the saving water, are not re-baptized but baptized by us.—*L.F.* xvii. 242 *sq.*

No. 155.—Firmilian, Bishop of Cæsarea in Cappadocia, 232–†72, in support of Cyprian

From Cyprian, *Ep.* lxxv. §§ 5, 6, 24, 25 (*C.S.E.L.* III. ii. 812–4, 825–7).

[§ 5] But since your messenger was in haste to return to you, and the winter season was close at hand, we have answered your letter to the best of our power. As regards then what Stephen has said, as though the Apostles forbade those to be baptized who came over from heresy, and that they delivered this to be observed by posterity, you have answered most fully, that no one can be so foolish as to believe that the Apostles delivered this, in that it is known that these very execrable and detestable heresies arose afterwards. For Marcion, the disciple of Cerdon, may be proved to have introduced his profane doctrine against God, much later than the Apostles and long after their times. Apelles, too, consenting to his blasphemy, added many other new and more heinous articles, in enmity to faith and truth. Moreover, the period of Valentinus and Basilides is evident that they, too, after the Apostles, and after a long period, rebelled with their wicked falsehoods against the Church of God. It is known also that the other heretics long after introduced their wicked sects and perverse intentions, as each was led astray by error; of all whom it is evident that they are self-condemned, and that even before the Day of Judgment they have pronounced against themselves an irreversible sentence. Whoso then confirmeth their baptism, what else does he than adjudge himself with them, and condemn himself by making himself a partaker with them?

[§ 6] But that they who are at Rome do not in all respects observe the things handed down from the beginning, and that they in vain pretend the authority of the Apostles, any one may know even from this, that in celebrating Easter and in many other divine and sacramental ordinances, we may see that there are certain diversities among them, and that all things are not alike observed by them, which are observed at Jerusalem. As in very many other provinces also, there are many differences according to the diversity of places and names [? men]; nor yet has there on this account been any departure from the peace and unity of the Catholic Church. This Stephen has now dared to make, breaking the peace with you which his predecessors ever maintained with you in mutual affection and respect; moreover herein defaming the blessed Apostles Peter and Paul, as if they had handed this down; whereas in their Epistles they execrated heretics, and warned us to avoid them. Whence it is apparent that this tradition is human which upholds heretics, and maintains that they have baptism which belongs to the Church alone.

[§ 24] . . . What "strifes" and dissensions hast thou [*sc.* Pope Stephen] "stirred up" [Prov. xxix. 22] through the Churches of the whole world! And how great "sin" hast thou "heaped up," when thou didst cut thyself off from so many flocks. For thou didst cut thyself off; deceive not thyself; for he is truly the schismatic, who has made himself an apostate from the communion of the unity of the Church. For while thou thinkest that all may be excommunicated by thee, thou hast excommunicated thyself alone from all. Nor have even the precepts of an Apostle been able to keep thee to the rule of truth and peace, when thus admonishing: "I therefore, the prisoner," etc. [Eph. iv. 1–6].

[§ 25] How diligently has Stephen fulfilled these salutary commands and warnings of the Apostle, keeping, in the first place, "lowliness and meekness"! For what can be more "lowly" and "meek" than to have disagreed with so many bishops throughout the whole world, breaking peace with them severally in various modes of discord; now with the Eastern Churches, as we feel confident you are aware, now with yourselves who are in the South! From whom he received episcopal legates with such "long-suffering and meekness" that he would not admit them even to the common intercourse of speech; so mindful, however, of "love" and charity that he commanded the whole brotherhood that no one admit them to their house; so that when they came not only "peace" and communion but shelter and hospitality were denied them. This is to have "kept the unity of the Spirit in the bond of peace," to cut himself off from the unity of charity, and in all things to make himself an alien to the brethren, and with the fury of contumacious discord to rebel against the Sacrament and the Faith. With such an one can there be "one body and one Spirit"; in whom, perhaps, there is not one mind, so slippery is it, so shifting, so uncertain? But as concerns him, let us quit the subject.—*L.F.* xvii. 272 *sqq.*

No. 156.—The Seventh Council of Carthage (and third on Baptism) under Cyprian, Sept. 1, 256.

From Cyprian (*C.S.E.L.* III. i. 435 *sq.*).

When, on the kalends of September, very many bishops [87] from the provinces of "Africa," Numidia and Mauretania, with their presbyters and deacons, had met together at Carthage, a great part of the laity being also present, and when the letter addressed by Jubaianus to Cyprian, as also the answer of Cyprian to Jubaianus, on the subject of baptizing heretics had been read, Cyprian said:—

Ye have heard, most beloved colleagues, what Jubaianus our fellow-bishop has written to me, consulting my moderate ability concerning the unlawful and profane baptism of heretics; and what answer I gave him; giving a judgment which we have once and again and often given, that heretics coming to the Church ought to be baptized and sanctified with the baptism of the Church. Another letter of Jubaianus has likewise been read to you, in which, agreeably to his sincere and religious devotion, in answer to our Epistle, he not only expressed his assent, but returned thanks also, acknowledging that he had received instruction. It remains that we severally declare our opinion on this same subject, judging no one, nor depriving any one of the right of communion, if he differ from us. For no one of us setteth himself up as a bishop of bishops, or by tyrannical terror forceth his colleagues to a necessity of obeying; inasmuch as every bishop in the free use of his liberty and power, has the right of forming his own judgment, and can no more be judged by another than he can himself judge another. But we must all await the judgment of our Lord Jesus Christ, who alone has the power both of setting us in the government of His Church, and of judging of our acts therein.

. . . .

[§ 87] Cyprian of Carthage said: The letter written to our colleague Jubaianus very fully expresses my opinion; that according to the testimony of the Gospel and the Apostles, heretics being called the adversaries of Christ and antichrists, when they come to the Church, are to be baptized with the one only baptism of the Church, that they may be made of adversaries friends and of antichrists Christians.—*L.F.* xvii. 286 *sq.*, 303.

No. 157.—The Trial of St. Cyprian, 258

From the *Acta Proconsularia* of St. Cyprian, §§ 1, 2 (*C.S.E.L.* III. iii. pp. cx *sq.*).

[§ 1] When the Emperor Valerian was Consul for the fourth, and Gallienus for the third time, on the third of the kalends [Aug. 30] of September, Paternus, proconsul at Carthage, in his council-chamber thus spoke to Cyprian, bishop:—

P. The most sacred Emperors Valerian and Gallienus have honoured me with letters, wherein they enjoin that all those who use not the religion of Rome, shall formally make profession of their return to the use of Roman rites; I have made accordingly enquiry of your name; what answer do you make to me?

C. I am a Christian, and bishop; I know no other gods beside the one and true God, who made heaven and earth, the sea, and all things therein; this God we Christians serve, to Him we pray day and night, for ourselves, for all mankind, for the health of the Emperors themselves.

P. Do you persist in this purpose?

C. That good purpose, which hath once acknowledged God, cannot be changed.

P. Will you then, obeying the mandate of the Emperors, depart into exile to the city of Curubis?

C. I go.

P. The letters, wherewith I have been honoured by the Emperors, speak of presbyters as well as of bishops; I would know of you, therefore, who be they, who are presbyters in this city?

C. By your laws you have righteously and with great benefit forbidden any to be informers; therefore they cannot be discovered and denounced by me; but they will be found in their own cities.

P. I am accordingly inquisitor in this place.

C. Our rules forbid any man to offer himself for punishment, and your ordinances discourage the same; they may not therefore offer themselves, but they will be discovered by your inquisition.

P. They shall be discovered by me. They [*sc.* the Emperors] further ordain that no conventicles be held in any place, and that the Christians shall not enter their cemeteries; if any transgress this wholesome ordinance, it shall be capital.

C. Do as you have been instructed.

[§ 2] Then Paternus the proconsul bade them lead away the bishop Cyprian into exile.—*L.F.* iii. pp. xix, xx.

No. 158.—The Rescript of Valerian, July 258

From Cyprian, *Ep.* lxxx. § 1 (*C.S.E.L.* III. ii. 839 *sq.*).

[§ 1] . . . Many various and uncertain rumours are afloat, but the truth is as follows: Valerian had sent a Rescript to the Senate directing that bishops, presbyters and deacons should forthwith be punished; that senators and men of rank, and Roman knights should lose their dignity and be deprived of their property, and if, when deprived of their possessions, they should still continue to be Christians, then they should lose their heads also; that matrons should be deprived of their property and banished; that whosoever of Cæsar's household had either before confessed, or should now confess, should forfeit their property, and be sent in chains as conscripts to Cæsar's farms.—*L.F.* xvii. 314.

No. 159.—The Martyrdom of St. Cyprian, Sept. 14, 258

From the *Acta Proconsularia*, §§ 2-4 (*C.S.E.L.* III. iii. pp. cxii *sq.*).

[§ 2] Then Paternus the proconsul bade them lead away the bishop Cyprian into exile. During his long abode in this place, Aspasius Paternus was succeeded by Galerius Maximus, who bade the bishop Cyprian be recalled from exile, and brought before him. Cyprian, the holy Martyr, chosen of God, returned from Curubis, to which he had been exiled by order of Aspasius Paternus, then proconsul, and by sacred command abode in his own gardens. There he was in daily expectation that he should be visited, as it had been shown him. While he dwelt there, suddenly on the Ides of September [Sept. 13] there came to him two chief officials; one the chief gaoler in the proconsular court of Galerius, the other marshal of the guard in the same court; they placed him between them in a chariot, and carried him to Sexti, whither the proconsul had retired for the recovery of his health. By order of the proconsul he was reserved for hearing on another day; so the blessed Cyprian was privately lodged in the house of the chief gaoler of the court of the most honourable Galerius Maximus, proconsul, in the street which is called Saturn's, between the temples of Venus and of Salus. Thither flocked the whole multitude of the brethren; which, when holy Cyprian knew, he bade that the young women should be protected, seeing they all continued in the open street before the gate of the officer's house.

[§ 3] So on another day, the eighteenth of the kalends of October [Sept. 14], a great crowd was collected early at Sexti, as the proconsul commanded. And the same day Cyprian was brought before him as he sat for judgment in the court called Sauciolum [*i. e.* the criminal court].

G. M. Are you Thascius Cyprianus?

C. I am he.

G. M. The most sacred Emperors have commanded you to conform to the Roman rites.

C. I refuse to do so.

G. M. Take heed for yourself.

C. Execute the Emperors' orders; in a matter so manifest, I may not deliberate.

Galerius, after briefly conferring with his judicial council, with much reluctance pronounced the following sentence: "You have long lived an irreligious life, and have drawn together a number of men bound by an unlawful association, and professed yourself an open enemy to the gods and the religion of Rome; and the pious, most sacred and august Emperors, Valerian and Gallienus, and the most noble Cæsar Valerian, have endeavoured in vain to bring you back to conformity with their religious observances;—whereas then you have been apprehended as principal and ringleader in these infamous crimes, you shall be made an example to those whom you have wickedly associated with you; the authority of law shall be ratified in your blood." He then read the sentence of the court from a written tablet: "It is the will of this court that Thascius Cyprianus be immediately beheaded."

C. Thanks be to God.—*L.F.* iii. pp. xx–xxii.

No. 160.—Dionysius, Bishop of Alexandria [247–†65], on Novatian

From Eus., *H.E.* VII. viii.

For with Novatian we are reasonably indignant, seeing that he has cut the Church in two and dragged certain of the brethren into impieties and blasphemies and introduced the most unholy teaching about God and accuses the most gracious Jesus Christ our Lord of being without pity, and besides all this sets at nought the holy laws and overthrows the confession of faith before baptism, and altogether banishes the Holy Spirit from them, even though there were some hope of His remaining or even of His returning to them.—C. L. Feltoe, *St. Dionysius of Alexandria*, 58.

No. 161.—Dionysius of Alexandria to Novatian

[? In reply to a letter from him announcing his election to the See of Rome.]

From Eus., *H.E.* VI. xlv.

If it was against thy will, as thou sayest, that thou wast promoted, thou wilt prove this by retiring of thine own accord. It were good to suffer anything and everything so to escape dividing the Church of God. And martyrdom to avoid schism is no less glorious than martyrdom to avoid idolatry. Nay, it is to my mind greater. In one case a man is a martyr for his own single soul's sake. But this is for the whole Church. Even now wast thou to persuade or constrain the brethren to come to one mind, thy true deed were greater than thy fall. This will not be reckoned to thee, the other will be lauded. And if thou shouldest be powerless to sway disobedient spirits, save, save thine own soul.—*Ibid.* 50.

No. 162.—Dionysius of Alexandria to Fabius, Bishop of Antioch, ? 251–†2

From Eus., *H.E.* VI. xliv. §§ 2–6.—The absolution of the lapsed (but penitent) Serapion *in articulo mortis*, by means of the Reserved Sacrament.

I will set out the following single example that happened amongst us. There was a certain aged believer amongst us, Sarapion, who had lived blamelessly for a long time but yielded to temptation. This man often begged to be restored, but no one heeded him; for he had sacrificed. But he fell ill, and for three days in succession he remained speechless and unconscious. Then recovering a little on the fourth day, he called to him his nephew and said: "How long, my child, do ye keep me back? hasten ye, I pray, and let me go speedily. Call thou one of the elders (presbyters)." After this he became speechless again. The boy ran for the elder, but it was night and he was ill and could not come. Now I had given instructions that if those who were departing life asked and especially when they chanced to have made supplication even before, they should be absolved in order that they might depart in good hope; he gave the boy, therefore, a morsel of the Eucharist, bidding him moisten it and drop it into the old man's mouth. The lad went back with it. When he drew near, before he entered, Sarapion revived again and said: "Hast come, child? The presbyter could not come, but do thou quickly what he bade thee, and let me go." So the boy moistened it and dropped it into his mouth: and the other shortly after swallowing it straightway gave up the ghost. Was he not clearly sustained and kept alive until he was absolved that, with his sin wiped out, he might be acknowledged (by the Lord) for the many good things he had done?—*Ibid.* 42 *sq.*

No. 163.—Dionysius of Alexandria on Valerian and Macrianus

From Eus., *H.E.* VII. x. §§ 2–7.

To John also it is revealed in like manner, when he says: "There was given him a mouth speaking great things and blasphemy, and there was given him authority and forty-two months. And both these things are to be wondered at in the case of Valerian, and of them it is especially to be observed how his prosperity lasted so long as he was gentle and well disposed towards the men of God. For none of the Emperors before him were so kindly and favourably affected towards them, not even those who were said to have been openly Christians, as he manifestly was, receiving them at the beginning in a most familiar and friendly spirit: indeed, his whole house was filled with devout persons and was a veritable Church of God. But he was persuaded to abandon this treatment by that tutor and chief ruler of Egyptian magicians, who instructed him to slay or persecute, as adversaries and hinderers of his vile

[1] Fabius inclined to Novatianism.—Eus., *H.E.* VI. xliv. § 1.

and detestable sorcerers, the pure and holy persons, who are and were able to confound the devices of accursed demons by being present and seen and merely breathing on them and uttering words, while he also incited him to perform unholy rites and detestable juggleries and abominable sacrifices such as the killing of wretched boys and the slaying of unhappy fathers' children and the dividing of new-born entrails asunder and the cutting up and mutilating of bodies which are God's creation, in the hope that such doings would bring them Divine favour.

And to this he adds as follows—

Fine offerings at all events did Macrianus make to them (*sc.* the demons) to propitiate them for the Empire which he hoped for, when, in his former position as so-called officer in charge of the Emperor's general (καθόλου) accounts, he entertained no reasonable (εὔλογον) nor catholic (καθολικόν) sentiments, but fell under the prophet's curse, who says: "Woe to those who prophesy out of their own heart and see not the general (τὸ καθόλου) view." For he did not understand the workings of Universal (καθόλου) Providence, nor suspect the approach of Judgment on the part of Him who is before all things and through all things and over all things. Wherefore he has become also the enemy of His universal (καθολικῆς) Church and has alienated and estranged himself from God's mercy and banished himself as far as possible from his own salvation, verifying in this his personal name.

And again further on he says—

For Valerian, through being persuaded to this policy by him, exposed himself to insults and injuries.—*Ibid.* 65 *sq.*

No. 164.—Dionysius of Alexandria on the Persecution at Alexandria

From Eus., *H.E.* VII. xi. §§ 6–11.

[§ 6] Dionysius, Faustus, Maximus, Marcellus and Chæremon being arraigned, Æmilianus the Prefect said: I have reasoned verbally with you concerning the clemency which our rulers have shown to you, [§ 7] for they have given you the opportunity to save yourselves, if you will turn to that which is according to nature, and worship the gods that preserve their empire, and forget those that are contrary to nature. What then do you say to this? For I do not think that you will be ungrateful for their kindness, since they would turn you to a better course.

[§ 8] D. Not all people worship all gods; but each one those whom he approves. We therefore reverence and worship the one God, the Maker of all; who hath given the empire to the divinely favoured and august Valerian and Gallienus; and we pray to Him continually for their empire that it may remain unshaken.

[§ 9] A. But who forbids you to worship Him if He is a God, together with these who are gods by nature. For ye have been commanded to reverence the gods, and the gods whom all know.

[§ 10] D. We worship no other.

A. I see that you are at once ungrateful, and insensible to the kindness of our Sovereigns. Wherefore ye shall not remain in this city. But ye shall be sent into the regions of Libya, to a place called Kephro. For I have chosen this place at the command of our Sovereigns; and it shall by no means be permitted you or any others either to hold assemblies or to enter into the so-called cemeteries.

[§ 11] But if any one shall be seen without the place which I have commanded, or be found in any assembly, he will bring peril on himself. For suitable punishment shall not fail. Go therefore where you have been ordered.

And he hastened me away, though I was sick, not granting even a day's respite. What opportunity then did I have either to hold assemblies or not to hold them?—*N. & P.-N.F.* 300.

No. 165.—The Authorship of the Apocalypse

From Dionysius of Alexandria, *On the Promises*, *ap.* Eus., *H.E.* vii. xxv. §§ 17–27.

Again, from the thoughts and from the actual words and their arrangement this John may be reasonably reckoned different from the other. For the Gospel and the Epistle agree with each other and begin in a similar way. The one says "In the beginning was the Word:" and the other

"That which was from the beginning." The one says "And the Word became flesh and tabernacled in us, and we beheld his glory, glory as of the Only-begotten from the Father:" the other uses the same or almost equivalent expressions, "That which we have heard, that which we have seen with our eyes, that which we beheld and our hands handled concerning the Word of Life, and the Life was manifested." For he starts in this way because he is dealing, as he shows in what follows, with those who say that the Lord has not come in the flesh. For which reason he is careful to add also: "And we have seen and bear witness and announce unto you the eternal Life which was with the Father and was manifested unto us. That which we have seen and heard we announce also unto you." He is consistent with himself and does not diverge from his own propositions, but treats them throughout under the same heads and in the same terms. Certain of which we will briefly recall; for instance, the attentive reader will find in each book frequent mention of the Life, the Light, the turning from darkness, constant reference to the Truth, Grace, Joy, the Flesh and the Blood of the Lord, the Judgment, the Forgiveness of sins, the Love of God towards us, the command to us to love one another and that we must keep all the commandments: again, there is the conviction of the world, of the devil, of the antichrist, God's adoption of us as Sons, the Faith, which is everywhere required of us, the Father and the Son everywhere: and generally throughout in describing the character of the Gospel and the Epistle one and the same complexion is to be observed in both. But the Revelation is quite different from them, foreign, out of touch and affinity with them, not having, one might almost say, one syllable in common. The Epistle contains no reminiscence nor subject dealt with in the Revelation nor the Revelation in the Epistle (to say nothing of the Gospel), whereas Paul in his Epistles did give some indication even about those revelations which he has not actually described.

And yet once more one can estimate the difference between the Gospel and Epistle and the Revelation from the literary style. For the first two books are not only written in irreproachable Greek, but are also most elegant in their phrases, reasonings and arrangements of expression. No trace can be found in them of barbarous words, faulty construction or peculiarities in general. For St. John seems to have possessed both words, the Lord having graciously vouchsafed them to him; viz. both the word and knowledge of the word of speech. That this John had seen a Revelation and received knowledge and the gift of prophecy, I do not deny, but I observe his dialect and inaccurate Greek style, which employs barbaric idioms and sometimes even faulty constructions, which it is not now necessary to expose. For I have not mentioned this in order to scoff, let no one think so, but simply to point out the dissimilarity of the writings.—C. L. Feltoe, *St. Dionysius of Alexandria*, 89 *sq.*

No. 166.—The Filial Subordination

From Athanasius, *De Sententia Dionysii*, § 18.

However, when I spoke of certain things that had an origin and certain things that were made, I did indeed casually mention examples of such things, recognizing that they were not altogether useful for my purpose: for instance, I said that neither was the plant the same as the husbandman, nor the boat as the shipwright. But afterwards I dwelt at length on those which were more to the point and cognate to the subject, and went more into detail about these truer examples, seeking out various additional evidences which I set out for you also in another letter: and in them I refuted as false the accusation also which they bring against me, as not stating that Christ is of one substance (ὁμοούσιος) with the Father. For even if I say that this word is not found nor read anywhere in Holy Writ, yet these later attempts of mine to explain which they have ignored are not inconsistent with this conception. For I compared human generation, which is clearly a transmission of the parents' own nature, saying that the parents were different from their children in this single point, that they were not themselves the children: or else it must needs be that neither parents nor children should exist. The letter itself I cannot, as I have said before, owing to circumstances, lay my hand on: otherwise I would have sent you my exact words, or rather a copy of the whole letter: and I will do so, if I have the opportunity. But I know from memory that I added several illustrations from things kindred to one another: for instance, I said that a plant coming up from a seed or a root was different from that whence it sprang and yet was absolutely of one nature with it: and a river flowing from a source partakes of a different shape and name; for neither is the source called river nor the river source, and both these things exist, and the source is, in a sense, the father and the river is the water from the source. But these and similar remarks they pretend never to have seen written, but act as if they were blind. They only try to pelt me from afar with those poor ill-fitting phrases of mine as with stones, failing to recognize that where a subject is obscure and requires to be brought within our understanding, not only do diverse but even quite contradictory illustrations convey the meaning sought for.—*Ibid.* 103 *sq.*

No. 167.—The Rescript of Gallienus, 261

From Eusebius, *H.E.* VII. xiii. § 2.

[§ 2] The Emperor Cæsar Publius Licinius Gallienus, Pius, Felix, Augustus, to Dionysius, Pinnas, Demetrius and the other bishops. I have ordered the bounty of my gift to be declared through all the world, that they may depart from the places of religious worship. And for this purpose you may use this copy of my Rescript, that no one may molest you. And this which you are now enabled lawfully to do, has already for a long time been conceded by me. Therefore Aurelius Cyrenius, who is the chief administrator of affairs, will observe this ordinance which I have given.—*N. & P.-N.F.* i. 302.

No. 168.—Dionysius, Bishop of Rome, 259–†68

From the *Epistola Dionysii adversus Sabellianos*, *ap.* Athanasius, *De decretis Nicænæ Synodi*, § 26 (*Op.* i. 181–3: *P.G.* xxvi. 461–6).—On the teaching of Dionysius of Alexandria.

Next, I may reasonably turn to those who divide and cut to pieces and destroy that most sacred doctrine of the

Church of God, the Divine Monarchy, making it as it were three powers and partitive subsistences and godheads three. I am told that some among you who are catechists and teachers of the Divine Word, take the lead in this tenet, who are diametrically opposed, so to speak, to Sabellius's opinions; for he blasphemously says that the Son is the Father, and the Father the Son, but they in some sort preach three Gods, as dividing the sacred Monad into three subsistences foreign to each other and utterly separate. For it must needs be that with the God of the Universe the Divine Word is united, and the Holy Ghost must repose and habitate in God; thus in one as in a summit, I mean the God of the Universe, must the Divine Triad be gathered up and brought together. For it is the doctrine of the presumptuous Marcion to sever and divide the Divine Monarchy into three origins—a devil's teaching, not that of Christ's true disciples and lovers of the Saviour's lessons. For they know well that a Triad is preached by Divine Scripture, but that neither Old Testament nor New preaches three Gods. Equally must one censure those who hold the Son to be a work, and consider that the Lord has come into being, as one of the things which really came to be: whereas the Divine Oracles witness to a generation suitable to Him and becoming, but not to any fashioning or making. A blasphemy then is it, not ordinary but the highest, to say that the Lord is in any sort a handiwork. For if He came to be Son, once He was not; but He was always, if (that is) He be in the Father, as He says Himself, and if the Christ be Word, and Wisdom, and Power (which, as ye know, divine Scripture says), and these attributes be powers of God. If then the Son came into being, once these attributes were not; consequently there was a time when God was without them; which is most absurd. [He then discusses:—Prov. viii. 22; Deut. xxxii. 6; Col. i. 15 and Ps. cx. 3; Prov. viii. 25; and concludes] In many passages of the Divine Oracles is the Son said to have been generated, but nowhere to have come into being; which manifestly convicts those of misconception about the Lord's generation, who presume to call his divine and ineffable generation a making. Neither then may we divide into three Godheads the wonderful and divine Monad: nor disparage with the name of "work" the dignity and exceeding majesty of the Lord; but we must believe in God the Father Almighty, and in Christ Jesus His Son, and in the Holy Ghost, and hold that to the God of the Universe the Word is united. For "I," says He, "and the Father are one," and "I in the Father and the Father in me." For thus both the Divine Triad and the holy preaching of the Monarchy will be preserved.—Athanasius in *N. & P.-N.F.* iv. 167–8.

No. 169.—The Teaching of Paul of Samosata, Bishop of Antioch, *c.* 260–70

From "The Sayings of Paul of Samosata," in *J. T. S.*, xix. 20–45.

Fragment I.—The Word was conjoined to him who came of [the seed of] David, *i.e.* Jesus Christ, who was begotten of the Holy Ghost. Jesus Christ indeed was born of the Virgin, through the Holy Ghost. But the Word was begotten of God, apart from the Virgin and apart from any other but God. Thus it was that the Word had being.

Fragment II.—Man is anointed: the Word is not anointed. The Nazarene is anointed, [not] our Lord. For the Word was greater than Christ: since Christ became great through Wisdom. Let us not disparage the dignity of Wisdom. The Word is from above: but Jesus Christ is man from hence. Mary did not give birth to the Word: she was not before the ages. Mary became a receptacle for the Word: and Mary is not older than the Word but she gave birth to a man, like us though better in every way [than we], since of the Holy Ghost and in accordance with the promises and the Scriptures [came] the grace that was upon him: so that the Christ who was [of the seed] of David was no stranger to Wisdom and never did Wisdom dwell so richly in any other. It is true that Wisdom dwelt in the prophets; and to a greater degree in Moses and in many a saint. But in greatest degree of all, it dwelt in Christ as in a temple. Hence in Christ there are two natures existing separately, and absolutely without intercommunion with each other: for Jesus Christ is one person, and the Word is another. . . .

Fragment III.—"If, as you [*sc.* orthodox] say, Wisdom

was united to Christ in the womb, this is consistent" [says Paul] "with the view that it was united to a human person."

Fragment IV.—Wisdom was not united to a human person essentially but as a quality.

Fragment VII (a).—If the Christ was not one who from being a man became God, then he is of one essence with the Father; and it follows of necessity that there are three essences: one prior, and the other two partaking thereof [Ath., *De Synodis*, § 45].

(This expression "of one essence," Paul construed to mean that Father and Son were a solitary Unit [Hilary, *De Synodis*, § 81]).

Fragment IX (a).—God [Father, Son, and Holy Spirit] is one God: but in God there is ever His Word and His Spirit, as in the heart of man is his own word. The Son of God is not a person, but is in God Himself. The Word came and dwelt in Jesus, who is a man. And thus there is one God, as may be gathered from passages such as these: "The Lord thy God is one Lord" [Deut. vi. 4]. . . . "I am in my Father, and my Father in me" [John xiv. 10 *sq.*]. When the Word came, He did His work alone, and then returned to the Father.

Fragment XI.—He was anointed by the Holy Spirit and called Christ. He suffered in accordance with nature, and did miracles in consequence of grace. By an unswerving will, he was made like unto God; and by remaining pure from sin, he became united to Him. By the divine operation, he acquired the power to do miracles; with the result that he was shown to possess one and the same operation of will with God, and so became known as the Redeemer and Saviour of mankind.

Fragment XII.—The different natures and the different persons have a single and only manner of union, viz. a harmony of will: whence appears the unity of operation between elements so brought into harmony with each other.

Fragment XIII.—Our Saviour became holy and righteous, inasmuch as, through struggle and effort, he overcame the sins of our first parent. And so, by attaining to virtue, he was conjoined to God, having one and the same will and operation with Him, by progress in goodness. This conjunction he maintained inseparable; and so inherited "the

Name that is above every name" [Phil. ii. 9], which was given him as a reward for his devotion.—K.

No. 170.—The Condition of the Church on the Eve of the Last Persecution, A.D. 303–13

From *The Canons of the Council of Elvira, c.* 300.

c. 3. Item, in the case of *Flamens* who have not sacrificed but merely given the games, inasmuch as they have abstained from the fatal sacrifices, we decree that they may be received into communion at the last: provided, however, that they first submit to suitable penance. . . .

c. 8. Item, women who, without cause, leave their husbands and marry again, are not to be received into communion even at the last.

c. 9. Item, a baptized woman who leaves a baptized husband on the ground of his adultery and marries again, is to be prohibited from marrying; if she marry, she is not to be received into communion, until the husband whom she has left be departed out of this life, unless perchance extremity of sickness require it to be given her.

c. 13. If virgins who have dedicated themselves to God, violate their vow of virginity and give themselves over to lust, without recognizing what they have done, we decree that they are not to be received into communion even at the last. If, however, after having once been seduced and defiled by a fall due to frailty of the flesh, they do penance all their life and abstain from intercourse, then, inasmuch as they rank the rather as lapsed, we decree that they ought to be received into communion at the last.

c. 18. If bishops, presbyters and deacons, after promotion to the ministry be found guilty of fornication, we decree that, on account of the scandal and the lewdness of the crime, they ought not to be admitted into communion, even at the last.

c. 19. Bishops, presbyters and deacons are not to leave their places in order to engage in trade; nor are they to go the round of the provinces in search of profitable markets. To gain their living, let them send a son, a freedman, an agent, a friend or somebody; and, if they want to trade, let them trade within the province.

c. 20. If any cleric be found taking usury, we decree that he be deposed and excommunicated. If, moreover, a layman be proved to have taken usury; and promise, on being reproved for it, to cancel the debt and not exact it further, we decree that he be pardoned; but that, if he persist in that iniquity, he be cast out of the Church.

c. 33. We decree, by a total prohibition, that bishops, presbyters and deacons—indeed, all clerics who have a place in the ministry [of the altar]—abstain from their wives and do not beget children: whoever does so, let him forfeit his rank among the clergy.

c. 56. We decree that a magistrate, during the year in which he holds office, be required to refrain from entering the church.

c. 57. Married women or their husbands are not to lend their apparel to deck a procession after the manner of the world; if they do, they are to be excommunicated for three years.

c. 60. If any one break an idol and be put to death on the spot; then, since there are no instances of such conduct in the Gospel nor are the Apostles found ever to have behaved after this fashion, we decree that he shall not be reckoned among the number of the martyrs.

c. 61. If any one, after the death of his wife, marry her sister and she be a baptized woman, we decree that they be excommunicated for five years—unless extremity of sickness require that reconciliation be granted them sooner.

c. 65. If the wife of a cleric be guilty of adultery, and her husband know that she is so and do not at once put her away, she is not to be received into communion even at the last—lest those who ought to be models of good conversation turn out to be examples of evil doing.—K.: tr. from C. J. Hefele, *Histoire des Conciles*, i. 212 *sqq.*

No. 171.—Origen and his Allegorism

From Porphyry [†304], *Against the Christians, ap.* Eus., *H.E.* VI. xix. §§ 4–8.

[§ 4] Some persons, desiring to find a solution of the baseness of the Jewish Scriptures, rather than abandon them, have had recourse to explanations inconsistent and incongruous with the words written; which explanations, instead of supplying a defence of the foreigners, contain rather approval and praise of themselves. For they boast that the plain words of Moses are enigmas, and regard them as oracles full of hidden mysteries; and having bewildered the mental judgment by folly, they make their explanations. . . .

[§ 5] As an example of this absurdity take a man whom I met when I was young, and who was then greatly celebrated, and still is, on account of the writings which he has left. I refer to Origen, who is highly honoured by the teachers of these doctrines.

[§ 6] For this man, having been a hearer of Ammonius, who had attained the greatest proficiency in philosophy of any in our day, derived much benefit from his teacher in the knowledge of the sciences; but as to the correct choice of life he pursued a course opposite to this.

[§ 7] For Ammonius, being a Christian and brought up by Christian parents, when he gave himself to study and to philosophy, straightway conformed to the life required by the laws. But Origen, having been educated as a Greek in Greek literature, went over to the barbarian recklessness. And carrying over the learning which he had obtained, he hawked it about: in his life conducting himself as a Christian and contrary to the laws, but in his opinions of material things and of the Deity being like a Greek, and mingling Grecian teachings with foreign fables.

[§ 8] For he was continually studying Plato, and he busied himself with the writings of Numenius . . . and those famous among the Pythagoreans. And he used the books of Chæremon the Stoic, and of Cornutus. Becoming acquainted through them with the figurative interpretation of the Grecian mysteries, he applied it to the Jewish Scriptures.—*N. & P.-N.F.* i. 265 *sq.*

No. 172.—Passion of the XLIX Martyrs of Abitina, Feb. 12, 304

From the *Acta SS. Saturnini*, etc., *ap.* Migne, *P.L.* viii. 689.

[§ 1] If a man exults in the faith of our most holy religion and makes his boast in Christ; and if he rejoices in the truth of the Lord, condemning error in order that he may hold fast to the Catholic Church and distinguish holy fellowship from profane, let him read the acts of the martyrs which, as need requires, have been committed to the memorial archives [*sc.* of the Church], lest, as years go by, the glory of the Martyrs and the condemnation of the Traditors should be forgotten. Hence my attempt to write the heavenly conflicts and the recent contests sustained by the brave soldiers of Christ, invincible warriors and glorious martyrs. I attempt it with the help of the public archives not so much because of any qualifications with which I am endowed, but out of a fellow-citizen's affection which I feel for the martyrs. . . .

[§ 2] In the times of Diocletian and Maximian, the devil declared war against the Christians, by searching for the holy Testaments of the Lord, by destroying the Lord's churches, and by forbidding sacred rites and holy assemblies to be kept to the Lord. But the holy army of the Lord God could not tolerate so monstrous a command, and shrank in horror from an order so sacrilegious. They seized the arms of faith, and went down to battle in order to fight not against men but against the devil. It is true that by giving up the Lord's Scriptures to the heathen and by handing over the divine Testaments to be burned in profane fires some fell from the fixed principles of the faith. Numbers, however, by preserving them and by gladly shedding their blood in defence of them, proved their constancy to the end. Filled with God, they conquered the devil and laid him low; they bore off the victor's palm by their sufferings; martyrs all, they sealed with their own blood a verdict against Traditors and their accomplices, whereby they rejected them from the communion of the Church. For it was not right that, in the Church of God, Martyrs and Traditors should exist side by side. Great hosts of confessors, therefore, hastened from all sides towards the field of battle; and, wherever they found the enemy, there they pitched the Lord's camp. In the city of Abitina, in the house of Octavius Felix, the clarion of war rang out, and the martyrs set up their standards. There, as they were duly celebrating the Eucharist, there were arrested by the magistrates of the colony and the commandant of the district, Saturninus a presbyter with his four children, *i.e.* Saturninus the younger and Felix who were Readers, Mary a consecrated Virgin, and the lad Hilarian [with others, forty-nine in all].

[§ 3] They were arrested, and were taken, rejoicing, to the Forum. . . . There the elements fought at once for the Lord's Scriptures. Fundanus, formerly bishop of the city, gave up the Lord's Scriptures to be burned: but no sooner had the . . . magistrate had them thrown on the fire, than, all of a sudden, the rain poured down out of a clear sky; the fire that had been kindled on the Scriptures was put out; the hail descended; and the whole place became a scene of desolation in defence of the Lord's Scriptures, for the fury of the elements. In this city, then, the martyrs of Christ were first put into the bonds they desired. Thence they were dispatched to Carthage, with joy and gladness: and all the way they sang hymns and psalms to the Lord; till they reached the Court of Anulinus, who was then proconsul. . . .

[§ 4] As soon then as they were presented by the Court before the proconsul, on a charge of having been sent by the magistrates of Abitina, as Christians who, contrary to the decree of the Emperors and Cæsars, had frequented the Lord's assembly, the proconsul began by questioning Dativus as to his condition in life and as to whether he had taken part in the assembly. He confessed himself a Christian, and admitted that he had been one of the congregation. . . .

[§ 10] . . . Felix then came forward to the contest. . . . "I need not ask" [said the proconsul] "whether you are a Christian: but were you one of the congregation? and have you any Scriptures?" A foolish and ridiculous question on the part of the judge! "You can hold your tongue about being a Christian: but, tell me, were you one of the congregation?" Felix replied: "As if a Christian could exist without the Eucharist, or the Eucharist without a Christian. . . . We attended our assembly right gloriously: for we always assemble to read the Lord's Scriptures at the Eucharist." Seriously perturbed at this confession, Anulinus had him beaten to death with clubs. . . .

[§ 15] Hilarian alone remained. . . . "I will cut off your

hair, your nose and your ears" [said the proconsul] "and then let you go." . . . "Do as you please," replied the lad: "I am a Christian." He was sent back to gaol, crying, with great joy, "Thanks be to God." And so the conflict ended, and the devil was beaten. . . .—K.

No. 173.—Meletianism

From Routh, *Rell. Sacr.*[2], iv. 91–3.—*The Letter of Phileas, Bishop of Thmuis, and others, to Meletius, Bishop of Lycopolis.*

Hesychius, Pachomius, Theodorus and Phileas, to Meletius our friend and fellow-minister in the Lord, greeting.

Some reports having reached us concerning thee, which, on the testimony of certain individuals who came to us, spake of certain things foreign to divine order and ecclesiastical rule which are being attempted, yea, rather which are being done by thee, we, in an ingenuous manner, held them to be unreliable, regarding them to be such as we would not willingly credit, when we thought of the audacity implied in their magnitude and their uncertain attempts. But since many who are visiting us at the present time have lent some credibility to these reports, and have not hesitated to attest them as facts, we, to our exceeding surprise, have been compelled to indite this letter to thee. And what agitation and sadness have been caused to us all in common and to each of us individually by [the report of] the ordination carried through by thee in parishes having no manner of connection with thee, we are unable sufficiently to express. We have not delayed, however, by a short statement to prove your practice wrong.

There is the law of our fathers and forefathers, of which neither art thou thyself ignorant, established according to divine and ecclesiastical order; for it is all for the good pleasure of God and the zealous regard of better things. By them it has been established and settled that it is not lawful for any bishop to celebrate ordinations in parishes other than his own; a law which is exceedingly important and wisely devised. For, in the first place, it is but right that the conversation and life of those who are ordained should be examined with great care; and, in the second place, that all confusion and turbulence should be done away with. For every one shall have enough to do in managing his own parish, and in finding with great care and many anxieties suitable subordinates [among those] with whom he has passed his whole life, and who have been trained under his hands. But thou, neither making any account of these things, nor regarding the future, nor considering the law of our sainted fathers and those who have been taken to Christ time after time, nor the honour of our great bishop and Father Peter, on whom we all depend in the hope which we have in the Lord Jesus Christ, nor softened by our imprisonments and trials, and daily and multiplied reproach, hast ventured on subverting all things at once. And what means will be left thee for justifying thyself with respect to these things?

But perhaps thou wilt say: I did this to prevent many being drawn away with the unbelief of many, because the flocks were in need and forsaken, there being no pastor with them. Well, but it is most certain that they are not in such destitution: in the first place, because there are many going about them and in a position to act as visitors; and, in the second place, even if there was some measure of neglect on their side, then the proper way would have been for the representation to be made promptly by the people, and for us to take account of them according to their desert. But they knew that they were in no want of ministers, and therefore they did not come to seek them. They knew that we were wont to discharge them with an admonition from such inquisition for matter of complaint, or that everything was done with all carefulness which seemed to be for their profit; for all was done under correction, and all was considered with well-approved honesty. Thou, however, giving such strenuous attention to the deceits of certain parties and their vain words, hast made a stealthy leap to the celebrating of ordinations. For if indeed those with thee were constraining thee to this, and in their ignorance were doing violence to ecclesiastical order, thou oughtest to have followed the common rule and have informed us by letter; and in that way, what seemed expedient would have been done. And if perchance some persuaded you to credit their story that it was all over with us (a thing of which thou couldst not have been ignorant, because there were many passing and re-passing by us who might visit you), even although, I say, this had been the case, yet thou oughtest to have waited for the judgment of the superior father, and for his allowance of this practice. But without giving heed to these matters, but indulging in a different expectation, yea rather, indeed, denying all respect to us, thou hast provided certain rulers for the people. For now we have learned too that there were also divisions, because thy unwarrantable exercise of the right of ordination displeased many.

And thou wert not persuaded to delay such procedure or restrain thy purpose readily even by the word of the Apostle Paul, the most blessed seer, and the man who put on Christ, who is the Christ of all of us no less; for he, in writing to his dearly-beloved son Timothy, says: "Lay hands suddenly on no man, neither be partaker of other men's sins." And thus he at once shows his own anxious consideration for him, and gives him his example and exhibits the law according to which, with all carefulness and caution, parties are to be chosen for the honour of ordination. We make this declaration to thee, that in future thou mayest study to keep within the safe and salutary limits of the law.—*A.-N.C.L.* xiv. 443–6.

No. 174.—The Anonymous Note about Meletius

From Routh, *Rell. Sacr.*² iv. 94.

After receiving and perusing this epistle, he neither wrote any reply nor repaired to them in the prison, nor went to the blessed Peter. But when all these bishops and presbyters and deacons had suffered martyrdom in the prison at Alexandria, he at once entered Alexandria. Now in that city there was a certain person, by name Isidorus, turbulent in character and possessed with the ambition of being a teacher. And there was also a certain Arius, who wore the habit of piety, and was in like manner possessed with the ambition to be a teacher. And when they discovered the object of Meletius's passion, and what it was that he sought, hastening to him and looking with an evil eye on the episcopal authority of the blessed Peter, that the aim and desire of Meletius might be made patent, they discovered to Meletius certain presbyters, then in hiding, to whom the blessed Peter had given power to act as parish-visitors. And Meletius recommending them to improve the opportunity given them for rectifying their error, suspended them for the time, and by his own authority ordained two persons in their place, namely, one in prison and another in the mines. On learning these things, the blessed Peter, with much endurance, wrote to the people of Alexandria an epistle in the following terms.—*A.-N.C.L.* xiv. 446.

No. 175.—The Letter of Peter, Bishop of Alexandria, 303-†11, to his Flock

From Routh, *Rell. Sacr.*[2] iv. 94.

Peter, to the brethren beloved and established in the faith of God, peace in the Lord. Since I have found out that Meletius acts in no way for the common good—for neither is he contented with the letter of the most holy bishops and martyrs—but, invading my parish, hath assumed so much to himself as to endeavour to separate from my authority the priests and those who had been entrusted with visiting the needy; and, giving proof of his desire for pre-eminence, has ordained in the prison several unto himself; now take ye heed to this and hold no communion with him until I meet him in company with some wise and discreet men, and see what the designs are which he has thought upon. Fare ye well.—*A.-N.C.L.* xiv. 323.

No. 176.—A Petition to Maximin, 312

From O. von Gebhardt, *Ausgewählte Märtyrerakten*, 185; *The Inscription of Aricanda.*

To the saviours of the whole human race, to the divinities, the Augusti, the Cæsars, Galerius Valerius Maximinus [Flavius Valerius] Constantinus, and Valerius Licinianus Licinius, the petition and supplication of the people of Lycia and Pamphylia.

The gods, your kinsmen, most illustrious emperors, having always shown manifest favour to all who have their religion earnestly at heart and pray to them for the perpetual health of you, our invincible Lords, we have thought it well to have recourse to your immortal sovereignty, and to request that the Christians, who long ago were disloyal, and still persist in the same mischievous intent, should at last be put down and not be suffered, by any absurd novelty, to offend against the honour due to the gods. This end will best be attained, if by your divine and perpetual decree, commandment be laid upon all that the malpractices of the detestable devotion of the atheists be forbidden and prevented; and all be required to attend constantly upon the cult of the gods your kinsmen, invoking them on behalf of your eternal and incorruptible sovereignty, as is most patently to the advantage of all your subjects.—K. [For the reply of Maximin, cf. Eus., *H.E.* IX. vii. §§ 13, 14.]

No. 177.—The Neronian Persecution, 64

From Lactantius, *De mortibus persecutorum* [303–5], c. ii. §§ 5–8.

[§ 5] And while Nero reigned, the Apostle Peter came to Rome, and through the power of God committed unto him, wrought certain miracles, and, by turning many to the true religion, built up a faithful and steadfast temple unto the Lord. [§ 6] When Nero heard of those things, and observed that not only in Rome, but in every other place, a great multitude revolted daily from the worship of idols, and, condemning their old ways, went over to the new religion, he, an execrable and pernicious tyrant, sprang forward to raze the heavenly temple and destroy the true faith. He it was who first persecuted the servants of God; he crucified Peter and slew Paul. Nor did he escape with impunity. [§ 7] For God looked on the affliction of His people, and therefore the tyrant, bereaved of authority and precipitated from the height of empire, suddenly disappeared, and even the burial-place of that noxious wild beast was nowhere to be seen. [§ 8] This has led some persons of extravagant imagination to suppose that, having been conveyed to a distant region, he is still reserved alive; and to him they apply the Sibylline verses concerning "the fugitive, who slew his own mother, being to come from the uttermost boundaries of the earth"; as if he, who was the first, should be the last persecutor, and thus prove the forerunner of Antichrist. But we ought not to believe those who, affirming that the two prophets Enoch and Elias have been translated into some remote place that they might attend our Lord when He shall come to judgment, also fancy that Nero is to appear hereafter as the forerunner of the devil, when he shall come to lay waste the earth and overthrow mankind.—*A.-N.C.L.* xxii. 166 *sq.*

No. 178.—The Misgovernment of Diocletian

From Lactantius, *De mort. pers.* c. vii.

[§ 1] While Diocletian, that author of ill, and deviser of misery, was ruining all things, he could not withhold his insults, not even against God. [§ 2] This man by avarice partly, and partly by timid counsels, overturned the Roman empire: for he made choice of three persons to share the government with him; and thus the empire having been quartered, armies were multiplied, and each of the four princes strove to maintain a much more considerable military force than any sole emperor had done in times past. [§ 3] There began to be fewer men who paid taxes than there were who received wages, so that the means of the husbandmen, being exhausted by enormous impositions, the farms were abandoned, cultivated grounds became woodland [§ 4] and universal dismay prevailed. Besides, the provinces were divided into minute portions, and many presidents and a multitude of inferior officers lay heavy on each territory, and almost on each city. There were also many stewards of different degrees, and deputies of presidents. Very few civil causes came before them: but there were condemnations daily, and forfeitures frequently inflicted; taxes on numberless commodities, and those not only often repeated, but perpetual; and, in exacting them, intolerable wrongs.

[§ 5] Whatever was laid on for the maintenance of the soldiery might have been endured; but Diocletian, through his insatiable avarice, would never allow the sums of money in his treasury to be diminished: he was constantly heaping together extraordinary aids and free gifts that his original hoards might remain untouched and inviolable. [§ 6] He also when, by various extortions, he had made all things exceedingly dear, attempted by an ordinance to limit their prices. [§ 7] Then much blood was shed for the veriest trifles, men were afraid to expose aught for sale, and the scarcity became more excessive and grievous than ever; until, in the end, the ordinance, after having proved destructive to multitudes, was from mere necessity abrogated. [§ 8] To this there were added a certain endless passion for building; and, on that account, endless exactions from the provinces for furnishing wages to labourers and artificers, and supplying carriages and whatever else was requisite to the works which he projected. [§ 9] Here public halls, there a circus, here a mint and there a workhouse for making implements of war; in one place an habitation for his empress, and in another for his daughter. Presently a great part of the city was quitted and all men removed with their wives and children, as from a town taken by enemies; [§ 10] and when those buildings were completed, to the destruction of whole provinces, he said: "They are not right, let them be done on another plan." Then they were to be pulled down, or altered, to undergo perhaps a future demolition. By such folly was he continually endeavouring to equal Nicomedia with the city Rome in magnificence.

[§ 11] I omit mentioning how many perished on account of their possessions or wealth; for such evils were exceedingly frequent, and through their frequency appeared almost lawful. [§ 12] But this was peculiar to him, that, whenever he saw a field remarkably well cultivated, or a house of uncommon elegance, a false accusation and a capital punishment were straightway prepared against the proprietor; so that it seemed as if Diocletian could not be guilty of rapine without also shedding blood.—*A.-N.C.L.* xxii. 168–70.

No. 179.—Diocletian consents to Persecute

From Lactantius, *De mort. pers.* c. xi.

[§ 1] The mother of Galerius, a woman exceedingly superstitious, was a votary of the gods of the mountains.

Being of such a character, she made sacrifices almost every day, and she feasted her servants on the meat offered to idols; but the Christians of her family would not partake of these entertainments; and while she feasted with the Gentiles, they continued in fasting and prayer. [§ 2] On this account she conceived ill-will against the Christians, and by woman-like complaints instigated her son, no less superstitious than herself, to destroy them. [§ 3] So, during the whole winter, Diocletian and Galerius held councils together, at which no one else assisted; and it was the universal opinion that their conferences respected the most momentous affairs of the empire. The old man long opposed the fury of Galerius, and showed how pernicious it would be to raise disturbances throughout the world and to shed so much blood; that the Christians were wont, with eagerness, to meet death; and that it would be enough for him to exclude persons of that religion from the court and the army. [§ 4] Yet he could not restrain the madness of that obstinate man. He resolved, therefore, to take the opinion of his friends. [§ 5] Now this was a circumstance in the bad disposition of Diocletian that whenever he determined to do good, he did it without advice, that the praise might be all his own; but whenever he determined to do ill, which he was sensible would be blamed, he called in many advisers that his own fault might be imputed to other men; [§ 6] and therefore a few civil magistrates and a few military commanders were admitted to give their counsel; and the question was put to them according to priority of rank. Some, through personal ill-will towards the Christians, were of opinion that they ought to be cut off, as enemies of the gods and adversaries of the established religious ceremonies. Others thought differently; but, having understood the will of Galerius, they, either from dread of displeasing him, or from a desire of gratifying him, concurred in the opinion given against the Christians. [§ 7] Yet not even then could the Emperor be prevailed upon to yield his assent. He determined, above all, to consult his gods, and to that end he despatched a soothsayer to enquire of Apollo at Miletus, whose answer was such as might be expected from an enemy of the divine religion. [§ 8] So Diocletian was drawn over from his purpose. But although he could struggle no longer against his friends and against Cæsar and Apollo, yet still he attempted to observe such moderation as to command the business to be carried through without bloodshed; whereas Galerius would have had all persons burnt alive who refused to sacrifice.—tr. *A.-N.C.L.* xxii. 173 *sq.*

No. 180.—The Outbreak of the Persecution at Nicomedia, Feb. 23, 303

From Lactantius, *De mort. pers.* c. xii.

[§ 1] A fit and auspicious day was sought for the accomplishment of this undertaking, and the festival of the god Terminus, celebrated on the seventh of the kalends of March (Feb. 23), was chosen, in preference to all others, to terminate, as it were, the Christian religion.

> That day, the harbinger of death, arose,
> First cause of ill, and long-enduring woes.

[§ 2] Of woes which befel not only the Christians, but the whole earth. When that day dawned, in the eighth consulship of Diocletian and seventh of Maximian, suddenly, while it was yet hardly light, the prefect, together with chief commanders, tribunes and officers of the treasury, came to the church in Nicomedia, and the gates having been forced open, they searched everywhere for an image of the Divinity. The books of the Holy Scriptures were found, and they were committed to the flames; the utensils and furniture of the church were abandoned to pillage: all was rapine, confusion, tumult. [§ 3] That church, situated on rising ground, was within view of the palace, and Diocletian and Galerius stood as if on a watch-tower, disputing long whether it ought to be set on fire. [§ 4] The sentiment of Diocletian prevailed, who dreaded lest so great a fire, being once kindled, some part of the city might be burnt; for there were many and large buildings that surrounded the church. [§ 5] Then the Prætorian Guards came in battle array, with axes and other iron instruments, and having been let loose everywhere, they, in a few hours, levelled that very lofty edifice with the ground.—*A.-N.C.L.* xxii, 174.

No. 181.—The Edict of Toleration issued by Galerius, April 30, 311

From Lactantius, *De mort. pers.* c. xxxiv.

[§ 1] Amongst our other regulations for the permanent advantage of the common weal, we have hitherto studied to reduce all things to a conformity with the ancient laws and public discipline of the Romans. It has been our aim in an especial manner that the Christians also who had abandoned the religion of their forefathers, should return to right opinions.

[§ 2] For such wilfulness and folly had, we know not how, taken possession of them that, instead of observing those ancient institutions, which possibly their own forefathers had established, they, through caprice, made laws to themselves, and drew together into different societies many men of widely different persuasions.

[§ 3] After the publication of our edict, ordaining the Christians to betake themselves to the observance of the ancient institutions, many of them were subdued through the fear of danger, and, moreover, many of them were exposed to jeopardy.

[§ 4] Nevertheless, because great numbers still persist in their opinions, and because we have perceived that at present they neither pay reverence and due adoration to the gods, nor yet worship their own God, therefore we, from our wonted clemency in bestowing pardon on all, have judged it fit to extend our indulgence to those men, and to permit them again to be Christians, and to establish the places of their religious assemblies; yet so as that they offend not against good order.

[§ 5] By another mandate we purpose to signify unto magistrates how they ought herein to demean themselves. Wherefore it will be the duty of the Christians, in consequence of this our toleration, to pray to God for our welfare, and for that of the public, and for their own; that the commonweal may continue safe in every quarter, and that they themselves may live securely in their habitations. —*A.-N.C.L.* xxii. 195 *sq*.

No. 182.—The Edict of Milan, March 313

From Lactantius, *De mort. pers.* c. xlviii.

[§ 2] When we, Constantine and Licinius, emperors, had an interview at Milan, and conferred together with respect to the good and security of the commonweal, it seemed to us that, amongst those things that are profitable to mankind in general, the reverence paid to the Divinity merited our first and chief attention, and that it was proper that the Christians and all others should have liberty to follow that mode of religion which to each of them appeared best; so that that God who is seated in heaven, might be benign and propitious to us, and to every one under our government.

[§ 3] And therefore we judged it a salutary measure, and one highly consonant to right reason, that no man should be denied leave of attaching himself to the rites of the Christians, or to whatever other religion his mind directed him, that thus the supreme Divinity, to whose worship we freely devote ourselves, might continue to vouchsafe his favour and beneficence to us.

[§ 4] And accordingly we give you to know that, without regard to any provisos in our former orders to you concerning the Christians, all who choose that religion are to be permitted, freely and absolutely, to remain in it, and not to be disturbed any way, or molested.

[§ 5] And we thought fit to be thus special in the things committed to your charge, that you might understand that the indulgence which we have granted in matters of religion to the Christians is ample and unconditional.

[§ 6] And perceive at the same time that the open and free exercise of their respective religions is granted to all others, as well as to the Christians; for it befits the well-ordered state, and the tranquillity of our times that each individual be allowed, according to his own choice, to worship the Divinity; and we mean not to derogate aught from the honour due to any religion or its votaries.

[§ 7] Moreover with respect to the Christians, we formerly gave certain orders concerning the places appropriated for their religious assemblies; but now we will that all persons who have purchased such places, either from our exchequer or from any one else, do restore them to the Christians, without money demanded or price claimed, and that this be performed peremptorily and unambiguously.

[§ 8] And we will also that they who have obtained any right to such places by form of gift do forthwith restore them to the Christians; reserving always to such persons, who have either purchased, or gratuitously acquired them, to make application to the judge of the district, if they look on themselves as entitled to any equivalent from our Beneficence. All these places are, by your intervention, immediately to be restored to the Christians.

[§ 9] And because it appears that, besides the places appropriated to religious worship, the Christians did possess other places, which belonged not to individuals, but to their society in general, that is, to their churches, we comprehend all such within the regulation aforesaid, and we will that you cause them all to be restored to the society or churches, and that without hesitation or controversy; provided always that the persons making restitution without a price paid shall be at liberty to seek indemnification from our bounty.

[§ 10] In furthering all which things for the behoof of the Christians, you are to use your utmost diligence, to the end that our orders be speedily obeyed, and our gracious purpose in securing the public tranquillity promoted.

[§ 11] So shall that divine favour which, in affairs of the mightiest importance, we have already experienced, continue to give success to us, and in our successes make the commonweal happy.

[§ 12] And that the tenor of this our gracious Ordinance may be made known unto you all, we will that you cause it by your authority to be published everywhere.—*A.-N.C.L.* xxii. 207–9.

No. 183.—The Canon of the New Testament

(*a*) From Eusebius, bishop of Cæsarea, 314–†40, *H.E.* III. iii. §§ 3–6.

[§ 3] But in the course of my history, I shall be careful to show in addition to the official succession, what ecclesiastical writers have from time to time made use of any of the disputed works, and what they have said in regard to the canonical and accepted writings, as well as in regard to those which are not of this class. [§ 4] Such are the writings that bear the name of Peter, only one of which I know to be genuine and acknowledged by the ancient elders. [§ 5] Paul's fourteen epistles are well known and undisputed. It is not indeed right to overlook the fact that some have rejected the Epistle to the Hebrews, saying that it is disputed by the church of Rome, on the ground that it was not written by Paul. . . . In regard to the so-called Acts of Paul, I have not found them among the undisputed writings. [§ 6] But, as the same Apostle, in the salutation at the end of the Epistle to the Romans, has made mention among others of Hermas, to whom the book called the *Shepherd* is ascribed, it should be observed that this, too, has been disputed by some, and on their account cannot be placed among the acknowledged books; while by others it is considered quite indispensable, especially to those who need instruction in the elements of the faith. Hence, as we know, it has been publicly read in churches, and I have found that some of the most ancient writers use it.

(β) From Eusebius, *H.E.* III. xxv.

[§ 1] Since we are dealing with this subject it is proper to sum up the writings of the New Testament, which have been already mentioned. First then must be put the holy quaternion of the Gospels; following them the Acts of the Apostles. [§ 2] After this must be reckoned the Epistles of Paul; next in order the extant former Epistle of John, and likewise the Epistle of Peter, must be maintained. After them is to be placed, if it really seem proper, the Apocalypse of John, concerning which we shall give the different opinions at the proper time. These then belong among the accepted writings. [§ 3] Among the disputed writings which are nevertheless recognized by many, are extant the so-called Epistle of James, and that of Jude, also the second Epistle of Peter, and those that are called the second and third of John, whether they belong to the evangelist or to another person of the same name. [§ 4] Among the rejected writings must be reckoned also the Acts of Paul, and the so-called *Shepherd*, and the Apocalypse of Peter, and in addition to these the extant Epistle of Barnabas, and the so-called Teachings of the Apostles; and besides, as I said, the Apocalypse of John, if it seem proper, which some, as I said, reject, but which others class with the accepted books. [§ 5] And among these some have placed also the Gospel according to the Hebrews, with which those of the Hebrews that have accepted Christ are especially delighted. And all these may be reckoned among the disputed books. [§ 6] But we have nevertheless felt compelled to give a catalogue of these also, distinguishing those works which, according to ecclesiastical tradition, are true and genuine and commonly accepted, from others which, although not canonical but disputed, are yet at the same time known to most ecclesiastical writers—we have felt compelled to give this catalogue in order that we might be able to know both these works and those that are cited by the heretics under the name of the Apostles, including, for instance, such books as the Gospels of Peter, of Thomas, of Matthias, or of any others besides them, and the Acts of Andrew, and John and the other Apostles, which no one belonging to the succession of ecclesiastical writers has deemed worthy of mention in his writings. [§ 7] And further, the character of the style is at variance with Apostolic usage, and both the thoughts and the purpose of the things that are related in them are so completely out of accord with true orthodoxy that they clearly show themselves to be the fictions of heretics. Wherefore they are not to be placed even among the rejected writings, but are all of them to be cast aside as absurd and impious.—*N. & P.-N.F.* i. 134 *sq.*, 155 *sqq.*

No. 184.—The Extrusion of Paul, Bishop of Antioch, *c.* 270

From Eusebius, *H.E.* VII. xxx. §§ 18, 19.

[§ 18] As Paul had fallen from the episcopate, as well as from the orthodox faith, Domnus, as has been said, became bishop of the church at Antioch. [§ 19] But as Paul refused to surrender the church-house, the Emperor Aurelian was petitioned; and he decided the matter most equitably, ordering the house to be given to those to whom the bishops of Italy and the city of Rome should adjudge it.—*N. & P.-N.F.* i. 316.

No. 185.—The Edicts of Diocletian, 303-4

From Eusebius, *H.E.* IX. x. § 8 and VIII. ii. §§ 4, 5.

[IX. x. § 8] Diocletian and Maximian enjoined that the meetings of the Christians should be abolished.

[VIII. ii § 4] It was in the nineteenth year of the reign of Diocletian, in the month Dystrus, called March by the Romans, when the feast of the Saviour's passion was near at hand, that imperial edicts were published everywhere, commanding that the churches be levelled to the ground and the Scriptures be destroyed by fire, and ordering that those who held places of honour be degraded, and that they of Cæsar's household, if they persisted in the profession of Christianity, be deprived of freedom.

[§ 5] Such was the first edict against us. But not long after, other decrees were issued, commanding that all the rulers of the churches in every place be first thrown into prison, and afterwards by every artifice be compelled to sacrifice.—*N. & P.-N.F.* i. 324 *sq.* (with slight alterations).

No. 186.—The Fourth Edict, April 30, 304

From Eusebius, *Mart. Pal.* iii. § 1.

In the course of the second year, the persecution against us increased greatly. And at that time, Urbanus being governor of the Province [*sc.* Palestine], imperial edicts were first issued to him, commanding by a general decree that all the people should sacrifice at once in the different cities, and offer libations to the idols.—*N. & P.-N.F.* i. 344.

No. 187.—The Fifth Edict, Autumn, 308

From Eusebius, *Mart. Pal.* ix. § 2.

Immediately letters from Maximin against us were published everywhere in every province. The governors and the military prefect urged by edicts and letters and public ordinances, the magistrates and generals and notaries in all the cities to carry out the imperial decree which ordered that the altars of the idols should with all speed be rebuilt; and that all—men, women and children, even infants at the breast—should sacrifice and offer oblations; and that with diligence and care they should cause them to taste of the execrable offerings; and that the things for sale in the market should be polluted with libations from the sacrifices; and that guards should be stationed before the baths in order to defile with the abominable sacrifices those who went to wash in them.—*N. & P.-N.F.* i. 350.

No. 188.—Maximin's attempted revival of Paganism, 311

From Eusebius, *H.E.* VIII. xiv. § 9.

[§ 9] Therefore Maximin persecuted us more violently and incessantly than his predecessors. He ordered temples to be erected in every city, and the sacred groves which had been destroyed through lapse of time to be speedily restored. He appointed idol-priests in every place and city; and he set over them in every province, as high priest, some political official who had especially distinguished himself in every kind of service, giving him a band of soldiers and a body-guard. And to all jugglers, as if they were pious and beloved of the gods, he granted governments and the greatest privileges.—*N. & P.-N.F.* i. 337.

No. 189.—The Letter of Sabinus to the provincial governors, conveying the instructions of Maximin, April 30, 311

From Eusebius, *H.E.* IX. i. §§ 4–6.

[§ 4] With continuous and most devoted earnestness, their Majesties, our most divine masters, the Emperors, formerly directed the minds of men to follow the holy and correct course of life, that those also who seemed to live in a manner foreign to that of the Romans, should render the worship due to the immortal gods. But the obstinacy and most unconquerable determination of some went so far that they could neither be turned back from their purpose by the just reason of the command, nor be intimidated by the impending punishment.

[§ 5] Since, therefore, it has come to pass that by such conduct many have brought themselves into danger, their Majesties, our most powerful masters, the Emperors, in the exalted nobility of piety, esteeming it foreign to their Majesties' purpose to bring men into so great danger for such a cause, have commanded their devoted servant myself to write to thy wisdom, that if any Christian be found engaging in the worship of his own people, thou shouldst abstain from molesting and endangering him, and shouldst not suppose it necessary to punish any one on this pretext. For it has been proved by the experience of so long a time that they can in no way be persuaded to abandon such obstinate conduct.

[§ 6] Therefore it should be thy care to write to the curators and magistrates and district overseers of every city, that they may know that it is not necessary for them to give further attention to this matter.—*N. & P.-N.F.* i. 357.

No. 190.—Constantine to Anulinus, proconsul of Africa, 313, on the restitution of goods to the Church

From Eusebius, *H.E.* X. v. §§ 15–17: cf. Duchesne, *Dossier*,[1] No. 8.

[§ 15] Greeting to thee, our most esteemed Anulinus. It is the custom of our Benevolence, most esteemed Anulinus, to will that those things which belong of right to another should not only be left unmolested, but should also be restored. [§ 16] Wherefore it is our will that when thou receivest this letter, if any such things belonged to the Catholic Church of the Christians, in any city or other place, but are now held by citizens or by any others, thou shalt cause them to be restored immediately to the said churches. For we have already determined that those things which these same churches formerly possessed shall be restored to them. [§ 17] Since, therefore, thy Devotedness perceives that this command of ours is most explicit, do thou make haste to restore to them, as quickly as

[1] "Le Dossier du Donatisme," *ap. Mélanges d'archéologie* x. 630 (Paris, 1890).

possible, everything which formerly belonged to the said churches—whether gardens, or buildings, or whatever they may be—that we may learn that thou hast obeyed this decree of ours most carefully. Farewell, our most esteemed and beloved Anulinus.—*N. & P.-N.F.* i. 380.

No. 191.—First Investigation at the Council of Rome, Oct. 2, 313

From Eusebius, *H.E.* X. v. §§ 18–20: Duchesne, *Dossier*, No. 19.—The letter of Constantine to Miltiades, bishop of Rome, 310–†4.

[§ 18] Constantine Augustus to Miltiades, bishop of Rome, and to Marcus. Since many such communications have been sent to me by Anulinus, the most illustrious proconsul of Africa, in which it is said that Cæcilian, bishop of the city of Carthage, has been accused by some of his colleagues in Africa, in many matters; and since it seems to me a very serious thing that in those provinces which Divine Providence has freely entrusted to my devotedness, and in which there is a great population, the multitude are found following the baser course, and dividing, as it were, into two parties, and the bishops are at variance, [§ 19] it has seemed good to me that Cæcilian himself with ten of the bishops that appear to accuse him, and with ten others whom he may consider necessary for his defence, should sail to Rome, that there, in the presence of yourselves and of Rheticius and Maternus and Marinus [bishops of Autun, Cologne and Arles], your colleagues, whom I have commanded to hasten to Rome for this purpose, he may be heard as you may understand to be in accordance with the most holy law. [§ 20] But in order that you may be able to have most perfect knowledge of these things, I have subjoined to my letter copies of the documents sent to me by Anulinus, and have sent them to your above-mentioned colleagues. When your Firmness has read these, you will consider in what way the above-mentioned case may be most accurately investigated and justly decided. For it does not escape your Diligence that I have such reverence for the legitimate Catholic Church that I do not wish you to leave schism or division in any place. May the Divinity of the great God preserve you, most honoured sirs, for many years.—*N. & P.-N.F.* i. 381.

No. 192.—Constantine to Cæcilian, Bishop of Carthage, making a grant of money to the Catholic Clergy of Africa and Numidia, 313

From Eusebius, *H.E.* X. vi.: Duchesne, *Dossier*, No. 10.

[§ 1] Constantine Augustus to Cæcilianus, bishop of Carthage. Since it is our pleasure that something should be granted, in all the provinces of Africa and Numidia and Mauretania, to certain ministers of the legitimate and most holy Catholic Religion, to defray their expenses, I have written to Ursus, the illustrious finance-minister of Africa, and have directed him to make provision to pay to thy Firmness three thousand *folles*. [§ 2] Do thou, therefore, when thou hast received the above sum of money, command that it be distributed among all those mentioned above, according to the brief sent to thee by Hosius. [§ 3] But if thou shouldest find that anything is wanting for the fulfilment of this purpose of mine in regard to all of them, thou shalt demand without hesitation from Herællides, our treasurer, whatever thou findest to be necessary. For I commanded him, when he was present, that if thy Firmness should ask him for any money, he should see to it that it be paid without delay. [§ 4] And since I have learned that some men of unsettled mind wish to turn the people from the most holy and Catholic Church by a certain method of shameful corruption, do thou know that I gave command to Anulinus the proconsul, and also to Patricius, Vicar of the Prefects, when they were present, that they should give proper attention not only to other matters but also above all to this, and that they should not overlook such a thing when it happened. [§ 5] Wherefore, if thou shouldest see any such men continuing in this madness, do thou without delay go to the above-mentioned judges and report the matter to them; that they may correct them as I commanded them when they were present. The Divinity of the great God preserve thee for many years.—*N. & P.-N.F.* i. 382 *sq.*

No. 193.—Constantine to Anulinus, proconsul of Africa, 313, on exemptions for the Catholic Clergy

From Eusebius, *H.E.* X. vii.: Duchesne, *Dossier*, No. 9.

[§ 1] Greeting to thee, our most esteemed Anulinus. Since it appears from many circumstances that when that religion is despised, in which is preserved the chief reverence for the most holy celestial Power, great dangers are brought upon public affairs; but that, when legally adopted and observed, it affords the most signal prosperity to the Roman name and remarkable felicity to all the affairs of men, through the divine beneficence—it has seemed good to me, most esteemed Anulinus, that those men who give their services with due sanctity and with constant observance of this law, to the worship of the divine religion, should receive recompense for their labours.

[§ 2] Wherefore it is my will that those within the province entrusted to thee, in the Catholic Church, over which Cæcilianus presides, who give their services to this holy religion, and who are commonly called clergymen, be entirely exempted from all public duties, that they may not by any error or sacrilegious negligence be drawn away from the service due to the Deity, but may devote themselves without any hindrance to their own law. For it seems that, when they show greatest reverence to the Deity, the greatest benefits accrue to the State. Farewell, our most esteemed and beloved Anulinus.—*N. & P.-N.F.* i. 383.

No. 194.—The Meletians

From Athanasius, *Apologia contra Arianos* [350], §§ 11, 59, 71; (*Op.* i. 105, 140, 148; *P.G.* xxv. 268, 356 *sq.*, 373).

[§ 11] However, what was the cup, and where and before whom was it broken? It is the Meletians who make the accusation, who are not worthy of the least credit; for they have been schismatics and enemies of the Church, not of a recent date, but from the times of the blessed Peter, Bishop and Martyr. They formed a conspiracy against

Peter himself; they calumniated his successor Achillas; they accused Alexander even before the Emperor; and being thus well versed in these arts, they have now transferred their enmity to Athanasius, acting altogether in accordance with their former wickedness. For as they slandered those that have been before him, so now they have slandered him. But their calumnies and false accusations have never prevailed against him until now that they have got Eusebius and his fellows for their assistants and patrons, on account of the impiety which these have adopted from the Arian madmen, which has led them to conspire against many bishops, and, among the rest, Athanasius. . . .

[§ 59] Peter was bishop among us before the persecution, and during the course of it he suffered martyrdom. When Meletius, who held the title of bishop in Egypt, was convicted of many crimes and among the rest of offering sacrifice to idols, Peter deposed him in a general council of the bishops. Whereupon Meletius did not appeal to another council, or attempt to justify himself before those who should come after, but made a schism so that they who espoused his cause are even yet called Meletians instead of Christians. He began immediately to revile the bishops and made false accusations, first against Peter himself, and against his successor Achillas, and, after Achillas, against Alexander. . . . While Meletius was thus employed, the Arian heresy also had arisen. But in the Council of Nicæa, while the heresy was anathematized, and the Arians were cast out, the Meletians, on whatever grounds (for it is not necessary now to mention the reason), were received. Five months, however, had not passed when, the blessed Alexander having died, the Meletians, who ought to have remained quiet, and to have been grateful that they were received on any terms, like dogs unable to forget their vomit, were again troubling the churches.

Upon learning this, Eusebius, who had the lead in the Arian heresy, sends and buys the Meletians with large promises, becomes their secret friend, and arranges with them for their assistance on any occasion when he might wish for it. . .

[§ 71] . . . When Meletius was admitted into communion (would that he had never been so admitted) the blessed Alexander, who knew his craftiness, required of him a schedule of the bishops whom he said he had in Egypt, and of the presbyters and deacons that were in Alexandria itself, and if he had any in the country district. This the Pope Alexander has done lest Meletius, having received the freedom of the Church, should tender many and thus, continually, by a fraudulent procedure, foist upon us whomsoever he pleased. Accordingly he has made out the following schedule of those in Egypt. "I, Meletius, of Lycopolis," etc.[twenty-nine bishops in Egypt, four presbyters and three deacons in Alexandria, and one country-presbyter]. —*N. & P.-N.F.* iv. 106, 131, 137.

No. 195.—The Coalition of Meletians and Arians

From Athanasius, *Ad episcopos Ægypti* [356], § 22 (*Op.* i. 232; *P.G.* xxv. 589 B.).

[§ 22] And thus by this coalition they are able to assist one another in their malicious designs. . . . The wickedness and falseness of the Meletians were, indeed, even before this, evident unto all men; so too the impiety and godless heresy of the Arians have long been known everywhere and to all; for the period of their existence has not been a short one. The former became schismatics five-and-fifty years ago, and it is thirty-six years since the latter were pronounced heretics, and they were ejected from the Church by the judgment of the whole Ecumenic Council. . . .—*N. & P.-N.F.* iv. 234.

No. 196.—The Origin of Donatism

From Optatus, *De schismate Donatistarum* [c. 370], i. §§ 15–19 (*C.S.E.L.* xxvi. 17–21).

[§ 15] It was not long after this that those very persons whom I have mentioned [*sc.* Secundus, bishop of Tigisis, and his fellow-bishops of the Council of Cirta], of the character I have described, men who had offered incense to idols, and murderers, proceeded to Carthage, and there, although

Cæcilian was already the bishop, made the schism by consecrating Majorinus—on whose chair, Parmenian,[1] you sit. And since I have shown that men who were guilty of Betrayal were your first fathers, it follows that Betrayers were also the originators of your schism.

In order to make this matter clear and beyond doubt to all, we shall have to prove from what root the branches of error have stretched themselves forth to the present day, and from what fountain this your rivulet of noxious water, creeping stealthily along, has flowed down even to our times. We shall have to point out whence, and where, and from whom this evil of schism has arisen; what were the causes which met together to produce it; who were the persons who effected it; who were the authors of this wicked thing; who fostered it; by whom appeal was made to the Emperor, that he should judge between the parties; who were they that sat in judgment; where the Council was held; what were its decrees.

The question is about a division. Now in Africa, as in other parts of the world, the Church was one before it was divided by those who consecrated Majorinus—whose chair you have inherited, and now occupy. We shall have to see who has remained in the root, with the whole world; who went forth; who sits on a second chair, which had no existence before the schism; who has raised altar against altar; who has consecrated a bishop when another was in undisturbed possession; who it is that lies under the judgment of John the Apostle, when he declared that many antichrists should go forth without "because they were not of us, for if they had been of us they would have remained with us."[2] Therefore he who was unwilling to remain with his brethren in unity, has followed the heretics, and gone forth without, as an antichrist.

[§ 16] No one is unaware that the schism, after the consecration of Cæcilian, was effected at Carthage through a certain mischief-making woman named Lucilla. When the Church was still in tranquillity, before her peace had been disturbed by the storms of persecution, this woman could not put up with the rebuke which she received from the archdeacon Cæcilian. It was said that she kissed a bone

[1] Donatist bishop of Carthage, *c.* 350–†92.

[2] 1 John ii. 19.

of some martyr or other—if he was a martyr—before she received the spiritual Food and Drink. Having then been corrected for thus touching, before she touched the sacred chalice, the bone of a dead man (if he was a martyr, at least he had not been acknowledged as such), she went away in confusion, full of wrath. This was the woman upon whom, whilst she was angry and afraid that she might fall under the discipline of the Church, on a sudden the storm of persecution broke.

[§ 17] It was at this time also that a deacon called Felix, who had been summoned before the tribunals on account of a much-spoken-of letter which he had written concerning the usurping Emperor [*sc.* Maxentius], fearing his danger, is said to have lain hidden in the house of bishop Mensurius. When Mensurius publicly refused to give him up, an account of the matter was despatched. A rescript came back that unless Mensurius would surrender the deacon Felix, he should be himself sent to the palace. On receiving this summons he found himself in no small difficulty, for the Church possessed very many gold and silver ornaments, which he could neither hide underground nor take away with him. So he confided them to the care of some of the seniors, whom he believed to be worthy of trust; not, however, before he had made an inventory, which he is said to have given to a certain old woman. He charged her that, when peace was restored to Christians, she should hand this over, if he himself did not return home, to whomsoever she found sitting on the bishop's chair. He went away, and pleaded his cause; he was commanded to return, but was not able to reach Carthage.

[§ 18] The storm of persecution passed over, and subsided. By the disposition of God, Maxentius sent pardon, and liberty was restored to Christians. Botrus and Celestius—so it is said—wishing to be consecrated bishops at Carthage, arranged that, without inviting the Numidians, only the neighbouring bishops should be asked to perform the ceremony at Carthage. Then, by the vote of the whole people, Cæcilian was chosen and was consecrated bishop, Felix of Autumna laying his hand upon him. Botrus and Celestius were disappointed of their hope. The inventory of the gold and silver, as had been ordered by Mensurius was handed over, in the presence of witnesses, to Cæcilian, who was now in possession of the see. The above-mentioned seniors were summoned; but they had swallowed up in the jaws of their avarice, as booty, that which had been entrusted to their keeping. When they were commanded to make restitution, they withdrew from communion with Cæcilian. The ambitious intriguers, who had failed to obtain their consecration, did likewise. Lucilla, too, that influential, mischief-making woman, who had before been unwilling to brook discipline, together with all her retainers, separated herself from her bishop. Thus wickedness produced its effect through the meeting together of three different causes and sets of persons.

[§ 19] In this way it came to pass that, at that time, the schism was brought to birth by the anger of a disgraced woman, was fed by ambition, and received its strength from avarice.

It was by these three that the accusations were concocted against Cæcilian, so that his consecration might be declared void. They sent to Secundus of Tigisis[1] to come to Carthage, whither the Betrayers, of whom we have already made mention, proceeded. They received hospitality—not from Catholics at whose request Cæcilian had been consecrated—but from the avaricious, from the ambitious, from those who had been unable to govern their tempers. Not one of them went to the Basilica, where all the people of Carthage had assembled with Cæcilian.

Then Cæcilian demanded: "If there is anything to be proved against me, let the accuser come out and prove it." Nothing could at that time be got up against him by all these enemies of his; they imagined, however, that he might be blackened by his consecrator being falsely alleged to have been a Betrayer. So Cæcilian gave a second demand—that since—so they thought—Felix had bestowed nothing upon him, they should themselves ordain him, as if he were still a deacon.

Then Purpurius, relying upon his usual ribaldry, thus spoke, as though Cæcilian had been his sister's son: "Let him stand forth as if he were to be consecrated bishop, and let his head be well smacked in penance."

[1] Because he was primate of Numidia.

When the bearing of all this was seen, the whole Church [of Carthage] retained Cæcilian, in order not to hand itself over to murderers.

The alternatives were, either that he should be expelled from his see as guilty, or that the Faithful should communicate with him as innocent.

The church was crowded with people; Cæcilian was sitting in his episcopal chair; the altar was set up in its own place—that very altar upon which bishops, acknowledged by all, had in past times offered sacrifice—Cyprian, Carpophorius, Lucian and the rest.

In this manner they went forth, and altar was raised against altar; and there was an unlawful consecration; and Majorinus, who had been *lector* when Cæcilian was archdeacon—Majorinus, a member of the household of Lucilla, at her instigation, and through her bribes, was consecrated bishop by Betrayers, who in the Numidian Council[1] had, as we have already said, acknowledged their crimes and granted pardon to one another. It is, therefore, clear that both the Betrayers who consecrated, and Majorinus who was consecrated, went forth from the Church.—O. R. Vassall-Phillips, *St. Optatus*, 15–37.

No. 197.—The Petition of the Donatists [*i.e.* The Unsealed Document of No. 217]

From Optatus, *De Schismate Donatistarum*, i. § 22 (*C.S.E.L.* xxvi. 25 *sq.*), Duchesne, *Dossier*, No. 18.

O Constantine, most excellent Emperor, since thou dost come of a just stock, and thy father (unlike other Emperors) did not persecute the Christians, we beseech thee that thy piety may command that we be granted judges from Gaul; for between us and other bishops in Africa disputes have arisen. Given by Lucianus, Dignus, Nasutius, Capito, Fidentius and the rest of the Bishops who adhere to Donatus [? Majorinus: cf. Duchesne, "Le Dossier du Donatisme," *ap. Mélanges d'archéologie*, x. 609; and V.-Phillips, *St. Optatus* 43, n. 3].—*Ibid.* 43.

[1] *sc.* of Cirta, March 5, 305.

No. 198.—Donatism: the fifth investigation, before the Consular Zenophilus, at Tamugada [Timgad, in Algiers], December 13, 320

From the *Gesta apud Zenophilum* in Optatus, *De schismate Donatistarum,* App. I. (*C.S.E.L.* xxvi. 192 *sq.*), or Routh, *Rell. Sacr.*[2] iv. 329 *sq.*

After these documents had been read, Zenophilus said: "From the acts and letters which have been read aloud, it is clear that Silvanus is a Betrayer."

And he said to Victor: "Frankly confess whether you know that he betrayed anything."

Victor said: "He did betray, but not in my presence."

Z.: "What office did Silvanus hold at the time amongst the clergy?"

V.: "The persecution broke out when Paul was bishop; Silvanus was then a sub-deacon."

Nundinarius the deacon replied: "When he came here, as he said, to be made Bishop, the people answered, 'Let it be another. Hear us, O God.'"

Z. to V.: "Did the people cry out 'Silvanus is a Betrayer'?"

V.: "I myself fought against his being made Bishop."

Z.: "So you did know that he was a Betrayer! Confess to this."

V.: "He was a Betrayer."

Nundinarius the deacon said: "You seniors cried out 'Hear us, O God! We want our fellow-citizen. This man is a Betrayer.'"

Z. to V.: "So you cried out with the people that Silvanus was a Betrayer and ought not to be made Bishop?"

V.: "I did cry out, and so did the people. For we wanted our fellow-citizen, a man of integrity." . . .—*Ibid.* App. II. pp. 365 *sq.*

No. 199.—Donatism: the second investigation, at Carthage, before the proconsul Ælianus, February 15, 314

From the *Acta purgationis Felicis* in Optatus, App. II. (*C.S.E.L.* xxvi. 203 *sq.*), or Routh, *Rell. Sacr.*[2] iv. 294.

Ælianus the proconsul said: "Through the evidence of Cæcilianus [not the bishop of Carthage, but the *Duovir* of Aptunga], who tells us that the Acts have been falsified, and many additions made to his letter, the purpose of Ingentius in doing these things has been made clear. So let him be committed to gaol, for we shall require him for stricter examination. Moreover, it is manifest that Felix the holy Bishop has been cleared from the charge of burning the Divine writings, since no one has been able to prove anything against him to show that he gave up or burned the most sacred Scriptures. For through all the evidence it has been made clear on the interrogatories that no Divine Scriptures were either discovered, or corrupted, or burnt by him. It is shown by the Acts that Felix the holy Bishop was neither present when these things were done, nor was privy to them, nor did he order anything of the kind.—*Ibid.* App. I. p. 345.

No. 200.—Donatism: the third investigation at the Council of Arles, August 1, 314

From Optatus, *De sch. Don.* App. III. (*C.S.E.L.* xxvi. 204–6), or Routh, *Rell. Sacr.*[2] iv. 297–9: Duchesne, *Dossier*, No. 26.—Constantine to Ælafius [? Ælius Paulinus], Vicar of Africa, *c.* 313–4.

Already some time back, since it was brought to my knowledge that many persons in our dominion of Africa had begun to separate from one another with mad fury, and had brought purposeless accusations against each other about the keeping of the most holy Catholic law, I thought it well, in order to settle this quarrel, that Cæcilian, the bishop of Carthage, against whom especially they all often petitioned me, should go to the city of Rome, and that some of these who had deemed fit to bring certain charges against him, should appear as well. I also ordered some bishops from the Gauls to proceed to our above-mentioned city of Rome, that, by the integrity of their lives and praiseworthy manner of living, together with seven bishops of the same communion, and the bishop of the city of Rome, and their assessors, they might give due attention to the questions which had been raised. Now they brought to my knowledge, by the written Acts of their meeting, all that had been done in their presence, affirming also by word of mouth that their judgment was based upon equity, and declaring that not Cæcilian, but those who brought charges against him, were guilty—so that, after giving their judgment, they forbade the latter to go back to Africa. Wherefore, in consequence of all this, I once hoped that, in accordance with the probable issue of events, a fitting end had been made to all the seditions and contentions of every kind which had been suddenly called into being by the other party. But after I had read your letters which you had deemed it your duty to send to Nicasius and the rest, about the crafty pretext of these men, I recognized clearly that they would not place before their eyes either considerations of their own salvation or (what is of more importance) the reverence which is due to Almighty God—for they are persisting in a line of action which not merely leads to their shame and disgrace, but also gives an opportunity of detraction to those who are known to turn their minds away from the keeping of the most holy Catholic law. I write thus because—and this is a thing which it is well that you should know—some have come from these men, asserting that the above-mentioned Cæcilian is deemed not to be worthy of the worship of our most holy religion, and in answer to my reply that they were making an empty boast (since the affair had been terminated in the city of Rome, by competent men of the highest character who were bishops) they thought fit to answer with persistent obstinacy that the whole case had not been heard, but that these bishops had shut themselves up somewhere and given the judgment as was most convenient to themselves. Wherefore, since I perceived that these numerous and important affairs were being pertinaciously delayed by discussions, so that it appeared that no end could be made of them without both Cæcilian and three of those who are making a schism against him, coming to the town of Arles, for the judgment of those who are opposed to Cæcilian and are bound to accept him as bishop, I have deemed it well to impose upon your care to provide, as soon as you receive this letter of mine, that the above-mentioned Cæcilian, with some of those whom he himself shall choose—and also some from the provinces of Byzacium, Tripolis, the Numidias and the Mauritanias, and each of the provinces (and these must bring a certain number of their clergy whom they shall choose)—and also some of those who have made a schism against Cæcilian (public conveyance being provided through Africa and Mauritania), shall travel thence by a short course to Spain. In the same way you shall provide in Spain each bishop with a single right of conveyance so that they may all arrive at the above-mentioned place by August 1. Furthermore, you will be pleased to convey to them without delay that it is their duty to provide, before they depart, for suitable discipline in their absence, in order that no sedition or contention of disputing parties may arise—a thing which would be the greatest disgrace. As to the rest, after the matter has been fully enquired into, let it be brought to an end. For when they shall all have come together, those things which are now known to be subjects of contention should with reason receive a timely conclusion, and be forthwith finished and arranged. I confess to your Lordship, since I am well aware that you are a worshipper of the most high God, that I consider it by no means right that contentions and altercations of this kind should be hidden from me by which, perchance, God may be moved not only against the human race but also against me myself to whose care, by His heavenly decree, He has entrusted the direction of all human affairs, and may in His wrath provide otherwise than heretofore. For then shall I be able to remain truly and most fully without anxiety, and may always hope for all most prosperous and excellent things from the ever-ready kindness of the most powerful God, when I shall know that all, bound together in brotherly concord, adore the most holy God with the worship of the Catholic religion that is his due.—*Ibid.* App. III.

No. 201.—Donatism: the third investigation: Synodal Letter of the Council of Arles to Silvester, Bishop of Rome, 314-†35

From Optatus, *De schism. Don.*, App. IV. (*C.S.E.L.* xxvi. 206–8), or Routh, *Rell. Sacr.*[2] iv. 304: cf. Duchesne, *Dossier*, No. 27.

To the most beloved Pope Silvester: Marinus, etc. [thirty-three in all], eternal health in the Lord.

Being united by the common tie of charity, and by that unity which is the bond of our mother, the Catholic Church, we have been brought to the city of Arles by the wish of the most pious Emperor, and we salute thee with the reverence that is thy due, most glorious Pope. Here we have suffered from troublesome men, dangerous to our law and tradition—men of undisciplined mind, whom both the authority of our God, which is with us, and our tradition and the rule of truth reject, because they neither have reasonableness in their argument, nor any moderation in their accusations, nor was their manner of proof to the point. Therefore by the judgment of God and of Mother Church, who knows and approves her own, they have been either condemned or rejected. And would, most beloved Brother, that you had deemed it well to be present at this great spectacle. We believe surely that in that case a more severe sentence would have been passed against them; and our assembly would have exulted with a greater joy, had you passed judgment together with us; but since you were by no means able to leave that region where the Apostles daily sit, and their blood without ceasing bears witness to the glory of God, it did not seem to us that by reason of your absence, most well-beloved brother, we ought to deal exclusively with those matters, on account of which we had been summoned, but we judged that we also should take counsel on our own affairs; because, as the countries from which we come are different, so events of various kinds will happen which we think that we ought to watch and regulate. Accordingly, we thought well in the presence of the Holy Spirit and His Angels that from among the various matters which occurred to each of us, we should make some decrees to provide for the present state of tranquillity. We also agreed to write first to you who hold [the government of] the greater dioceses that by you especially they should be brought to the knowledge of all. What it is that we have determined on, we have appended to this writing of our insignificance. But in the first place we were bound to discuss a matter that concerned the usefulness of our life. Now since one died and rose again for many, the same season should be observed with a religious mind by all at the same time, lest divisions or dissensions might arise in so great a service of devotion.

We judge therefore [c. 1] that the Pasch of the Lord should be observed throughout the world upon the same day. [c. 2] Also concerning those who have been ordained clerics in any places whatsoever, we have decreed that they remain fixed in the same places. [c. 3] Concerning those, too, who throw down their arms in time of peace, we have decreed that they should be kept from communion. [c.4] Concerning the wandering agitators who belong to the faithful, we have decreed that, as long as they continue their agitation, they be debarred from communion. [c. 5] Concerning the strolling players, we have decreed that, as long as they act, they be debarred from communion. [c. 6] Concerning these [heretics] who are weighed down by illness, and wish to believe, we have decreed that hands be laid upon them. [c. 7] Concerning magistrates, who belong to the Faithful and are appointed to office, we have determined that, when they are promoted, they should receive ecclesiastical letters of communion, but in such a way that in whatever place they may be living, the bishop of that place shall have a heed to them, and if they begin to act against discipline, they be then excluded from communion. We have decreed similarly with regard to those who wish to hold state offices. [c. 8] Moreover, with regard to the Africans, forasmuch as they use their own law of re-baptizing, we have decreed that, if any heretic comes to the Church, he should be questioned concerning the Creed; and, if it be found that he has been baptized in the Father and the Son and the Holy Ghost, hands shall be laid upon him, and no more. But if, on being questioned as to the Creed, he does not give the Trinity in answer, then let him rightly be baptized. And the rest. . . .

Then, being sick of the affair, he [*sc.* Constantine] commanded all to return to their homes. Amen.—*Ibid.* App. IV.

No. 202.—Gnostic Ebionites

From Epiphanius, Bishop of Salamis, *Panarion* [*c.* 374–7], *Hær.* xxx. § 16 (*Op.* i. 139 *sq.* : *P.G.* xli. 432 *sq.*).

They also receive Baptism, apart from the daily ablutions with which they baptize themselves. And in imitation of Christians within the Church, they celebrate the Mysteries yearly in unleavened bread, while for the other part of the Mystery they use water only. As I have already said, they affirm two powers constituted of God, viz.: Christ and the devil. Christ, they say, received for His portion the age to come, but to the devil was entrusted this age that now is—in either case, by command of the Almighty and at the request of each. To this end, they say that Jesus was born of the seed of a man, and chosen, and so, in accordance with this choice, called Son of God because of the Christ descending upon Him from above in the form of a dove. They deny that He was begotten of God the Father, asserting that He was created like one of the archangels but that He was greater than they: that He rules over Angels and all things made by the Almighty; and that He came and taught according to the contents of the Gospel called by that name among them, saying "I came to put an end to sacrifices; and, if ye cease not from sacrificing, the divine wrath shall not cease from you." These are their principles, and such as these. They have another *Acts of the Apostles*, as they call it. It is choke-full of impiety; and it is, in the main, with it that they arm themselves against the truth. They allege certain "ascents" and "instructions," among them the *Ascents of James*: whom they represent as condemning, by his expositions, the Temple and its sacrifices and the fire that is upon its altar.

There is also a good deal else that is full of nonsense: for therein they lay accusation against St. Paul, and are not ashamed to dish up stories merely invented by the villainy and lying of false apostles. Pointing out that he was of

Tarsus, as he himself confesses and denies not, they assume that he was a Gentile; taking occasion from the place where, for love of truth, he says: "I am of Tarsus, a citizen of no mean city" [Acts xxi. 30]. Then they pretend that he was a Gentile, the son of a Gentile mother and a Gentile father; that he went up to Jerusalem and stayed there for some time; that he wanted to marry the daughter of the High Priest, and so became a proselyte and was circumcised; and that, at last, because he failed to obtain the girl, he gave vent to his indignation by writing against Circumcision and the Sabbath and the Law.—K.

No. 203.—Modalist Monarchianism, or Sabellianism

From Epiphanius, *Hær.* lxii. §§ 1, 2 (*Op.* i. 513 *sq.*: *P.G.* xli. 1052).

[§ 1] Not many years ago, one Sabellius made his appearance; indeed, within recent times; and from him the Sabellians take their name. With some slight exceptions, his opinions were like those of the Noëtians. Most of his followers are to be found in Mesopotamia and in Rome; and they are the victims of folly.

Their tenet is as follows: that one and the same Being is Father, Son and Holy Spirit, in such sense that to one substance belong three names, much as in a man [we find] body, soul and spirit. The body, so to say, is the Father; the soul, so to say, the Son; and the Spirit in the Godhead is what the spirit is in a man. Or as in the sun: it is one substance but has three activities; I mean light, heat and orb. The heat, whether warmth or fervour, is the Spirit; the light is the Son; and the Father Himself is the form of the whole substance. Once on a time the Son was sent forth, like a ray; and, after accomplishing in the world all that had to do with the dispensation of the Gospel and human salvation, was then received back again into heaven; just as a ray is emitted by the sun and is then withdrawn into the sun again. The Holy Spirit is still being sent forth into the world; and, successively and severally, into every one of those who are worthy to receive it. The Spirit re-creates him; fills him with fresh fervour; and supplies him, so to say, with heat and warmth, infusing fresh power and influence into his spirit. Such are the tenets they inculcate.

[§ 2] They make use of all the Scriptures of the Old and the New Testament; or, rather, of such phrases as they select to suit their own perverse insanity and folly. They start off with the terms in which God spake to Moses: "Hear, O Israel, the Lord thy God is one Lord;[1] thou shalt not make to thyself other gods."[2] "There shall no strange gods be in thee."[3] "I am the first and I am the last and beside me there is no God,"[4] and any other texts they can find to suit their own notions. These they adopt to prove their position. Or again, from the Gospel: "I am in the Father and the Father in Me."[5] "I and the Father are one."[6]—K.

No. 204.—The Old Roman Creed, *c.* 100

From Epiphanius, *Hær.* lxxii. § 3 (*Op.* ii. 836; *P.G.* xlii. 385–8).—The Creed of Marcellus of Ancyra, 341.

1. I believe in God [the Father[7]] Almighty
2. And in Christ Jesus, his only Son, our Lord
3. Who was born of the Holy Ghost and the Virgin Mary
4. Who was crucified under Pontius Pilate and was buried
5. And the third day rose again from the dead
6. He ascended into heaven
   And sitteth on the right hand of the Father
7. From thence he cometh to judge the quick and the dead
8. And in the Holy Ghost
9. The holy Church
10. The remission of sins

[1] Deut. vi. 4.
[2] Exod. xx. 3.
[3] Ps. lxxxi. 10.
[4] Is. xliv. 6.
[5] John x. 38.
[6] John x. 30.
[7] Omitted by Marcellus; but found in Rufinus, *Comment. in Symb. Apost.* [*c.* 400], § 4 (*Op.* 57; *P.L.* xxi. 340 B).

11. The resurrection of the flesh
[12. The life everlasting [1]].

No. 205.—The Neronian Persecution, 64

From Sulpicius Severus, *Chronica* [*c.* 403],
II. xxviii. § 3–xxix. § 4.

[xxviii. § 3] He [Nero] first attempted to abolish the name of Christian, in accordance with the fact that vices are always inimical to virtues, and that all good men are ever regarded by the wicked as casting reproach upon them. [§ 4] For at that time our divine religion had obtained a wide prevalence in the city. Peter was there executing the office of bishop, and Paul too, after he had been brought to Rome, on appealing to Cæsar from the unjust judgment of the governor. Multitudes then came together to hear Paul, and these, influenced by the truth which they were given to know, and by the miracles of the Apostles which they then so frequently performed, turned to the worship of God. [§ 5] For then took place the well-known and celebrated encounter of Peter and Paul with Simon [*sc.* Magus]. He, after he had flown up into the air by his magical arts, and supported by two demons (with the view of proving that he was a god), the demons being put to flight by the prayers of the Apostles, fell to the earth in the sight of all the people, and was dashed to pieces.

[xxix. § 1] In the meantime, the number of the Christians being now very large, it happened that Rome was destroyed by fire, while Nero was stationed at Antium. But the opinion of all cast the odium of causing the fire upon the emperor, and he was believed in this way to have sought for the glory of building a new city. [§ 2] And in fact Nero could not, by any means he tried, escape from the charge that the fire had been caused by his orders. He therefore turned the accusation against the Christians, and the most cruel tortures were accordingly inflicted upon the innocent. Nay, even new kinds of death were invented, so that, being covered in the skins of wild beasts, they perished by being devoured by dogs, while many were crucified or

[1] Found in Marcellus; but not in Rufinus: see § 41 (*Op.* 105; *P.L.* xxi. 378 A).

slain by fire, and not a few were set apart for this purpose, that, when the day came to a close, they should be consumed to serve for light during the night. [§ 3] In this way, cruelty first began to be manifested against the Christians. Afterwards, too, their religion was prohibited by laws which were enacted; and by edicts openly set forth it was proclaimed unlawful to be a Christian. At that time Paul and Peter were condemned to death, the former being beheaded with a sword, while Peter suffered crucifixion.—*N. & P.-N.F.* xi. 110 *sq.*

No. 206.—Origen's Works on the Scriptures

From Jerome [†420], *Translatio Hom. Origenis in Jer. et Ezech.* Præfatio (*Op.* V. 741–2 [*P.L.* xxv. 583–6]).

It is a good deal to ask of me, my friend, that I should put Origen into Latin, and give to Roman ears the man who, in the opinion of Didymus, able to see [well enough on this point], is, next to the Apostles, a second teacher of the churches. As you know, I have been suffering, of late, from pain in the eyes. I got it from too close application to reading, and from a dearth of *amanuenses*. Small means have deprived me of this assistance. So what you are right in desiring of me, I cannot get done as urgently as you desire it. Some time ago I translated fourteen homilies of his on Jeremiah, without keeping their order. Since then, I have, at intervals, dictated [the translation] of these fourteen on Ezekiel. My chief aim has been that my translation should preserve the style of the man aforesaid in that simplicity of diction which alone is of any profit to the churches. So I have scorned all glitter of rhetoric. Not words but things are what I wish to commend; and I would briefly remind you that Origen's works on the Scriptures as a whole are of three kinds. The first class of his works are the Excerpts or *Scholia*, as the Greeks call them. In these he summarily and briefly explains any obscurities or difficulties he may find in the text. Second come his *Homilies:* some of which are contained in this present translation. A third class are his *Tomes,* or volumes as we might call them. In these he spreads the full sail of his genius to all the breezes that blow; and casting off from shore, sails out into the open sea. I know you would like me to translate his utterances of each kind. I have already explained why I cannot manage it. But I promise you that if, at your prayers, Jesus should give me back my health, I will translate not all—that would be too rash a promise—but a good selection of his works, on the condition which I have often made with you, that, if I do the dictating, you do the writing !—K.

No. 207.—An Account of Montanism

From Jerome, *Ep.* xli. [385], to Marcella (*Op.* i. 188–90: *P.L.* xxii. 474–6).

[§ 1] As regards the passages brought together from the Gospel of John, with which a certain votary of Montanus has assailed you, in which our Saviour promises that He will go to the Father, and that He will send the Paraclete [John xiv. 28; xv. 26], as regards these the Acts of the Apostles inform us both for what time the promises were made, and at what time they were actually fulfilled. Ten days had elapsed, we are told, from the Lord's ascension and fifty from His resurrection, when the Holy Spirit came down, and the tongues of the believers were cloven, so that each spoke every language. Then it was that, when certain persons of those who as yet believed not declared that the disciples were drunk with new wine, Peter standing in the midst of the apostles and of all the concourse said: "Ye men of Judæa . . . I will pour out of my Spirit" [Acts ii. 14–18].

[§ 2] If, then, the apostle Peter, upon whom the Lord has founded the Church, has expressly said that the prophecy and promise of the Lord were then and there fulfilled, how can we claim another fulfilment for ourselves? If the Montanists reply that Philip's four daughters prophesied [Acts xxi. 9] at a later date, and that a prophet is mentioned named Agabus [Acts xi. 28; xxi. 10, 11], and that in the partition of the Spirit, prophets are spoken of as well as apostles, teachers and others [1 Cor. xii. 28; Eph. iv. 11], and that Paul himself prophesied many things concerning heresies still future, and the end of the world; we tell them that we do not so much reject prophecy—for this is attested by the passion of the Lord—as refuse to receive prophets whose utterances fail to accord with the Scriptures old and new.

[§ 3] In the first place, we differ from the Montanists regarding the rule of faith. We distinguish the Father, the Son and the Holy Spirit as three Persons, but unite them as one Substance. They, on the other hand, following the doctrine of Sabellius, force the Trinity into the narrow limits of a single personality. We, while we do not encourage them, yet allow second marriages, since Paul bids the younger widows to marry [1 Tim. v. 14]. They suppose a repetition of marriage a sin so awful that he who has committed it is to be regarded as an adulterer. We according to the apostolic tradition (in which the whole world is at one with us) fast through one Lent yearly; whereas they keep three in the year as though three saviours had suffered. I do not mean, of course, that it is unlawful to fast at other times through the year—always excepting Pentecost[1]—only that while in Lent it is a duty of obligation, at other seasons it is a matter of choice. With us, again, the bishops occupy the place of the apostles, but with them a bishop ranks not first but third. For while they put first the patriarchs of Pepuza in Phrygia, and place next to these the ministers called stewards, the bishops are relegated to the third or almost the lowest rank. No doubt their object is to make their religion more pretentious by putting that last which we put first. Again, they close the doors of the Church to almost every fault, whilst we read daily, "I desire the repentance of a sinner rather than his death" [Ezek. xviii. 23] . . . Their strictness does not prevent them from themselves committing grave sins, far from it; but there is this difference between us and them, that, whereas they in their self-righteousness blush to confess their faults, we do penance for ours, and so more readily gain pardon for them.

[§ 4] I pass over their sacraments of sin, made up, as they are said to be, of sucking children subjected to a triumphant martyrdom. I prefer, I say, not to credit these: accusations of blood-shedding may well be false. But I

[1] *i.e.* The fifty days from Easter to Whit-Sunday.

must confute the open blasphemy of men who say that God first determined in the Old Testament to save the world by Moses and the prophets, but that finding Himself unable to fulfil His purpose He took to Himself a body of the Virgin, and preaching under the form of the Son in Christ, underwent death for our salvation. Moreover, that when by these two steps He was unable to save the world, He last of all descended by the Holy Spirit upon Montanus and those demented women Prisca and Maximilla; and that thus the mutilated and emasculate Montanus possessed a fulness of knowledge such as was never claimed by Paul; for he was content to say, "We know in part, and we prophesy in part," and again, "Now we see through a glass darkly" [1 Cor. xiii. 9, 12]. . . .—*N. & P.-N.F.* vol. VI. 55 *sq.*

No. 208.—The Anniversary of the Overthrow of Jerusalem, *c.* 392

From Jerome, *In Sophoniam,* c. i., commenting on *Dies iræ, dies illa* of *Zeph.* i. 15 (*Opera* vi. 692: *P.L.* xxv. 1354 A–C).

We have only to read Josephus, side by side with the prophecy of Zephaniah, to see the truth of his account. It is true not only of what happened at the taking of the city but of what goes on at the present day. The treacherous labourers for having killed God's servants, and at last, His Son, are forbidden, except for the purpose of wailing, to set foot in Jerusalem. In order to obtain leave to bewail the ruin of their city, they pay for the privilege at a price: so that they who once bought the blood of Christ, now buy their tears; and even their weeping they cannot get for nothing. On the day on which Jerusalem was captured and destroyed, you may see the people coming to mourn—a stream of decrepit women-folk and of old men, laden with rags and years, giving proof in body and mien of the wrath of God. With the Cross of the Lord gleaming, the Church of the Resurrection shining, and the standard of the Cross shimmering from the Mount of Olives, the wretched crowd foregathers to bemoan the ruins of their Temple—a piteous people yet deserving no pity. Tears are on their cheeks. Their arms are wan. Their hair is dishevelled. A soldier demands money, to let them weep a little longer. Can any one doubt, when he sees all this, what is meant by the "day of trouble and distress, a day of wasteness and desolation, a day of darkness and gloominess, a day of clouds and thick darkness, a day of the trumpet and alarm" [Zeph. i. 15, 16]? For they have trumpets even in their grief; and, according to the prophecy, the voice of "your feast" is turned to "mourning" [Amos viii. 10]. They wail over the ashes of the sanctuary, and over the altar ruined, and over cities once fenced, and over the lofty corners of the Temple, from which, in days gone by, they threw down James the brother of the Lord. So much then for the captivity of the Jews.—K.

No. 209.—The Mysteries of Mithra

From Jerome, *Ep.* cvii. [403], § 2 (*Op.* i. 678 *sq.*; *P.L.* xxii. 868 *sq.*).

[§ 2] I speak thus to you, Læta, my most devoted daughter in Christ, to teach you not to despair of your father's [1] salvation. My hope is that the same faith which has gained you your daughter [2] may win your father too, and that so you may be able to rejoice over blessings bestowed upon your entire family. You know the Lord's promise: "The things which are impossible with men are possible with God." It is never too late to mend. The robber passed even from the cross to paradise. . . . And . . . did not your own kinsman Gracchus, whose name betokens his patrician origin, when a few years back he held the Præfecture of the City,[3] overthrow, break in pieces, and shake to pieces the grotto of Mithras and all the dreadful images therein? Those I mean by which the Worshippers were initiated as Raven, Bridegroom [or, the Hidden One], Soldier, Lion, Perseus [or, the Persian], Sun, Crab [or, the Courser of the Sun] and Father? Did he not, I repeat, destroy these; and then, sending them before him as hostages, obtain for himself Christian baptism?

[1] Albinus, a heathen pontiff (Jerome, *Ep.* cvii. § 1).
[2] The infant Paula.
[3] Furius Maecius Gracchus was prefect of the city, A.D. 376–7.

Even in Rome itself paganism is left in solitude. They who once were the gods of the nations remain under their lonely roofs with horned owls and birds of night. The standards of the military are emblazoned with the sign of the Cross. The emperor's robes of purple and his diadem sparkling with jewels are ornamented with representations of the shameful yet saving gibbet. Already the Egyptian Serapis has been made a Christian.[1]—*N. & P.-N.F.* vi. 190.

No. 210.—Nazarenes and Ebionites

From Jerome, *Ep.* cxii. § 13 (*Op.* i. 746 *sq.*; *P.L.* xxii. 924), of A.D. 404: Augustine, *Ep.* lxxv. § 13 (*Op.* ii. 174; *P.L.* xxxiii. 257 *sq.*): [Jerome to Augustine].

The matter in debate, therefore, or I should rather say your opinion regarding it, is summed up in this: that since the preaching of the Gospel of Christ, the believing Jews do well in observing the precepts of the Law, *i.e.* in offering sacrifices as Paul did, in circumcising their children, as Paul did in the case of Timothy, and keeping the Jewish Sabbath, as all the Jews have been accustomed to do. If this be true, we fall into the heresy of Cerinthus and Ebion, who, though believing in Christ, were anathematized by the fathers for this one error that they mixed up the ceremonies of the Law with the Gospel of Christ, and professed their faith in that which was new, without letting go what was old. Why do I speak of the Ebionites, who make pretension to the name of Christian? In our own day there exists a sect among the Jews throughout all the synagogues of the East, which is called the sect of the Minei, and is even now condemned by the Pharisees. The adherents to this sect are known commonly as Nazarenes. They believe in Christ the Son of God, born of the Virgin Mary; they say that He who suffered under Pontius Pilate and rose again, is the same as the one in whom we believe. But while they desire to be both Jews and Christians, they are neither one nor the other. I therefore beseech you, who think that you are called upon

[1] Theophilus, archbishop of Alexandria, 385–†412, destroyed the Serapeum, 391: see Gibbon, *Decline and Fall,* c. xxviii.

to heal my slight wound, which is no more, so to speak, than a prick or a scratch from a needle, to devote your skill in the healing art to this grievous wound, which has been opened by a spear driven home with the impetus of a javelin. For there is surely no proportion between the culpability of him who exhibits the various opinions held by the fathers in a commentary on Scripture, and the guilt of him who re-introduces within the Church a most pestilential heresy. If, however, there is for us no alternative but to receive the Jews into the Church, along with the usages prescribed by their Law; if, in short, it shall be declared lawful for them to continue in the Churches of Christ what they have been accustomed to practise in the synagogues of Satan, I will tell you my opinion of the matter; they will not become Christians, but they will make us Jews.—J. G. Cunningham, *The Letters of St. Augustine*, i. 289 *sq.*

No. 211.—The Appointment of the Bishop at Alexandria to *c.* 250

(*a*) From Jerome, *Ep.* cxlvi. [? date], § 1 (*Op.* i. 1080–3; *P.L.* xxii. 1192–4).

[§ 1] We read in Isaiah, "A fool will speak folly." I hear that a certain person has broken out into so great madness as to place deacons before presbyters, that is, bishops. For when the apostle plainly teaches that presbyters and bishops are the same, what happens to the server of tables and widows that he sets himself up arrogantly over those at whose prayers the body and blood of Christ are made? Do you ask for authority? Listen to the proof. . . . That afterwards one was chosen to preside over the rest, this was done as a remedy for schism, and to prevent one individual from rending the Church of Christ by drawing it to himself. For even at Alexandria, from the time of Mark the Evangelist to the episcopates of Heracles and Dionysius, the presbyters used always to appoint as bishop one chosen out of their number, and placed on the higher grade, as if an army should make a commander, or as if deacons should choose one of themselves whom they should know to be diligent, and call him archdeacon. For, with the exception of ordaining, what does a bishop do which a presbyter does not? The church of the city of Rome is not to be thought one church, and that of the whole world another. Gaul and Britain, and Africa and Persia, and the East and India, and all foreign nations worship one Christ, and observe one rule of truth. If authority is asked for, the world is greater than the city. Wherever there is a bishop, whether at Rome, or Eugubium, or Constantinople, or Rhegium, or Alexandria, or Tanis, he is of the same dignity and of the same priesthood. The power of riches or the lowliness of poverty does not make him a higher bishop or a lower bishop. But all are successors of the apostles.—D. Stone, *Episcopacy and Valid Orders*, 43 *sqq*.

No. 212.—Papias on St. John

Philip of Side, *Historia Christiana*, *c.* A.D. 430.

Papias, Bishop of Hierapolis, who was a disciple of John the Divine, and a companion of Polycarp, wrote five books of Oracles of the Lord, wherein, when giving a list of the apostles, after Peter and John, Philip and Thomas and Matthew, he included among the disciples of the Lord Aristion and a second John, whom he also called "the Elder." [He says] that some think that this John is the author of two short and Catholic Epistles, which are published in the name of John; and he gives as the reason that the primitive (fathers) only accept the first Epistle. Some, too, have wrongly considered the Apocalypse also to be his (*i. e.* the Elder John's) work. Papias, too, is in error about the Millennium, and from him Irenæus also. Papias in his second book says that John the Divine and James his brother were killed by the Jews. The aforesaid Papias stated on the authority of the daughters of Philip that Barsabas, who is also called Justus, when challenged by the unbelievers drank serpents' poison in the name of the Lord, and was shielded from all harm. He makes also other marvellous statements, and particularly about the mother of Manaim who was raised from the dead. As for those who were raised from the dead by Christ, (he states) that they survived till the time of Hadrian.—The "De Boor" Fragment: or Fragments of Papias, No. V. J. B. Lightfoot, *Apostolic Fathers* (abridged edition), 530 *sq*.

No. 213.—Manichæism

From Augustine, *De utilitate credendi* [391], § 2 (*Op*. viii. 45 *sq*.; *P.L.* xlii. 66).

[§ 2] I propose then to prove to you, if I can, that the Manichees sacrilegiously and rashly inveigh against those who, following the authority of the Catholic faith before that they are able to gaze upon that truth which is beheld by the pure mind, are forearmed by believing, and prepared for God who is about to illuminate them. For you know, Honoratus, that for no other reason I fell in with such men than because they used to say that, laying aside the fear of authority, they would by mere and simple reason lead to God those who would listen to them, and would deliver them from all error. For what else was impelling me for nearly nine years, spurning the religion which had been planted in me when a child by my parents, to follow and diligently listen to these men, except that they said that we were frightened by superstition, and that faith is enjoined on us before reason, but that they press no one to faith except when the truth has been first discussed and made clear? Who would not be enticed by these promises, especially the mind of a young man desirous of truth, and also proud and talkative through the disputations of certain learned men in the school, such as they then found me, despising indeed, as it were, old wives' fables, and desiring to grasp and drink in the sincere and open truth promised by them? But what reason again recalled me from wholly cleaving to them, so that I kept myself in that rank, which they call that of the Hearers, so that I did not give up the hope and business of this world, except that I remarked that they themselves were rather eloquent and full in refuting others, than abiding firm and sure in proving their own positions?—*Certain smaller treatises of St. Augustine*, tr. H. de Romestin, 96–7.

No. 214.—The Validity of the Sacraments Distinct from their Efficacy

From Augustine, *De Baptismo* [*c.* 400], i. § 18 (*Op.* ix. 89, B.C.; *P.L.* xliii. 119).

[§ 18] What if he approached baptism itself in deceit? Were his sins remitted, or were they not? Let them choose which they will. Whichever they choose will answer our purpose. If they say they were remitted, how then shall "the Holy Spirit of discipline flee deceit," if in him who was full of deceit He worked remission of sins? If they say they were not remitted, I ask whether, if he should afterwards confess his sin with contrition of heart and true sorrow, it would be judged that he ought to be baptized again? And if it is mere madness to assert this, then let them confess that a man can be baptized with the true baptism of Christ, and that yet his heart, persisting in malice or sacrilege, may not allow remission of sins to be given; and so let them understand that men may be baptized in communions severed from the Church, in which Christ's baptism is given and received in the said celebration of the sacrament, but that it will only then be of avail for the remission of sins when the recipient, being reconciled to the unity of the Church, is purged from the sacrilege of deceit, by which his sins were retained, and their remission prevented. For as in the case of him who had approached the sacrament in deceit there is no second baptism, but he is purged by faithful discipline and truthful confession, which he could not be without baptism, so that what was given before becomes then powerful to work his salvation, when the former deceit is done away by the truthful confession; so also in the case of the man who, while an enemy to the peace and love of Christ, received in any heresy or schism the baptism of Christ, which the schismatics in question had not lost from among them, though by his sacrilege his sins were not remitted, yet, when he corrects his error, and comes over to the communion and unity of the Church, he ought not to be again baptized, because by his very reconciliation to the peace of the Church he receives this benefit, that the sacrament now begins in unity to be of avail for the remission of his sins, which could not so avail him as received in schism.—J. R. King, *The Works of Augustine*, iii. 19 *sq*.

No. 215.—The Objectivity of the Sacraments

From Augustine, *De Baptismo*, iv. §§ 16, 18 (*Op*. ix. 130; *P.L.* xliii. 164).

[§ 16] Wherefore the same blessed Cyprian teaches us that baptism is to be considered as consecrated in itself by the words of the Gospel, as the Church has received, without joining to it or mingling with it any consideration of waywardness and wickedness on the part of either minister or recipients; since he himself points out to us both truths—both that there have been some within the Church who did not cherish kindly Christian love, but practised envy and unkind dissension, of whom the Apostle Paul spoke; and also that the envious belong to the devil's party, as he testifies in the most open way in the epistle which he wrote *about envy and malignity*. Wherefore, since it is clearly possible that, in those who belong to the devil's party, Christ's sacrament may yet be holy—not, indeed, to their salvation but to their condemnation—and that not only if they are led astray after they have been baptized, but even if they were such in heart when they received the sacrament, "renouncing the world," as the same Cyprian shows, "in words only and not in deeds;" [1] and since even if afterwards they be brought into the right way, the sacrament is not to be again administered which they received when they were astray; so far as I can see the case is clear and evident, that in the question of baptism we have to consider not who gives, but what he gives; not who receives, but what he receives; not who has, but what he has. For if the men of the party of the devil, and therefore in no way belonging to the one Dove, [2] can yet receive, and have and give baptism in all its holiness, in no way defiled by their waywardness, as we are taught by the letters of Cyprian himself, how are we ascribing to heretics

[1] Cyprian, *Ep*. xi. § 1 (*C.S.E.L.* III. ii. 496). [2] *Cant*. vi. 8.

what does not belong to them? How are we saying that what is really Christ's is theirs, and not rather recognizing in them the signs of our Sovereign, and correcting the deeds of deserters from him?

[§ 18] . . . Accordingly, neither without any more than within, can any one who is of the devil's party, either in himself or in any other person, stain the sacrament, which is of Christ. It is not, therefore, the case that "the word, which eats as a canker"[1] to the ears of those who hear it, gives remission of sins;[2] but when baptism is given in the words of the Gospel, however great be the perverseness of understanding on the part either of him through whom, or of him to whom it is given, the sacrament itself is holy in itself on account of Him whose sacrament it is. And, if any one receiving it at the hands of a misguided man, yet does not receive the perversity of the minister but only the holiness of the mystery, being closely bound to the unity of the Church in good faith and hope and charity, he receives remission of his sins—not by "the words which do eat as doth a canker," but by the sacraments of the Gospel flowing from a heavenly source. But if the recipient himself be misguided, on the one hand, what is given is of no avail for the salvation of the misguided man; and yet, on the other hand, that which is received remains holy in the recipient, and is not renewed to him if he be brought to the right way.—J. R. King, *The Works of Augustine,* iii. 94–8.

No. 216.—Donatism, 303–21. The Acts of the Council of Cirta, in Numidia, now Constantine in Algiers, March 5, 305

From Augustine, *Contra Cresconium* [406], iii. § 30 (*Op.* ix. 449 *sq.*; *P.L.* xliii., liii. 510 *sq.*), [Duchesne, *Dossier*, No. 5].

When Diocletian was Consul for the eighth and Maximian for the seventh time, on March 4, after Secundus, bishop of Tigisis and Primate, had taken his seat in the house of Urbanus Donatus, he said:

1 2 Tim. ii. 17.
2 Cyprian, *Ep.* lxxiii. § 15 (*C.S.E.L.* III. ii. 789).

"Let us first see that all are duly qualified to act, and thus we shall be able to consecrate a Bishop."

Secundus said to Donatus of Mascula: "It is alleged that you have been guilty of Betrayal."

Donatus replied: "You know how Florus searched for me to make me offer incense, and God did not deliver me into his hands, my brother; but since God has pardoned me, so do you too leave me to God."

Secundus said: "What, then, are we to do about the Martyrs? They have been crowned because they did not 'betray.'"

Donatus said: "Send me to God. Before Him I will render my account."

Secundus said: "Come to one side."

Secundus said to Marinus of the Waters of Tibilis: "It is alleged that you, too, were guilty of Betrayal."

Marinus answered: "I did give papers to Pollus. My codices are safe."

Secundus said: "Stand on one side."

Secundus said to Donatus of Calama: "It is alleged that you were guilty of Betrayal."

Donatus answered: "I gave them medical treatises."

Secundus said: "Stand on one side."

Secundus said to Victor of Rustica: "It is alleged that you 'betrayed' four Gospels."

Victor answered: "Valentianus was Curator. He forced me to throw them into the fire. I knew that they were lost. Pardon me this fault, and God also will pardon me."

Secundus said: "Stand on one side."

Secundus said to Purpurius of Limata: "It is alleged that you killed at Milevis the two sons of your sister."

Purpurius answered: "Do you think that I am frightened of you, like the rest? What have *you* done, who were forced by the Curator and the soldiers to give up the Scriptures? How did you come to be set free by them, unless you surrendered something, or ordered it to be surrendered? For they did not let you go at random. Yes, I did kill, and I intend now to kill those who act against me. So do not now provoke me to say anything more. You know that I interfere with nobody's affairs."

Secundus the Less said to Secundus his uncle: "Do you

hear what he is saying against you? He is ready to leave, and make a schism; and not only he, but also all those who are accused by you. I know that they intend to abandon you, and pronounce sentence against you. You will then remain alone, a heretic. So what business is it of yours what any one has done? He has to render an account to God."

Secundus said to Felix of Rotarium, [to Nabor] of Centurio, and Victor of Garba: "What do you think?"

They answered: "They have God, to whom they must render their account."

Secundus said: "You know, and God knows. Sit down."

And they all answered: "Thanks be to God."—O. R. Vassall-Phillips, *St. Optatus,* App. xi.

No. 217.—The Report of Anulinus to Constantine, April 15, 313

From Augustine, *Ep.* lxxxviii. [406], § 2 (*Op.* ii. 213 E.; *P.L.* xxxiii. 302); Duchesne, *Dossier,* No. 16.

[§ 2] My duty has caused me, among the acts of my insignificance, to send your Majesty's heavenly letter, after I had received and venerated it, to Cæcilian and his subordinate clerics; at the same time I exhorted them that—now that unity has been effected with general consent, since through the condescension of your Majesty their liberty was seen to be in every respect completely secure, and the Catholic Church was protected—they should apply themselves to the service of their holy Law and to the things of God, with due reverence. But a few days afterwards I was approached by certain persons, followed by a great throng of the populace, who held that Cæcilian must be opposed, and presented me in my official capacity with two documents, one bound in leather and sealed, the other a *libellus* unsealed, and demanded with insistence that I should send them to the sacred and venerable Court of your Highness. This my littleness has been careful to do (preserving Cæcilian in his position), and I have forwarded their Acts, that your Majesty may be in a position to determine everything. I have sent the two *libelli,* of which the one bound in leather has been endorsed, *Libellus Ecclesiæ Catholicæ criminorum Cæciliani traditus a parte Majorini.* Also the one without a seal together with that in leather. Given on the fifteenth of April at Carthage, when Constantine Augustus was for the third time Consul.—*Ibid.* App. xii.

No. 218.—Donatism: the second investigation, at Carthage, Feb. 15, 314

From Augustine, *Contra Cresconium* [406], iii. § 81 (*Op.* ix. 476; *P.L.* xliii. 540): Duchesne, *Dossier,* No. 58.—Constantine to Probianus, proconsul of Africa, A.D. 315.

Your predecessor Ælianus, at a time when he was discharging the duties of that most worthy man, Verus our Vicar, in consequence of his ill-health, thought well (and with reason), amongst other matters, to investigate and determine the business—that is, the charges—brought by envy against Cæcilian, a bishop of the Catholic Church. For after he had secured the presence of Superius the Centurion, and Cæcilianus the Magistrate of Aptunga, and Saturninus who was formerly *Curator*, and Calidius the younger *Curator*, and Solon a public official of that city, he gave them a fair hearing—so that when it was alleged as an objection against Cæcilian that he had been raised to the episcopate by Felix, who was accused of the Betrayal and burning of the Divine Scriptures, the innocence of Felix was proved. Finally, when Maximus charged Ingentius, a decurion of Liqua, with having falsified a letter of Cæcilianus formerly *Duovir,* we have learned from the Acts of the Proceedings that this Ingentius was prepared for torture, and was only saved by his statement that he was a decurion of Liqua. Wherefore it is our will that you should despatch this Ingentius, under suitable escort, to my Court of Constantine Augustus, so that it may be made quite clear, in the presence and hearing of those who are concerned with this affair, and for some time past have been incessantly appealing to me, that it is to no purpose that they show their malice against Cæcilian the bishop, and have been pleased to bestir themselves against him with violence. So will it be brought to pass that these disputes having ceased, as is right, the people may without any dissension serve their religion with the reverence that is its due.—*Ibid.* App. xiv.

No. 219.—Donatism: the fourth investigation: by Constantine, at Milan, Nov. 10, 316

From Augustine, *Contra Cresconium* [406], iii. § 82 (*Op.* ix. 476 *sq.*; *P.L.* xliii. 451): Routh, *Rell. Sacr.*[2] iv. 317: cf. Duchesne, *Dossier*, No. 34.—Constantine to Eumalius, Vicar of Africa.

"Whereat [*sc.* at the trial before him] I clearly perceived," says he [*sc.* Constantine], that Cæcilian was a man distinguished by entire blamelessness; one who observed the accustomed duties of his religion, and devoted himself to it as was required of him. It was clear also that no fault could be found in him, such as had been attributed to him in his absence, by the inventions of his enemies.—K.

No. 220.—The Issue between Stephen and Cyprian

From Augustine, *De unico baptismo,* § 23 (*Op.* ix. 538; *P.L.* xliii. 607), [written c. 410].

[§ 23] . . . There were two bishops of most eminent churches, the Roman namely and the Carthaginian, Stephen and Cyprian, both abiding in Catholic unity; of whom Stephen judged that the baptism of Christ was in no case to be repeated, and was heavily displeased with those who so did. But Cyprian thought that those baptized in heresy or schism, as not having the baptism of Christ, were to be baptized in the Catholic Church. Many thought with Stephen, some also with Cyprian; both, with them, abiding in unity.—*L.F.* xvii. 260, note.

No. 221.—The Appointment of the Bishop at Alexandria

From *Apophthegmata Patrum*, c. lxxviii. (*P.L.* lxv. 341).

Certain heretics once came to Pœmen [the hermit, *c.* 350–400] and began to abuse the archbishop [Athanasius] of Alexandria, as having received his ordination from presbyters. But the old man made no answer, and called his brother and said, "Lay the table and give them food, and send them away in peace."—D. Stone, *Episcopacy and Valid Orders*, 46.

No. 222.—The Appointment of the Bishop at Alexandria

From Severus, Patriarch of Antioch, 518–38, *ap. J. T. S.* ii. 612.

And the bishop also of the city renowned for its orthodox faith, the city of the Alexandrians, used in former days to be appointed by the presbyters; but, in later times, in accordance with the canon which has prevailed everywhere, the solemn institution of their bishop has come to be performed by the hand of bishops, and no one contemns the strictness which prevails in the holy Churches, and has recourse to the former practices, which have yielded to the later clear, strict, approved, and spiritual ordinances.—*Ibid.* 45 *sq.*

No. 223.—Our "Apostles' Creed," *c.* 750

From Pirminius, *De singulis libris canonicis Scarapsus* [†758], (*P.L.* lxxxix. 1034).

1. I believe in God the Father Almighty,
   Maker of *heaven* **and** *earth:*
2. And in Jesus Christ, his only Son, our Lord,
3. Who ***was conceived*** by the Holy Ghost,
   Born of the Virgin Mary,
4. **Suffered** under Pontius Pilate,
   Was crucified, **dead** and buried,
   He descended into hell;
5. The third day he rose again from the dead,
6. He ascended into heaven,
   And sitteth on the right hand of ***God*** the Father Almighty;
7. From thence he shall come to judge the quick and the dead.

8. ***I believe*** in the Holy Ghost;
9. The holy **Catholic** Church;
 The Communion of Saints;
10. The Remission of sins;
11. The resurrection of the flesh,
12. **And the life everlasting.**

[Words in black type are found in the *Fides Hieronymi*, A.D. 377, and in the creed commented on by Niketas, bishop of Remesiana, *De Symbolo*, c. A.D. 375; words in black italic are those in *Fides Hieronymi*, and those in italic are in the creed commented on by Niketas. What is common to the two may have come from the East.]

No. 224.—Papias on St. John

By Georgius Monachus [*seu.* Hamartolus], *Chronicon*, *c.* 866.

After Domitian, Nerva reigned one year, who recalled John from the island (*i.e.* Patmos), and allowed him to dwell in Ephesus. He was at that time the sole survivor of the twelve Apostles, and after writing his Gospel received the honour of martyrdom. For Papias, bishop of Hierapolis, who was an eye-witness of him, in the second book of the Oracles of the Lord, says that he was killed by the Jews, and thereby evidently fulfilled, together with his brother, Christ's prophecy concerning them, and their own confession and undertaking on His behalf. For when the Lord said unto them: "Are ye able to drink of the cup that I drink of?" and they readily assented and agreed, He said: "My cup shall ye drink, and with the baptism that I am baptized shall ye be baptized." And reasonably so, for it is impossible for God to lie. So too the learned Origen affirms in his interpretation of St. Matthew's Gospel that John was martyred, declaring that he had learnt the fact from the successors of the Apostles. And indeed the well-informed Eusebius also, in his *Ecclesiastical History*, says: "Thomas received by lot Parthia, but John, Asia, where also he made his residence and died at Ephesus."—J. B. Lightfoot, *The Apostolic Fathers*, 531.

No. 225.—The Appointment of the Bishop at Alexandria

From Eutychius, Melkite Patriarch of Alexandria [933–43]: *Annals*, 329–331 (*P.G.* cxi. 982 B., C.).

In the ninth year of Claudius Cæsar the Evangelist Mark in the city of Alexandria called men to believe in our Lord Jesus Christ. While he was going round the city, the string of his shoe broke, so he went to a shoemaker named Ananias that he might mend his shoe. He took up an awl to bore a hole in the shoe, and pierced his finger so as to draw much blood and cause great pain. Mark then said to him, If you believe in Jesus Christ the Son of God, your finger will be healed; and, taking hold of the finger, he said, In the name of Jesus Christ let your finger be healed: and at the same moment the finger was healed and no more blood flowed. From that time then Ananias believed in Christ, and Mark baptized him and made him Patriarch of Alexandria. He was the first of the patriarchs who presided at Alexandria. And the Evangelist Mark appointed together with Ananias the Patriarch twelve presbyters to be with the Patriarch; so that, when the Patriarchate was vacant, they should choose one of the twelve presbyters, and that the other eleven should lay their hands on his head and bless him and make him Patriarch, and afterward should choose some eminent man and make him presbyter with themselves in the place of him who had been made Patriarch, so that they might always thus be twelve. And this custom of the presbyters of Alexandria creating the Patriarch out of the twelve presbyters went on till the time of Alexander, Patriarch of Alexandria [? 312–†328], who was of the number of the three hundred and eighteen [*i. e.* the Council of Nicæa]. He forbade the presbyters to create the Patriarch any more. He also ordered that, when a Patriarch was dead, the bishops should assemble to appoint a Patriarch. Further, he ordered that when the Patriarchate was vacant, they should choose from some place, whether from among the twelve presbyters or from others, some eminent man of known goodness, and create him Patriarch. —D. Stone, *Episcopacy and Valid Orders*, 46 *sq.*

INDEX

Numbers in thick type refer to the numbers of the Documents.
Numbers in plain type refer to the pages.

PUBLICATIONS

OF THE

S. P. C. K. &

THE SHELDON PRESS

BOOKS FOR STUDENTS

AND

OTHERS

SOCIETY FOR PROMOTING CHRISTIAN KNOWLEDGE

AND

THE SHELDON PRESS

LONDON: NORTHUMBERLAND AVENUE, W.C. 2

43 QUEEN VICTORIA STREET, E.C. 4

BRIGHTON: 61 PRESTON STREET. BATH: 39 GAY STREET

New York and Toronto: THE MACMILLAN COMPANY

And of all Booksellers.

Translations of Early Documents

A Series of Texts important for the study of Christian origins. Under the Joint Editorship of the Rev. W. O. E. OESTERLEY, D.D., and the Rev. Canon G. H. BOX, D.D.

The Church Times says: "The names of the Editors are a guarantee of trustworthy and expert scholarship, and their work has been admirably performed."

FIRST SERIES—Palestinian-Jewish and Cognate Texts (Pre-Rabbinic)

Jewish Documents of the Time of Ezra

Translated from the Aramaic by A. E. COWLEY, Litt.D. 4*s.* 6*d.*

The Wisdom of Ben-Sira (Ecclesiasticus)

By the Rev. W. O. E. OESTERLEY, D.D., Examining Chaplain to the Bishop of London. 3*s.* 6*d.*

The Book of Enoch

By the Rev. R. H. CHARLES, D.D., Canon of Westminster. 3*s.* 6*d.*

The Book of Jubilees

By the Rev. Canon CHARLES. 5*s.* 6*d.*

The Testaments of the Twelve Patriarchs

By the Rev. Canon CHARLES. 3*s.* 6*d.*

The Ascension of Isaiah

By the Rev. Canon CHARLES. Together with *The Apocalypse of Abraham* in one volume. 4*s.* 6*d.*

The Apocalypse of Ezra (ii. Esdras)

By the Rev. Canon BOX. 3*s.* 6*d.*

The Apocalypse of Baruch

By the Rev. Canon CHARLES. Together with *The Assumption of Moses* in one volume. 3*s.* 6*d.*

The Apocalypse of Abraham

By the Rev. Canon BOX. Together with *The Ascension of Isaiah* in one volume. 4*s.* 6*d.*

The Assumption of Moses

By Rev. W. J. FERRAR, M.A. Together with *The Apocalypse of Baruch* in one volume. 3*s.* 6*d.*

The Biblical Antiquities of Philo

By M. R. JAMES, Litt.D., F.B.A., Hon. Litt.D., Dublin, Hon. LL.D., St. Andrews, Provost of King's College, Cambridge. 8*s.* 6*d.*

The Lost Apocrypha of the Old Testament

By M. R. JAMES, Litt.D. 5*s.* 6*d.*

Translations of Early Documents (continued).

SECOND SERIES—Hellenistic-Jewish Texts

The Testament of Abraham
By G. H. BOX, M.A., D.D. With an Appendix by S. GASELEE, M.A. 6*s*.

The Wisdom of Solomon
By W. O. E. OESTERLEY, D.D. 3*s*. 6*d*.

The Sibylline Oracles (Books iii-v)
By the Rev. H. N. BATE, M.A., Examining Chaplain to the Bishop of London. 3*s*. 6*d*.

The Letter of Aristeas
By H. ST. JOHN THACKERAY, M.A., King's College, Cambridge. 3*s*. 6*d*.

Selections from Josephus
By H. ST. J. THACKERAY, M.A. 5*s*.

The Third and Fourth Books of Maccabees
By the Rev. C. W. EMMET, B.D. 3*s*. 6*d*.

The Book of Joseph and Asenath
Translated from the Greek by E. W. BROOKS. 3*s*. 6*d*.

THIRD SERIES—Palestinian-Jewish and Cognate Texts (Rabbinic)

The Sayings of the Jewish Fathers (Pirke Aboth). Translated from the Hebrew by W. O. E. OESTERLEY, D.D. 5*s*

Tractate Berakoth (Benedictions). With Introduction and Notes by A. LUKYN WILLIAMS, D.D. 6*s*.

Tractate Sanhedrin. Mishnah and Tosefta. The Judicial procedure of the Jews as codified towards the end of the second century A.D. Translated from the Hebrew, with brief Annotations, by the Rev. HERBERT DANBY, M.A. 6*s*.

Tractate Shabbath. Mishnah. Translated from the Hebrew with Explanatory Notes by W. O. E. OESTERLEY, D.D. 6*s*.

Kimhi's Commentary on the Psalms (Book I, Selections). By Rev. R. G. FINCH, B.D. *7s. 6d.*

Midrash Sifre on Numbers. Selections from Early Rabbinic Scriptural Interpretations. Translated by PAUL P. LEVERTOFF. Introduction by Canon G. H. BOX, D.D. *7s. 6d.*

Sukkah, Mishna and Tosefta. With Introduction, Translation and Short Notes by A. W. GREENUP, D.D. 5s.

Select Passages Illustrating Neoplatonism. Translated with an Introduction by E. R. DODDS, University College, Reading. 5s.

A Short Survey of the Literature of Rabbinical and Mediæval Judaism. By W. O. E. OESTERLEY, M.A., D.D., and G. H. BOX, M.A., D.D. 12*s.* 6*d.*

Select Passages Illustrating Mithraism. Translated with an Introduction by the Rev. A. S. GEDEN, D.D. 3*s.* 6*d.*

The Uncanonical Jewish Books
A Short Introduction to the Apocrypha and the Jewish Writings 200 B.C.–A.D. 100. By W. JOHN FERRAR, M.A. 2*s.* 6*d.*

Barnabas, Hermas and the Didache
Being the Donnellan Lectures, 1920, by J. ARMITAGE ROBINSON, D.D., Dean of Wells. 6*s.*

The Acts of the Apostles
Translated from the Codex Bezae, with an Introduction on its Lucan Origin and importance by Canon J. M. WILSON, D.D. 3*s.* 6*d.*

Pistis Sophia
Literally Translated from the Coptic by GEORGE HORNER. With an Introduction by F. LEGGE, F.S.A. 16*s.*

Translations of Christian Literature

The Church Times says: "The splendid series of Translations."
The Tablet says: "Excellent translations series for which all students are so deeply indebted to the enterprise of the S.P.C.K."

A NUMBER of translations from the Fathers have already been published by the S.P.C.K. under the title "Early Church Classics." This series is now enlarged to include texts which are neither "early" nor necessarily "classics." The divisions at present proposed are given below. Volumes belonging to the original series are marked with an asterisk.

SERIES I.—GREEK TEXTS.

Eusebius. Bishop of Cæsarea. The Ecclesiastical History and the Martyrs of Palestine. Translated, with Introduction and Notes, by HUGH JACKSON LAWLOR, D.D., Litt.D., and JOHN ERNEST LEONARD OULTON, B.D. Volume I. Translation. Vol. II. Introduction, Notes and Appendix. Each 10*s.* 6*d.* net.

The Ascetic Works of St. Basil. Translated into English, with Introduction and Notes, by W. K. L. CLARKE, D.D. 12*s.* 6*d.*

Dionysius the Areopagite: The Divine Names and the Mystical Theology. By C. E. ROLT. 7*s.* 6*d.*

The Library of Photius. By J. H. FREESE, M.A. Vol. I. 10*s.*

The Apocriticus of Macarius Magnes. By T. W. CRAFER, D.D. 7*s.* 6*d.*

***The Epistle of St. Clement, Bishop of Rome.** By the Rt. Rev. J. A. F. GREGG, D.D. 1*s.* 9*d.* (*Out of print.*)

***Clement of Alexandria: Who is the Rich Man that is being saved?** By P. M. BARNARD, B.D. 1*s.* 9*d.*

***St. Chrysostom: On the Priesthood.** By T. A. MOXON. 2*s.* 6*d.*

The Doctrine of the Twelve Apostles. By C. BIGG, D.D. Revised by the Right Rev. A. J. MACLEAN, D.D. 3*s.* 6*d.*

***The Epistle to Diognetus.** By the Rt. Rev. L. B. RADFORD, D.D. 2*s.* 6*d.*

St. Dionysius of Alexandria. By C. L. FELTOE, D.D. 4*s.*

Translations of Christian Literature (continued).

SERIES I.—GREEK TEXTS (*continued*).

***The Epistle of the Gallican Churches: Lugdunum and Vienna.** With an Appendix containing Tertullian's Address to Martyrs and the Passion of St. Perpetua. By T. H. BINDLEY, D.D. 1*s.* 9*d.*

***St. Gregory of Nyssa: The Catechetical Oration.** By the Ven. J. H. SRAWLEY, D.D. 2*s.* 6*d.*

***St. Gregory of Nyssa: The Life of St. Macrina.** By W. K. LOWTHER CLARKE, D.D. 1*s.* 9*d*

Gregory Thaumaturgus (Origen the Teacher): the Address of Gregory to Origen, with Origen's Letter to Gregory. By W. METCALFE, B.D. 3*s.* 6*d.* [*Re-issue.*

***The Shepherd of Hermas.** By C. TAYLOR, D.D. 2 vols. 2*s.* 6*d.* each.

Eusebius: The Proof of the Gospel. By W. J. FERRAR 2 vols. 20*s.* (*Not sold separately.*)

Hippolytus: Philosophumena. By F. LEGGE. 2 vols. 20*s.* (*Not sold separately.*)

The Epistles of St. Ignatius. By the Ven. J. H. SRAWLEY, D.D. 4*s.*

***St. Irenaeus: Against the Heresies.** By F. R. M. HITCHCOCK, D.D. 2 vols. 2*s.* 6*d.* each.

Palladius: The Lausiac History. By W. K. LOWTHER CLARKE, D.D. 5*s.*

***St. Polycarp.** By B. JACKSON. 1*s.* 9*d.*

The Dialogue of Palladius concerning the Life of Chrysostom. By HERBERT MOORE. 8*s.* 6*d.*

Fifty Spiritual Homilies of St. Macarius the Egyptian. By A. J. MASON, D.D. 15*s.*

SERIES II.—LATIN TEXTS.

St. Augustine on the Spirit and the Letter. By W. J. SPARROW-SIMPSON, D.D. 5*s.*

Tertullian's Treatises concerning Prayer, concerning Baptism. By A. SOUTER, D.Litt. 3*s.*

Tertullian against Praxeas. By A. SOUTER, D.Litt. 5*s.*

Translations of Christian Literature (continued).

SERIES II.—LATIN TEXTS (*continued*).

Tertullian concerning the Resurrection of the Flesh. By A. Souter, D.Litt. 12*s.* 6*d.*

Novatian on the Trinity. By H. Moore. 6*s.*

St. Augustine: The City of God. By F. R. M. Hitchcock, D.D. 3*s.* [*Re-issue.*

***St. Cyprian: The Lord's Prayer.** By T. H. Bindley, D.D. 2*s.*

Minucius Felix: The Octavius. By J. H. Freese. 3*s.* 6*d.*

***Tertullian: On the Testimony of the Soul and On the Prescription of Heretics.** By T. H. Bindley, D.D. 2*s.* 6*d.*

***St. Vincent of Lerins: The Commonitory.** By T. H. Bindley, D.D. 2*s.* 6*d.*

St. Bernard: Concerning Grace and Free Will. By Watkin W. Williams. 7*s.* 6*d.*

The Life of Otto: Apostle of Pomerania, 1060-1139. By Ebo and Herbordus. Translated by Charles H. Robinson, D.D. 8*s.* 6*d.*

Anskar, the Apostle of the North, 801–865. By Charles H. Robinson, D.D. Translated from the Vita Anskarii by Bishop Rimbert, his fellow-missionary and successor. 4*s.* [Published by S.P.G.]

Select Epistles of St. Cyprian treating of the Episcopate. Edited with Introduction and Notes by T. A. Lacey, M.A. 8*s.* 6*d.*

SERIES III.—LITURGICAL TEXTS.

Edited by C. L. Feltoe, D.D.

St. Ambrose: On the Mysteries and on the Sacraments. By T. Thompson, B.D., and J. H. Srawley, D.D. 4*s.* 6*d.*

***The Apostolic Constitution and Cognate Documents, with special reference to their Liturgical elements.** By De Lacy O'Leary, D.D. 1*s.* 9*d.*

Translations of Christian Literature (continued).

SERIES III.—LITURGICAL TEXTS (*continued*).

The Anaphoras of the Ethiopic Liturgy. By J. M. HARDEN, D.D. 7*s.* 6*d.*

The Liturgy of the Eighth Book of the Apostolic Constitution, commonly called the Clementine Liturgy. By R. H. CRESSWELL. 3*s.*

The Pilgrimage of Etheria. By M. L. McCLURE. 6*s.*

Bishop Sarapion's Prayer-Book. By the Rt. Rev. J. WORDSWORTH, D.D. 2*s.* 6*d.*

The Swedish Rite. By E. E. YELVERTON. 8*s.* 6*d.*

Twenty-five Consecration Prayers. With Notes and Introduction by ARTHUR LINTON. 7*s.* 6*d.*

SERIES IV.—ORIENTAL TEXTS.

The Ethiopic Didascalia. By J. M. HARDEN, B.D. 9*s.*

The Apostolic Preaching of Irenaeus (Armenian). By J. A. ROBINSON, D.D. 7*s.* 6*d.*

SERIES V.—LIVES OF THE CELTIC SAINTS.

EDITED BY ELEANOR HULL.

St. Malachy of Armagh (St. Bernard). By H. J. LAWLOR, D.D. 12*s.*

The Latin and Irish Lives of Ciaran. Translated and Annotated by R. A. STEWART MACALISTER, Litt.D., F.S.A. 10*s.*

St. Patrick: Life and Works. By N. J. D. WHITE, D.D. 6*s.* 6*d.*

St. David. By A. W. WADE-EVANS. 7*s.* 6*d.*

The Life of St. Samson of Dol. By THOMAS TAYLOR, B.D. 5*s.*

The Life of St. Gall. By MAUD JOYNT. 7*s.* 6*d.* net.

SERIES VI.—SELECT PASSAGES.

Documents Illustrative of the History of the Church. Vol. I.: to A.D. 313. Vol. II.: A.D. 313–A.D. 461. Edited by B. J. KIDD, D.D. Vol. I. 8*s.* 6*d.* Vol. II. 10*s.*

Ante-Nicene Exegesis of the Gospels. By HAROLD SMITH, D.D. Vols. I.–V. Each 7*s.* 6*d.*

SERIES VII.

Lives of the Serbian Saints. By VOVESLAV YANICH, D.D., and C. P. HANKEY, M.A. 6*s.* 6*d.*

Handbooks of Christian Literature

The Letters of St. Augustine. By the Rev. Canon W. J. SPARROW SIMPSON, D.D. 10*s.*

The Early Christian Books. A Short Introduction to Christian Literature to the Middle of the Second Century. By the Rev. W. JOHN FERRAR, M.A. 3*s.* 6*d.*

The Inspiration and Authority of Holy Scripture. A Study in the Literature of the First Five Centuries. By G. DUNCAN BARRY, B.D. 4*s.* 6*d.*

The Eucharistic Office of the Book of Common Prayer. By the Rev. LESLIE WRIGHT, M.A., B.D. 3*s.* 6*d.*

An Introduction to Ethiopic Christian Literature. By J. M. HARDEN, B.D., LL.D. 5*s.*

Helps for Students of History

Edited by C. JOHNSON, M.A., H. W. V. TEMPERLEY, M.A., and J. P. WHITNEY, D.D., D.C.L.

The Times Educational Supplement says: "The S.P.C.K. has been fortunate in securing specialists of high rank for this series."

1. **Episcopal Registers of England and Wales.** By R. C. FOWLER, B.A., F.S.A. 6*d.*
2. **Municipal Records.** By F. J. C. HEARNSHAW, M.A., LL.D. 1*s.*
3. **Medieval Reckonings of Time.** By REGINALD L. POOLE, LL.D., Litt.D. 6*d.*
4. **The Public Record Office.** By C. JOHNSON, M.A. 6*d.*
5. **The Care of Documents.** By C. JOHNSON, M.A. 6*d.*
6. **The Logic of History.** By C. G. CRUMP. 8*d.*
7. **Documents in the Public Record Office, Dublin.** By R. H. MURRAY, Litt.D. 8*d.*
8. **The French Wars of Religion.** By ARTHUR A. TILLEY, M.A. 6*d.*

By Sir A. W. WARD, Litt.D., F.B.A.

9. **The Period of Congresses—I. Introductory.** 8*d.*
10. **II. Vienna and the Second Peace of Paris.** 1*s.*
11. **III. Aix-la-Chapelle to Verona.** 1*s.*
    Nos. 9, 10, and 11 in one volume, cloth, 3*s.* 6*d.*
12. **Securities of Peace: A Retrospect (1848–1914).** Paper, 2*s.*; cloth, 3*s.*

Helps for Students of History (continued).

13. **The French Renaissance.** By A. A. TILLEY, M.A. 8*d*.
14. **Hints on the Study of English Economic History.** By W. CUNNINGHAM, D.D., F.B.A., F.S.A. 8*d*.
15. **Parish History and Records.** By A. HAMILTON THOMPSON, M.A., F.S.A. 8*d*.
16. **A Short Introduction to the Study of Colonial History.** By A. P. NEWTON, M.A., D.Litt. 6*d*.
17. **The Wanderings and Homes of Manuscripts.** By M. R. JAMES, Litt.D., F.B.A. Paper, 2*s*.; cloth, 3*s*.
18. **Ecclesiastical Records.** By the Rev. CLAUDE JENKINS, M.A., Librarian of Lambeth Palace. 1*s*. 9*d*.
19. **An Introduction to the History of American Diplomacy.** By CARL RUSSELL FISH, Ph.D. 1*s*.
20. **Hints on Translation from Latin into English.** By ALEXANDER SOUTER, D.Litt. 6*d*.
21. **Hints on the Study of Latin (A.D. 125-750).** By ALEXANDER SOUTER, D.Litt. 8*d*.
22. **Report of the Historical MSS. Commission.** By R. A. ROBERTS, F.R.Hist.S. 2*s*. 6*d*.
23. **A Guide to Franciscan Studies.** By A. G. LITTLE. 1*s*. 6*d*.
24. **A Guide to the History of Education.** By JOHN WILLIAM ADAMSON. 8*d*.
25. **Introduction to the Study of Russian History.** By W. F. REDDAWAY. 6*d*.
26. **Monuments of English Municipal Life.** By W. CUNNINGHAM, D.D., F.B.A. 1*s*.
27. **La Guyenne Pendant la Domination Anglaise, 1152-1453.** Par CHARLES BÉMONT. 1*s*. 4*d*.
28. **The Historical Criticism of Documents.** By R. L. MARSHALL, M.A., LL.D. 1*s*. 3*d*.
29. **The French Revolution.** By G. P. GOOCH. 8*d*.
30. **Seals.** By H. S. KINGSFORD. 1*s*. 3*d*.
31. **A Student's Guide to the Manuscripts of the British Museum.** By JULIUS P. GILSON, M.A. 1*s*.

32. **A Short Guide to some Manuscripts in the Library of Trinity College, Dublin.** By R. H. MURRAY, Litt.D. 1*s.* 9*d.*

33-35. **Ireland.** No. 33, 1494–1603; No. 34, 1603–1714; No. 35, 1714–1829. By R. H. MURRAY, Litt.D. Each, 1*s.* Nos. 33–35 in one volume, 3*s.* 6*d.*

36. **Coins and Medals.** By G. F. HILL, M.A., F.B.A. 1*s.* 6*d.*

37. **The Latin Orient.** By W. MILLER, M.A. 1*s.* 6*d.*

38. **The Turkish Restoration in Greece, 1718-1797.** By WILLIAM MILLER, M.A. 1*s.* 3*d.*

39. **Sources for the History of Roman Catholics in England, Ireland and Scotland, 1533–1795.** By JOHN HUNGERFORD POLLEN, S.J. 1*s.* 3*d.*

40. **English Time Books.—Vol. I. English Regnal Years and Titles, Hand-lists, Easter Dates, etc.** Compiled by J. E. W. WALLIS, M.A. 4*s.*

41. **Knights of Malta, 1523–1798.** By R. COHEN. 2*s.*

42. **Records for the Early History of South Africa.** By C. GRAHAM BOTHA. 1*s.*

43. **The Western Manuscripts of the Bodleian Library.** By H. H. E. CRASTER, D.Litt. 1*s.* 3*d.*

44. **Geographical Factors.** By H. J. FLEURE. 6*d.*

45. **The Colonial Entry Books. A Brief Guide to the Colonial Records in the Public Record Office before 1696.** By C. S. S. HIGHAM, M.A. 1*s.* 6*d.*

46. **The University Library, Cambridge.** By H. GIDNEY ALDIS, M.A. 6*d.*

47. **A Students' Guide to the Manuscripts relating to English History in the Seventeenth Century in the Bodleian Library.** By G. DAVIES. 1*s.*

48. **History and Ethnology.** By W. R. H. RIVERS, M.D., LL.D., F.R.S. 6*d.*

49. **Some Aspects of Boundary Settlement at the Peace Conference.** By ALAN G. OGILVIE, B.Sc. 6*d.*

50. **The Mechanical Processes of the Historian.** By CHARLES JOHNSON, M.A., F.S.A. 6*d.*

51. **The Sources for the History of the Council in the Sixteenth and Seventeenth Centuries.** By E. R. ADAIR, M.A. 3*s.* 6*d.*

Texts for Students

1. **Select Passages from Josephus, Tacitus, Suetonius, Dio Cassius,** illustrative of Christianity in the First Century. Arranged by H. J. White, D.D. 3*d*.
2. **Selections from Matthew Paris.** By C. A. J. Skeel, D.Lit. 9*d*.
3. **Selections from Giraldus Cambrensis.** By C. A. J. Skeel, D.Lit. 9*d*.
4. **Libri Sancti Patricii.** The Latin Writings of St. Patrick, etc. By Newport J. D. White, D.D. 6*d*.
5. **A Translation of the Latin Writings of St. Patrick.** By Newport J. D. White, D.D. 6*d*.
6. **Selections from the Vulgate.** 9*d*.
7. **The Epistle of St. Clement of Rome.** 6*d*.
8. **Select Extracts from Chronicles and Records relating to English Towns in the Middle Ages.** By F. J. C. Hearnshaw, M.A., LL.D. 9*d*.
9. **The Inscription on the Stele of Méša.** Commonly called the Moabite Stone. Translated by the Rev. H. F. B. Compston, M.A. 6*d*.
10. **The Epistles of St. Ignatius.** 1*s*.
11. **Christian Inscriptions.** By H. P. V. Nunn, M.A. 1*s*.
12. **Selections from the "Historia Rerum Anglicarum" of William of Newburgh.** 1*s*. 3*d*.
13. **The Teaching of the Twelve Apostles.** By T. W. Crafer, D.D. 4*d*. 13A. **An English Translation.** 3*d*.
14. **The Epistle of Barnabas.** Edited by T. W. Crafer, D.D. 6*d*. 14A. **An English Translation.** 6*d*.
15. **The Code of Hammurabi.** By P. Handcock, M.A. 1*s*.
16. **Selections from the Tell El-Amarna Letters.** By Percy Handcock, M.A. 4*d*.
17. **Select Passages Illustrating Commercial and Diplomatic Relations between England and Russia.** By A. Weiner, M.A., F.R.Hist.S. 1*s*. 6*d*.
18. **The Early History of the Slavonic Settlements in Dalmatia, Croatia and Serbia.** By J. B. Bury. 2*s*.
19. **Select Extracts Illustrating Florentine Life in the 13th and 14th Centuries.** By E. G. Roper, B.A. 1*s*.
20. **Select Extracts Illustrating Florentine Life in the 15th Century.** By Esther G. Roper, B.A. 1*s*.
    Nos. 19 and 20 in one volume, 2*s*. 6*d*.
21. **Itinerarium Regis Ricardi.** By M. T. Stead. 1*s*. 9*d*.

Texts for Students (continued).

22. **The Second Epistle of Clement to the Corinthians.** 6*d.*

22A. **An English Translation of the above.** 6*d.*

23. **Extracts Illustrating Sports and Pastimes in the Middle Ages.** By E. L. GUILFORD, M.A. 1*s.* 9*d.*

24. **Babylonian Flood Stories.** 25. **Babylonian Penitential Psalms.** By P. HANDCOCK, M.A. 6*d.* each.

26. **The Hymn of Cleanthes.** Translated with Introduction and Notes by E. H. BLAKENEY, M.A. 6*d.*

27. **The Foundations of Modern Ireland.** The Civil Policy of Henry VIII. and the Reformation. By CONSTANTIA MAXWELL, M.A. 1*s.* 6*d.*

28. **Selections from the Qur'án.** Arranged by H. U. WEITBRECHT STANTON, M.D., D.D. 1*s.*

29. **The Tome of Pope Leo the Great.** Latin Text with Translation, Introduction, and Notes, by E. H. BLAKENEY, M.A. 1*s.*; duxeen boards, 1*s.* 6*d.*

30. **The Book of Amos.** Hebrew Text edited by THEODORE H. ROBINSON, M.A., D.D. 2*s.* 6*d.*

31. **Sukkah. (A Critical Hebrew Text.)** By A. W. GRËENUP, D.D. 2*s.* 6*d.*

32. **Readings from the Apocrypha.** Selected and Annotated by E. H. BLAKENEY, M.A. 1*s.*; cloth, 1*s.* 6*d.*

33 & 34. **English Social Life in the Eighteenth Century.** Illustrated from Contemporary Sources. By M. D. GEORGE. Each 1*s.* 6*d.* In one vol., cloth, 3*s.* 6*d.*

35. **Texts Illustrating Ancient Ruler-Worship.** Edited by C. LATTEY, S.J., M.A. 6*d.*

35A. **An English Translation of the above.** 6*d.*

36. **Select Passages Illustrative of Neoplatonism.** Greek edition. Edited by E. R. DODDS, B.A. 4*s.* 6*d.*

37. **Traders in East and West.** Some Aspects of Trade in the 17th and 18th Centuries. By FLORENCE L. BOWMAN and ESTHER G. ROPER. 2*s.*

38. **Travellers and Travelling in the Middle Ages.** By E. L. GUILFORD, M.A. 2*s.*

39. **St. Augustine: De Fide et Symbolo.** Edited by HAROLD SMITH, D.D. 2*s.* 6*d.*

40. **God and His Works.** Being Selections from Part I. of the "Summa Theologica" of St. Thomas Aquinas. Arranged, with an Introduction, by A. G. HEBERT, M.A. Paper cover, 2*s.* 6*d.* Duxeen boards, 3*s.* 6*d.* net.

41. **Village Life in the Fifteenth Century.** Illustrated from Contemporary Sources by H. M. DUNCAN and W. J. HAWARD. 3*s*. 6*d*. net.
42. **The Book of Ruth.** The Hebrew Text with Grammatical Notes and Vocabulary by A. R. S. KENNEDY, D.D. 2*s*. 6*d*. net.
43. **Cyprian De Unitate Ecclesiæ.** The Latin text, translated, with an Introduction and Brief Notes, by E. H. BLAKENEY, M.A. 1*s*. 6*d*. net.

The Bede Histories.

Edited by MISS H. L. POWELL, St. Mary's College, Lancaster Gate.

SERIES III.

History of the People of England. By ALICE DRAYTON GREENWOOD, F.R.Hist.Soc. With many Maps and Illustrations.

Vol. I. 55 B.C. to A.D. 1485. 7*s*. 6*d*.

History says: "The book is characterised by a general accuracy of detail."

The Birmingham Post says: "A characteristic of the book is the detailed account given of the people's social and economic condition, their occupations and recreations both in town and country."

Vol. II. 1485–1688. 7*s*. 6*d*.

History says: "Invaluable to the highest forms of schools and to undergraduates. . . One has the sense that everything is there which is wanted . . . a most useful instrument of teaching, not less to the teacher than the taught."

The Spectator says: "A readable and well-planned book by a competent scholar."

Vol. III. 1689–1834. 7*s*. 6*d*.

The Times Literary Supplement says: "Fully maintains the high standard of the earlier volumes . . . should be of great value to the young University student. The facts are accurate, well co-ordinated and clearly set forth. . . . The maps, illustrations and reproductions are numerous and excellent."

SERIES II.

History of the People of England from the Earliest Times to 1066. By ADELINE I. RUSSELL, M.A. With 122 Illustrations and 8 Maps. Vol. I. 2*s*. 6*d*.

[*The first volume of a junior series. With over* 100 *illustrations and* 308 *pages it is splendid value for money.*]

The Teachers' Times says: ". . . Presented in a most attractive form. The outline is brightly written. . . . Incidents and quotations are taken, where possible, from contemporary authorities. Illustrations are very plentiful."

The Journal of Education says: "Scholarly, well-balanced and thoroughly interesting."

Studies in Church History

Richard Baxter. Puritan and Mystic. By A. R. LADELL, M.A. Preface by W. H. FRERE, D.D., Bishop of Truro. 5*s.* net.

The Dominican Order in England before the Reformation. By BERYL E. R. FORMOY, M.A. 6*s.*

The Cathedral Church of Hereford: Its History and Constitution. By ARTHUR THOMAS BANNISTER, M.A. 7*s.* 6*d.*

The Christian Church in the Epistles of St. Jerome. By L. HUGHES, M.A., D.D. 4*s.* 6*d.*

The Prelude to the Reformation. By the Rev. R. S. ARROWSMITH. 8*s.*

The Albigensian Heresy. By H. J. WARNER, B.D. 3*s.* 6*d.*

The Early Franciscans and Jesuits. A Study in Contrasts. By ARTHUR S. B. FREER, M.A. 6*s.*

Some Eighteenth-Century Churchmen: Glimpses of English Church Life in the Eighteenth Century. By G. LACEY MAY, M.A. With Illustrations. 9*s.*

Christian Monasticism in Egypt to the Close of the Fourth Century. By W. H. MACKEAN, D.D. 8*s.*

The Venerable Bede. His Life and Writings. By the Rt. Rev. G. F. BROWNE, D.D. With Illustrations. 10*s.*

The Reformation in Ireland. A Study of Ecclesiastical Legislation. By H. HOLLOWAY, M.A. 7*s.* 6*d.*

The Emperor Julian. An Essay on His Relations with the Christian Religion. By EDWARD J. MARTIN, B.D. 3*s.* 6*d.*

The Importance of Women in Anglo-Saxon Times; The Cultus of St. Peter and St. Paul, and other Addresses. By the Right Rev. G. F. BROWNE, D.D. With two Illustrations. 7*s.* 6*d.*

Essays Liturgical and Historical. By J. WICKHAM LEGG, D.Litt., F.S.A. 5*s.*

French Catholics in the Nineteenth Century. By the Rev. W. J. SPARROW SIMPSON, D.D. 5*s.*

An Abbot of Vézelay. By ROSE GRAHAM, F.R.Hist.S. With eight Illustrations. 3*s.* 6*d.*

The Monastic Chronicler and the Early School of St. Albans. By CLAUDE JENKINS, M.A. 3*s.* 6*d.*

The Historic Monuments of England

Edited by A. HAMILTON THOMPSON, M.A. (Cantab.), Hon. D.Litt. (Durham), F.S.A., Professor of Mediæval History in the University of Leeds.

The Cathedral Churches of England. By A. HAMILTON THOMPSON, M.A., Hon. D.Litt. (Durham), F.S.A. With copious Illustrations. 8*s.* 6*d.* net.

Parish Church Architecture. By E. TYRRELL GREEN. With 64 Illustrations, chiefly from drawings by the Author, and a Map. 8*s.* 6*d.* net.

English Monumental Sculpture since the Renaissance. By KATHARINE A. ESDAILE. With many Illustrations. 10*s.* 6*d.* net.

The Painted Glass of York. An Account of the Mediæval Glass of the Minster and the Parish Churches. By the Rev. F. HARRISON, M.A., F.S.A., Librarian of the Dean and Chapter Library, York. With a Preface by W. FOXLEY NORRIS, D.D., Dean of Westminster. With four coloured Plates and numerous Illustrations. 12*s.* 6*d.* net.

English Mediæval Painted Glass. By J. D. LE COUTEUR. With about 50 Illustrations. 8*s.* 6*d.* net.

Sundials. Incised Dials and Mass-Clocks. A Study of the Time-Markers of Mediæval Churches, containing Descriptions, Photographs, Diagrams, and Analysis of Dials, chiefly in Hampshire, but also in various other counties. By ARTHUR ROBERT GREEN, M.R.C.S. (England), L.R.C.P. (London). 10*s.* 6*d.* net.

French Church Architecture. By E. TYRRELL GREEN. With about 70 Illustrations. 10*s.* 6*d.* net.

Baptismal Fonts. Classified and Illustrated. By E. TYRRELL GREEN. With over 100 Illustrations. 10*s.* 6*d.* net.

[20.6.29.

Printed in Great Britain by R. Clay & Sons, Ltd., Bungay, Suffolk.

GLADSTONE'S
LIBRARY